# IDEAL CITIZENS

SUNY SERIES IN AFRO-AMERICAN STUDIES
JOHN HOWARD AND ROBERT C. SMITH, EDITORS

# IDEAL CITIZENS

## The Legacy of the Civil Rights Movement

JAMES MAX FENDRICH

STATE UNIVERSITY OF NEW YORK PRESS

*Cover Photo*: Medical doctors protest in 1985 outside a Health Maintenance Organization. The four physicians in the photo are Edward Holifield, Joseph Webster, Harold Martin, and Charles Richardson. Two of them are FAMU graduates. (Florida Flambeau archives)

Published by
State University of New York Press, Albany

© 1993 State University of New York

All rights reserved

No part of this book may be used or reproduced
in any manner whatsoever without written permission
except in the case of brief quotations embodied in
critical articles and reviews.

For information, contact State University of New York Press
www.sunypress.edu

Production by E. Moore
Marketing by Bernadette LaManna

Library of Congress Cataloging-in-Publication Data

Fendrich, James Max, 1938–
   Ideal citizens : the legacy of the civil rights movement / James Max Fendrich.
     p.   cm. — (SUNY series in Afro-American studies)
   Includes bibliographical references (p.  ) and index.
   ISBN 0-7914-1323-3 (CH : acid-free). — ISBN 0-7914-1324-1 (PB : acid-free)
   1. Civil rights workers—Florida—Tallahassee—Political activity-
-Longitudinal studies.  2. Afro-American civil rights workers-
-Florida—Tallahassee—Political activity—Longitudinal studies.
3. Afro-Americans—Civil rights—Florida—Tallahassee—History—20th century.  4. United States—Politics and government—1945-
5. College students—Florida—Tallahassee—Political activity-
-Longitudinal studies.  6. Afro-American college students—Florida-
-Tallahassee—Political activity—Longitudinal studies.  7. Florida Agricultural and Mechanical University—Students—Longitudinal studies.  8. Tallahassee (Fla.)—Race relations.  I. Title.
II. Series.
F319.T14F46  1993
323'.092'273—dc20                                      92-2538
                                                            CIP

10 9 8 7 6 5 4 3 2 1

*For my children, Matthew, Kerrie, Christopher, and Alise*

# Contents

| | |
|---|---|
| Tables | ix |
| Acknowledgments | xi |
| Prologue: Misconceptions about Civil Rights Activists | xix |
| 1. The Civil Rights Movement: The River of Baptism | 1 |
| 2. Tracking the Civil Rights Activists: How the Research Was Done | 29 |
| 3. The Black Protest Generation in the 1970s and 1980s | 51 |
| 4. The Divergent Politics of the White Generation | 85 |
| 5. African American and White Activists Twenty-Five Years Later | 119 |
| 6. Conclusions: Taking Stock | 133 |
| Epilogue: Current Dilemmas and Future Prospects | 145 |
| Appendix | 151 |
| Notes | 163 |

References 179

Index 191

# TABLES

| | | |
|---|---|---|
| 3.1. | African American Attitudes in 1973 | 59 |
| 3.2. | African American Attitudes in 1988 | 73 |
| 3.3. | African American Political Participation in 1988 | 80 |
| 4.1. | White Political Participation in 1986 | 110 |
| A.1. | Regression Analysis of African American Separatism and Nationalism in 1973 | 152 |
| A.2. | Regression Analysis of African American Political Attitudes in 1973 | 153 |
| A.3. | Regression Analysis of African American Political Behavior in 1973 | 154 |
| A.4. | Regression Analysis of African American Political Behavior in 1988 | 155 |
| A.5. | Regression Analysis of White Political Attitudes in 1971 | 156 |
| A.6. | Regression Analysis of White Political Behavior in 1971 | 157 |

Tables

| | | |
|---|---|---|
| A.7. | Regression Analysis of White Political Attitudes in 1986 | 158 |
| A.8. | Regression Analysis of White Complete Political Activism in 1986 | 159 |
| A.9. | Regression Model for Citizenship | 160 |
| A.10. | Analysis of Variance by Race | 161 |
| A.11. | Regression Analysis of the Political Attitudes and Behavior for African American and White Activists | 162 |

# ACKNOWLEDGMENTS

I must acknowledge the assistance and cooperation of many people. Foremost I would like to thank the civil rights activists. In his review of books on the Kennedys and Martin Luther King, Jr., during the 1960s, Gary Wills (1988) states this period was the nation's finest hour, not because of the Kennedys, but because of King and the civil rights movement. I agree. All of us benefited from that long struggle. In one sense I am writing about my heroes. College protesters demonstrated great courage in challenging adult institutions. They began as rather ordinary young men and women who took upon themselves the challenge to change society. But African American and white students did not start the civil rights movement. As in most student movements, youths in college took their lead from small cadres of adults who mounted challenges against U.S. apartheid. Then, inspired by the Southern Christian Leadership Conference (SCLC) and the Congress of Racial Equality (CORE), college students began to make history by their direct actions. They changed themselves, the civil rights movement, and the country.

In 1956, five months after the Montgomery bus boycott was initiated, two Florida A&M University (FAMU) students—Wilhelmina Jakes and Carrie Patterson—started the second major bus boycott in Tallahassee, Florida. They were inspired by Martin Luther King, Jr.'s, challenge to antidemocratic, segregated institutions. Jakes and Patterson initiated a movement that witnessed eight years of sustained protest. In 1960, two sisters, Patricia and Priscilla Stephens, organized the first interracial CORE chapter in the Deep South, literally marching into the 1960s. The most intense period was between 1960 and 1963, with boycotts, picketing, mass marches, and mass arrests. The four courageous young women pioneered actions that mobilized thousands of black college students. They also inspired as many as two hundred white students who attended Florida State University (FSU) to join the civil rights struggle.

Tallahassee, Florida, is recognized as one of the leading centers of the black student movement (Killian 1984; Matthews and Prothro 1966; Morris 1984). Smith (1989) states that FAMU students led the first mass civil rights demonstration on an American college campus and the first student-initiated bus boycott. During the CORE-sponsored sit-ins in 1960, the protesters were the first students in the country to test being served at lunch counters and the first to accept a jail sentence rather than pay fines and go free (Rabby 1984). Their defiance generated national attention.

Threatened, beaten, jailed, and occasionally suspended or expelled from the universities, students fought for social justice. Vigilantes burned a cross in the front yard of Wilhelmina Jakes and Carrie Patterson. The black community had to provide protection. Suffering abhorrent conditions in jail, Patricia Stephens led CORE activists to defy the jailers and sing freedom songs. White prisoners, at the instigation of their jailers, attacked Jeff Poland, one of the white activists. He was severely beaten and suffered broken bones. Another activist, Alan Breitler, publicly announced he would be the first white to integrate FAMU. The student government at FSU dismissed him from office as undersecretary of student welfare for religious affairs. Rednecks burned a cross in his yard and someone stole and partially destroyed his car. Yet, facing daunting odds, the students persisted, building a broad base of support.

In tracing the life choices and politics of the black and white activists, I received their cooperation not once, but twice. In 1971 I conducted the first wave of a ten-year longitudinal study. The white cohort from this period was sent questionnaires. After acquiring a small grant from the Office of Education at HEW, I completed a similar study of African Americans in 1973. Twenty-five years after the student protest, both groups cooperated again. In 1986 a second white survey was completed and in 1988 a similar survey was completed for blacks.

I would also like to thank those white and black students who took no direct part in the civil rights protests. In designing the study, I realized the necessity of having baseline or control groups. The distinctiveness of the careers and politics of former activists could only be determined by comparing them with their nonactivist counterparts.

Because my primary interest is the long-term political consequences of student activism, I selected two control groups for each sample of black and white activists. Student government leaders who took no active part in the civil rights struggle and random samples of black and white students who were active in neither protests nor student politics were included in the survey. They, too, were very cooperative. Although occasionally grumbling about too many political questions, they shared their career developments and adult politics. The careers of these nonactivists were rich and varied, ranging from successful businessman to highly placed public official, to jail supervisor. Their careers and politics over their life cycles reflect the more normal trajectories of 1960s college graduates.

I owe a different kind of gratitude to Julian Samora. He affected my biographical involvement in race relations and social movements. When he asked me to work on his research project, I was propelled into the cauldron of the civil rights movement and the federal government's response. Samora received a grant from the U.S. Commission on Civil Rights, and I went to work for the commission in Washington, D.C., to gather the necessary information. The Eisenhower administration created the commission as part of the first civil rights legislation since Reconstruction. Its charge was gathering facts and making recommendations in five areas: justice, housing, education, employment, and voting. It is difficult to imagine a more exciting place to work in 1962–63. Although chronically understaffed and weak at data gathering, the commission was a nerve center of civil rights policy-making. The civil rights movement forced the federal government to take action, and the commission was in the center of the federal response.

Intense and vivid memories remain from that experience. In the summer of 1962 I shared an apartment with two black roommates. One was a co-worker at the commission, and the other was a medical student studying with a noted pathologist at Howard University. They forced me to confront the causes and residues of my own racism. In 1963, I chose to live in a poor, black neighborhood. It was a vibrant, religious, violent, apolitical community. My neighbors lived a day-to-day existence, whereas I could afford to buy two weeks of groceries. On August 27, 1963, the day of the massive civil rights march on Washington, the daily rhythms of life proceeded as usual, except for heavy patrolling by uniformed and plainclothes police. No attempt was made to mobilize poor African Americans for the march, but the police and army, with helicopter rotors running at a nearby military fort, stood by to stop anticipated forms of violent protest.

The commission assignment of which I am most proud was an internal memo written on African American social and economic progress in the United States. It started on the shaky premise of significant progress. Once I made black and white comparisons using 1940, 1950, and 1960 census data and other social indicators, I discovered I had committed the same mental error as most white Americans: I had forgotten the enormous gains of the white population during the post–World War II era. In effect, African Americans were the last group on the escalator. Over time living standards did improve, but the relative gaps between white Americans and African Americans remained nearly constant. Subsequently I received word that the memo was used by congressional staff developing civil rights legislation and Chief Justice Earl Warren in his preparation for a State Department–sponsored visit to Africa.

During the summer of 1963, I played a minor role in the events Robert Penn Warren (1965) describes in *Who Speaks for the Negro?* Warren begins with efforts by CORE to get black ministers to lead a voter registration drive in Plaquemine and West Feliciana parishes in Louisiana. I was at the end of desperate phone calls from CORE organizers. Two black ministers had tried to register to vote but had disappeared while in police custody. Although the commission did not have police powers, it had a good working relationship with the Justice Department. We pressured Justice to get federal marshals into the area to protect the black ministers. No one was hurt. Unfortunately, there were far too many times when the Justice Department did not provide protection for civil rights workers during this period of challenge and turmoil.

I became extremely critical of the Kennedy administration and the U.S. Senate. During the spring of 1963, the general counsel of the Civil Rights Commission recommended to President Kennedy that federal funds to state and private groups be cut if they continued to discriminate against minorities. A brilliant black attorney, the general counsel had all the potential for a promising judicial career. Although later implemented, this idea was initially too radical for the Kennedys. Up to that point the slow progress in opening opportunities for minorities was limited to programs directly under federal control. Once the initial recommendation leaked to the press, the Kennedy administration could not take the heat and fired the general counsel.

During the summer of 1963 the commission worked on drafting what became the 1964 Civil Rights Act. Events in the South and the planning for the march on Washington forced the president's hand, but the 1963 civil rights bill was killed by southern senators, who mounted a successful filibuster until the bill was withdrawn. The Senate also made sure that the commission's budget was halved. Forced to leave, many part-time and full-time employees, including myself, sought other opportunities. Even with the massive march on Washington in 1963, there was insufficient political momentum to pass a major piece of civil rights legislation. It took continued protest, highly publicized injustices, and the assassination of President Kennedy to generate the momentum needed to pass the 1964 Civil Rights Act. This experience convinced me that without the extensive pressure from the civil rights movement, elite reform from above would have been an insufficient force to secure basic rights and freedoms.

I am also indebted to Tallahassee's black ministers. They, along with a few other black community leaders, formed the Inter-Civic Council (ICC), which was modeled after King's Montgomery Improvement Association. Although black and white students initiated the battles against segregation, the ICC mobilized the local black community resources to sustain the protest. Ministers like Dr. James N. Hudson, the Reverend C. K. Steel, the Reverend K. S. Dupont, and the Reverend J. Metz Rollins, as well as businessmen like Dan B. Speed and G. W. Conoly, were also targeted for physical threats, harassment, and arrests. The Reverend Dr. Hudson was a small man missing one arm, but he was a giant in the local struggle. Years later I observed him in an oncology clinic waiting room. In a room filled with nervous patients he was calmly reading scripture.

Arriving in Tallahassee in 1965, I had the opportunity to work with these leaders as an active member of the Tallahassee Human Relations Committee. This interracial organization forced the city to reopen public facilities on an integrated basis. C. K. Steele became a leading figure during the sustained protest period. Today, in the center of Tallahassee, there is a monument dedicated to his memory. Many are proud to have marched behind his leadership.

After 1970 the country witnessed the rapid demobilization of student protest (Orcutt and Fendrich 1980). The question of the long-range consequences of political insurgency was beginning to surface. I knew that to assess accurately the consequences of student activism I had to go back into recent history. Significant effects or consequences could not be measured until sufficient time had elapsed. It takes years to complete educations and establish careers. Therefore, I decided to study the earliest waves of black and white civil rights activists who had protested during the early 1960s. Fortunately, Tallahassee provided accessible information.

I owe particular gratitude to Dean Charles U. Smith at FAMU. Dean Smith and I had collaborated on an earlier study of black leadership, and he helped to gather the African American data in 1973 and 1988. His contributions included securing access to FAMU alumni records, cosigning a cover letter encouraging alumni to cooperate in the study, providing funds for postage, and having the questionnaires returned to his office. A noted authority on the civil rights movement, Smith published *The Civil Rights Movement in Florida and the United States* (1989).

I am also indebted to Alison Tarleau and Ron Simmons, who, as research assistants, worked on the ten-year follow-up study and to Robert Turner and Kenneth Lovoy, who assisted in the twenty-five-year follow-up. The alumni offices of both FAMU and FSU were helpful in tracking down former students. FSU provided two small grants to pay for part of the research costs. This research was also supported in part by a National Institute of Mental Health Special Fellowship grant. A sabbatical during 1990 provided the opportunity to complete the research.

A number of people inspired the twenty-five-year, second-wave follow-up studies. Recognition of the historical significance of the movement and its effect on U.S. politics was growing. Excellent television documentaries, including, "Eyes on the Prize, I and II" by Henry Hampton and major books by Branch (1988) and Garrow (1986), demanded attention. Glenda Rabby's (1984) well-researched and well-written historical dissertation on the Tallahassee civil rights movement served as a primary source of inspiration. Reading it reinforced my desire to know what activists were doing in the 1980s. I dusted off the old files and started to track down subjects. I am also indebted to a number of activists who read the manuscript in draft form, suggesting clarifications and providing comments. Their comments enriched the text by providing personal examples of some of the major findings.

The book developed with more than a little help from my friends. Colleagues Bruce Bellingham, Leslie Inniss, and Jill Quadagno gave the early drafts a careful reading and provided helpful suggestions. The manuscript also benefited from the critical reading of early drafts by Dick Braungart, Joseph DeMartini, James Geschwender, Lewis Killian, Doug McAdam, Aldon Morris, Jack Whalen, Tunga Lergo, Larry Christiansen and Kim Kryter. Their special expertise, criticisms and suggestions kept me on track. Delores J. Bryant provided the initial editorial assistance and Joan Morris provided photographs from the Florida State Museum Archives.

My last thanks are more personal. I owe a deep sense of gratitude to my family. When they were younger I dragged my four children, Matt, Kerrie, Chris, and Alise, to marches, protests, and meetings. When they were grown, they strongly encouraged me to complete the book. Special credit goes to my wife, Mary Bryant. In addition to being a teacher, union activist, and political leader in the community, she spent long hours as the sounding board for many of the ideas. She also patiently endured the unusual time schedules and periods of single-mindedness spent at the word processor.

## PROLOGUE: MISCONCEPTIONS ABOUT CIVIL RIGHTS ACTIVISTS

Americans' views of the 1960s protest movements are today still as unsettled as their views of the Vietnam War. The popular media portrait of the sixties frequently denigrates the participants and trivializes the social movements demanding change (Bell 1976; Gitlin 1987; McAdam 1989a). Some popular appraisals of ex-activists characterize them as maturing middle-class yuppies who long ago abandoned the foolish ways of youth and have settled down as responsible Americans. Countless news stories and articles have told us what happened to those 1960s activists. We are told they are either like Yippie Jerry Rubin, now a stockbroker, or like former Black Panther Eldridge Cleaver, now a born-again Christian.[1] We have television sitcoms like "Family Ties" in which ex-activists raise their conservative son. The movie *The Big Chill* serves as the metaphor of conversion to normalcy. Youthful idealism wanes as adults face the responsibilities of establishing careers and supporting families. Although there may be fond memories of those crazy college days, ex-activists, regardless of the degree and type of their political participation, become just like everyone else as adults. Thus, ex-activists as adults are employed in the same type of occupations and belong to the same type of voluntary organizations as other college graduates. They maintain moderate political sentiments and behavior and live in the suburbs with two children. So we are told.

Our confusing interpretation of the 1960s is rooted in inadequate conceptual frameworks and tendencies to overgeneralize. There are three sources of confusion. One problem is failing to distinguish the student political movement from the counterculture movement. The struggle for political change began earlier and with fewer advocates than the counterculture movement. More importantly, each movement embodied distinguishable values, expectations, and experiences. Students in the political movement had deep personal commitments to social responsibility, and they worked to change adult institutions. The political movement demanded active involvement in public events and an effort to stay aware of the news and to deepen personal understanding of the forces of change. Although both movements shared a concern with personal integrity and conflicts with adult institutions, the counterculture movement was more expressive. It was disgusted with politics, tedious talk, and analysis of what needed to be done. It advocated turning on and dropping out rather than commitment to collective goals. The prime values of the counterculture were liberty and autonomy rather than equality and democracy (Whalen and Flacks 1989). Thus, when the leading social critic Daniel Bell (1976) leveled his broadside against the student generation of the 1960s, his aim was at the counterculture's excessive hedonism and expressiveness. He ignored the political activists' generation.

A second source of confusion over the 1960s concerns the nature of the participants, the timing of the movement's rise, and the issues being protested. The Berkeley "Free Speech" movement in 1964 is most often cited as the beginning of student protest. The uprising at Berkeley, which focused on university reform, preceded the mass mobilization of students opposed to the Vietnam War. But, the fact that black students already had been activists for eight years when Mario Savio mobilized students at Berkeley is often overlooked (Smith 1989). Despite the numbers of black students involved, social scientists have painted a picture of student activism that is almost totally white (Gurin and Epps 1975). Existing studies tend to be biased toward white students attending elite universities. If we generalize from the information gained from a limited sample of white students, we cannot hope to understand the full range of concerns of young people, both black and white, who felt compelled to try to change social institutions (Gurin and Epps 1975).

The absence of longitudinal research on black activists is both surprising and regrettable. Black Americans were the first to mount significant challenging movements in the post–World War II era. Not only was the civil rights movement the first major challenge to the postwar consensus, but it also had a profound effect on later waves of social movements both at home and abroad. At home, the civil rights movement had a direct impact on its own cadre of participants. It created a new African American leader and citizen (Killian and Smith 1960). The movement also laid the groundwork for a nationwide network of activists in a variety of civil rights and progressive organizations. That network forced the federal government to pass and implement a number of crucial laws guaranteeing equal opportunity for racial and ethnic minorities and women. There was the Civil Rights Act of 1964, the Voting Rights Act of 1965, and the Open Housing Act of 1968, as well as numerous executive orders and supplemental legislation. In addition, the civil rights movement was a catalyst for the antiwar, student rights, and women's movements (McAdam 1988). A movement that started in Montgomery, Alabama, in 1955 is still having dramatic effects. When the citizens of Czechoslovakia overthrew their Communist leaders in the spring of 1990, they sang their version of "We Shall Overcome" (Ash 1990). Martin Luther King, Jr.'s, birthday is celebrated in 144 countries.

A third source of confusion about the student politics of the 1960s concerns the hostility and threats elicited by students' demands for change. Protesters often heard the catcalls, "Get a job," "Grow up," and "Go back where you came from" from angry and frightened bystanders. Later we will see that white authorities considered civil rights activists, who were protesting for basic human rights, Communists or Communist dupes. President Richard Nixon's first reaction to the killings at Kent State was to call the students "bums." In order to discredit the activists, popular psychological theories of mindless, irrational contagion or the convergence of like-minded misfits were resurrected from outdated theories.[2] Focusing on worldwide student movements, Feuer (1969) provided a preposterous theory of Oedipal conflict. Students protested, he claimed, because they hated their fathers. This line of "research" was quickly discredited by the empirical research on activists (Flacks 1971; Keniston 1968). Yet the idea that activists are misfits remains popular. A young man interviewed on National Public Radio in 1990 was questioned about sending troops to fight in the Persian Gulf. He stated that current students are more conservative: "We don't run around naked protesting the war like during the 1960s." Such an event never occurred, yet his comments are a typical example of the prevailing distortion and confusion about the 1960s.

Distorted representations of the 1960s permeate the literature. In their book *Destructive Generation* (1989), Collier and Horowitz provide a selective and distorted picture of the 1960s. They focus on a few solitary events and individual leftists in the Berkeley area after 1968.

They conclude that the entire generation of college activists, exceeding three million students (Sale 1973), was a destructive force: destructive in that students hated everything America stood for. Moreover, this generation was totalitarian. In their thoughts and actions protesters set out to destroy democratic institutions and procedures. Collier and Horowitz are former leftists who became conservatives. Not only do they warn their readers about destructive youth caught up in their Oedipal conflicts, but they also go on to state there is a resurgence of the 1960s left in the contemporary United States. According to Collier and Horowitz, former activists want to continue their attack on America by destroying democracy. This view is clearly at odds with the view of scholars who studied the protest while activism was occurring. In their study of black college students in the 1960s, Matthews and Prothro (1966:446) made the following prediction:

> The current generation of Negro college students appears to offer prime candidates for political leadership. With but few exceptions, they already possess the political interest, record of political activity, and identification with other Negroes that adult leadership seems to require. And, if research on the political consequences of aging is a reliable guide, we should expect all these attributes to increase in strength and frequency as the students grow into adult roles.

This book focuses on the long-range consequences of intense, youthful, political experience. What happened to civil rights protesters? What kind of citizenship do they practice? How did their careers develop as they faced a variety of life choices? Our view is hampered because the media focus on a few, holding them to a high standard, and ignore the many.

Jesse Jackson, Andrew Young, and Marion Barry are three highly visible members of the African American activist generation. The relentless eye of the media holds them up to ideal standards and frequently finds them wanting. Jesse Jackson must tiptoe through a political mine field while the slips or political misjudgments of other politicians are forgiven by the press. Andrew Young, one of the lieutenants in Martin Luther King, Jr.'s, army, was ambassador to the United Nations, a U.S. congressman from Georgia, and mayor of Atlanta. Yet he is likely to be remembered as a failed candidate for governor of Georgia. Marion Barry, too, was a highly visible political figure. As a veteran of the civil rights movement, he moved to

Washington, D.C. He was elected to the school board in 1971, became chair of the City Council in 1975, and became mayor in 1978. While still mayor in 1990, the FBI entrapped him in a sting operation, charging him with a series of felonies and misdemeanors. The press portrayed him as a civil rights leader gone bad. Yet an interracial jury could not ignore the overzealous Justice Department entrapment and found Barry only guilty of a minor charge of drug use. Barry's case represents just one in a documented pattern of harassment of black public officials (Sawyer 1987).

Seldom do we read about a leading civil rights activist like U.S. Representative John Lewis, who came from the humblest of backgrounds. As a youth he was so isolated in a rural area in Alabama that he never saw a white person. As a rawboned, stammering teenager, he was inspired by Martin Luther King, Jr., and wanted to join the movement. Before winning a seat in the U.S. Congress, he was beaten and jailed many times on the road to freedom (Branch 1988). Lesser-known former black and white activists hold public office, from former U.S. congresswoman Elizabeth Holtzman to local officials. There are also those who direct important advocacy groups: Marian Wright Edelman at the Children's Defense Fund or Mary King, a white Student Nonviolent Coordinating Committee (SNCC) organizer, who became a highly placed federal official during the Carter administration. Our understanding of the important historical repercussions of the 1960s is unfortunately hampered by the media focus on a few, selectively chosen individuals. The real significance of the 1960s lies not in the lives of media stars but in the lives of the rank-and-file activists.

Looking ahead, I can say the 1960s activists turned out to be ideal American citizens. The central finding is that 1960s activists are fully exercising their citizenship rights and continue to be more active than other members of their generation. To use Milbrath and Goel's (1977) terms, ex-activists have become "complete activists," or political "gladiators," as adults. The details and significance of the long-range effects of the movement will be presented later. This book is about people like Willie Adams, who was president of the Florida A&M University student body and led a mass protest march. Met with armed resistance, he shouted to his fellow marchers, "If they kill me, march over my dead body." His action may not have the unforgettable dramatic impact of one Chinese man stopping a column of tanks in Beijing, but it was a dangerous and uncertain challenge to entrenched, powerful authorities. Willie Adams is now a successful physician. The ex-student activists are the kind of people you would want to have as friends and neighbors. They would be excellent contributors to your local and national organizations. Should they choose to run for office, they would be worthy of support. Finally, if you chose to march on city hall, almost the only people over forty joining the protest would be the activist cohort of the 1960s.

# 1

## THE CIVIL RIGHTS MOVEMENT: THE RIVER OF BAPTISM

*The greatness of America is the right to protest for right.*
—Martin Luther King, Jr., April 3, 1968,
the day before he was assassinated.

*I think that people aren't fully free until they're in a struggle for justice. And that means for everyone. It's a struggle of such importance that they are willing, if necessary, to die for it. I think that's what you have to do before you're really free, then you've got something to live for. You don't want to die, because you've got so much you want to do. This struggle is so important that it gives a meaning to life. Now that sounds like a contradiction, but I encourage people to push limits, to try to take that step, because that's when they are really free. I saw this happen during the time of the sit-ins and the formation of the Student Non-violent (sic) Coordinating Committee.*
—Myles Horton, 1989

*We've got to fill the jails in order to win our equal rights.*
—activist Patricia Stephens

*To think how little it required to be an activist in those days and what work it is today. Writing a column, dining with a Negro, carrying a sign in front of a rotten theater, going to A&M occasionally, even eating regularly in the old Soda Shoppe. No National Guard, just rednecks—how easy it seems—but I'll never forget the fear I experienced.*
—white activist 1971

*While a student at Florida A&M University during the 1960s, I experienced first hand the humiliation, frustration, anxiety and the hurt of being on the other side of bigotry, prejudice and discrimination. As one of African descent, I was not allowed to eat in any establishments in town; try on clothing in stores; or use a public facility. I could not enter the front door of a doctor's, dentist's or optometrist's office, nor could I sit in a city park; go to a movie theater or get a room at a hotel or motel... At the time, the only thing I enjoyed about Tallahassee was Florida A&M University and leaving Tallahassee.*
—black activist Bernard Hendricks, 1990.

What is this talk of protest, dying for justice, filling of jails, intense fear, frustration, and anxiety? A movement that began idealistically ran smack into a wall of prejudice and strong-willed action to resist change. Killings, beatings, jailings, terrorism, and state-sponsored repression or indifference were standard responses to citizens demanding equal treatment. The civil rights movement was a hard, tough fight against almost overwhelming odds. In thinking and reading about the 1960s, it is easy to forget that violent, confusing, and rapidly changing environment. The period was historically discontinuous. The protest era broke from the past and does not continue into the present. Confusing images abound because the intense struggle was so different from everyday life and politics. When our recent history gets retold, it tends to be smoothed out, sanitized, and structured in an orderly fashion.

On February 1, 1960, four black freshmen at North Carolina A&T—David Richmond, Franklin McCain, Joseph McNeil, and Ezell Blair—sat down at the lunch counter in a Greensboro F. W. Woolworth store and refused to leave until they were served. Without prompting from any existing civil rights organizations or adult black leadership, they launched a new phase of a student-led struggle for freedom.[1] Within a year and a half student sit-ins had spread to over twenty states and one hundred cities. At least 70,000 black and white students actively engaged in demonstrations and rallies. More than 3,600 people were arrested. At least 141 students and 58 faculty were dismissed. Hundreds of other students withdrew from universities to protest the expulsions (Matthews and Prothro 1966; Orum 1973).[2] The sit-ins were more than the typical youthful enthusiasm on college campuses during that period. One activist observed that businessmen may think sit-ins are like panty raids, but they haven't had their sociologists in the field recently (Moore 1960). Demonstrations could be mobilized quickly in different cities. Black students realized that disruptive politics could change patterns of southern segregation faster than a reliance on legal approaches. In many locations students became impatient with their elders and formed their own separate organizations to push militantly for change.[3]

Three major surveys provide insights about the protests. The level of protest participation was very high. Matthews and Prothro (1966) report that 39 percent of black students were taking part in the protest movement by 1962. Orum (1973) reports that 69 percent participated in protest. Orum's figure is higher because the survey was conducted during a period of rapid growth in the movement and his sample consisted of seniors who had four years to become involved in campus-based protests. Gurin and Epps (1975) found that during the 1960s about 20 percent of white students participated in various forms of student protest or political action; however, 70 percent of black college students participated. In the local movement center of Tallahassee 63 percent of Florida A&M University (FAMU) students participated in the protest movement during the 1960-63 period.

To fully understand how these dramatic events created an activists' generation and changed the larger society, it is necessary to step back in history. Student activists were baptized into adult politics by the protest movement. One out of six demonstrators was arrested; one out of twenty was thrown in jail; one out of ten was beaten, clubbed, gassed, pushed, spat upon, or harassed in other ways. Only 11 percent said that they experienced no negative effects from having protested (Matthews and Prothro 1966). The movement shaped their orientation and participation in politics. As Karl Mannheim ([1928] 1972:111) stated, "I only really possess those 'memories' which I have created directly for myself, only that 'knowledge' I have personally gained in real situations. This is the only sort of knowledge which really sticks and it alone has real binding power." The events covered in this chapter were the real political education for activists. Rather than having a vicarious, academic exposure, activists gained personal knowledge and learned about democracy from the streets, mass meetings, and jails.

In organizing this book I have structured it chronologically into three time periods: the protest era of the early 1960s, the activists ten years later in the early 1970s, and the activists twenty-five years later in the mid-1980s. Throughout I have tried to remain faithful to C. Wright Mills's (1959) dictum that all our lives represent the "intersection of biography and history." This is particularly important for members of social movements, whose political education is often intense and disjunctive. As Piven and Cloward (1979:xx) in their book *Poor People's Movements* state, "Once protest is acknowledged as a form of political struggle the chief question to be examined must inevitably be the relationship between what the protesters do, the context in which they do it, and the varying responses of the state."

During the period between 1955 and 1960 that led up to student protests, there were at least 487 movement actions.[4] Local black churches, colleges, and NAACP chapters played significant roles. Martin Luther King, Jr., and the Southern Christian Leadership Conference (SCLC) were involved in only 26 percent of these actions, suggesting an ever-widening base for the protest movement (McAdam 1982). Students, learning from their elders, were the last of the major organized groups in the African American community to initiate widespread insurgent activity.

In his analysis Morris (1984) shows that the four freshmen who sat-in in Greensboro had important organizational links to the adult protest movement. They knew about King's movement in Montgomery. They were familiar with previous sit-in demonstrations that occurred in Durham between 1957 and 1960. They belonged to the Youth Division of the NAACP, which was headed by Floyd McKissick. McKissick claims he knew all four men and that they studied the new tactics and strategies of the movement (Morris 1984). When students did become a major political force in 1960, they demonstrated the use of innovative tactics and the ability to use local resources to build strong organizations.

## BACKGROUND CHARACTERISTICS

Surprisingly, African American family background characteristics and individual orientations and psychological traits are not significantly different for protesters than for nonprotesters. Gurin and Epps (1975) found that black students who took part in the campus protest are not distinguished from nonparticipants by different demographic and family influences. Rather, the key influences on student activism tend to be campus based. The location of the university, the major issues on campus, the intellectual exposure to critical analysis, and campus organizations and support groups have stronger effects on student activism than other factors. Protest was likely to occur and participation was the highest in those environments where local movement centers provided structured opportunities to protest (Gurin and Epps 1975; Haines 1988; Morris 1984; Orum 1973).

From the third day of the sit-ins in Greensboro there was token white participation. Black and white civil rights protesters emerged from entirely different circumstances. The majority of black college students came from poor, working-class backgrounds, and most were the first generation to attend college. This largest segment of the black population—the working class—is frequently overlooked in research. The findings from research presented here support Gurin and Epps's (1975) study and Zinn's (1964) observations, which show that activists were disproportionately drawn from the "striving working class." FAMU students came from extremely modest families who had aspirations for upward mobility for their children. Black working-class families put an enormous value on education and made extraordinary sacrifices to support their children's college education.[5] In most families both parents of FAMU students worked. It was not unusual to find the father as a day laborer and the mother as a school cafeteria worker, or to have the father a career enlisted man in the military and the mother working in a dry cleaners. There was also a pattern of serving the rich, with the father working as a chauffeur or gardener and the mother as a maid. It was extremely rare to find both parents employed in "white-collar" occupations. Among the FAMU protesters, 69 percent had fathers with fewer than four years of high school education; 56 percent of nonparticipants had fathers with under four years of high school. Of those arrested, 71 percent had blue-collar fathers. Among the nonactivists, 79 percent had fathers in blue-collar occupations.[6] The activists did not come from priviledged, middle-class backgrounds. In 1964 the Geschwenders (1973) studied the relationship between measures of relative deprivation and protest participation among sociology students attending FAMU, and they also found that the students were primarily from working-class backgrounds. The middle-class students were not more likely to participate in protest activities than working-class students. In contrast, active white students came from highly educated, professional, higher-income families (Flacks 1971; Keniston 1968). Their mothers were generally employed in professional occupations and the families tended to be urban and somewhat secular in outlook.

The supportive environment for protesting was also much different for blacks and for whites. Only 3 percent of the southern black adult population disapproved of the sit-ins, and black college students protested within the context of a local black movement center. Not only did they have strong community support, but they also had firm backing from fellow students and many faculty within black universities. In contrast, only 1 percent of southern whites approved of the sit-ins, and as rare as they were, only 18 percent of southern white liberals approved of them (Matthews and Prothro 1966). In an interview one of the white activists reported leading a dual life: one as a member of a traditional southern family and another as a college demonstrator opposed to segregation.

Another major difference between black and white protesters during the early 1960s was the degree of integration into the mainstream of campus life. Black activists belonged to more campus organizations, held more offices, and participated more often in student government and policy groups on campus. In contrast, white civil rights activists were less integrated into the campus mainstream and less in control of student government. During the height of the civil rights struggle in Tallahassee, white student government leaders at Florida State University (FSU) did not necessarily approve of segregation practices, but they strongly disapproved of student demonstration tactics.

Some southern white civil rights activists had deep religious convictions that contradicted segregation; others were students who had "avant-garde" interests. They were committed to an existentialist philosophy that demanded acting and doing regardless of the likelihood of success. These beliefs were part of the intellectual culture on college campuses in the early 1960s (Gitlin 1987). Sandra Cason participated in an Austin, Texas, sit-in when she attended the University of Texas and lived in the Christian Faith and Life Community house. She captured the sense of white commitment when she addressed a National Student Association (NSA) convention:

> I cannot say to a person who suffers injustice, "Wait." Perhaps you can. I can't. And having decided that I cannot urge caution, I must stand with him. If I had known that not a single lunch counter would open as a result of my action, I could not have done differently than I did. If I had known violence would result, I could not have done differently than I did. I am thankful for the sit-ins if for no other reason than that they provided me with an opportunity for making a slogan into a reality, by making a decision into an action. It seems to me that this is what life is all about. While I would hope that the NSA congress will pass a strong sit-in resolution, I am more concerned that all of us, negro and white, realize the possibility of becoming less inhuman humans through commitment and action, with all their frightening complexities.
>
> When Thoreau was jailed for refusing to pay taxes to a government which supported slavery, Emerson went to visit him. "Henry David," said Emerson, "what are you doing in there?" Thoreau looked at him and replied, "Ralph Waldo, What are you doing out there?" (Hayden 1988: 41-42).

Cason's statement suggests that the early white southern activists were different from most students. They had deep moral and political commitments that they were willing to put into action. Although not social isolates or marginals, white civil rights activists could be found in progressive, politically oriented student groups, and in avant-garde literary or intellectually oriented groups (White 1964). On a more personal level, one of the white activists claims that white males all dated black women during the protest (interview). Demerath, Marwell, and Aiken (1971) found that early white civil rights activists were motivated by a progressive political ideology and humanistic values. They were not the mainstream, social conformist type of student, nor were they likely to control or be leaders in student government during the early 1960s.

White activists were distinct from both the black activists' generation and the other white students who did not support or participate in the civil rights struggle. There was only a smattering of thin support for white civil rights activists in the white community. A few liberal professors in the social sciences and liberal arts offered encouragement, guidance, and money for bail bonds. In an interview, one former activist commented that students participated if their major professors approved of the movement and avoided direct involvement otherwise. One church serving the campus ministry encouraged limited white involvement in the Tallahassee civil rights struggle. The student newspaper at FSU was staffed with moderately progressive reporters and writers whose views were reflected in editorials and news stories. There was also a small group of avant-garde students affected by the emerging beat generation and the questioning of social conventions. By and large, however, the white community strongly opposed the militant tactics of the protest movement.

In contrast, black students had almost universal support from the black community. Their professors, student government, local ministers, civil rights organizations, and parents were proud of the students' challenges to segregation. One exception to family support was the response to a Congress of Racial Equality (CORE) demonstrator who sat-in and was arrested. In an interview he explained that he came from an orphaned family of six children. His oldest brother sent money home while serving in the Army. His oldest sister, who kept the family together, told him when he was arrested, "The next time you want to sit-in, you can sit in our living room."

Tallahassee's white activists shared the characteristics of the Demerath, Marwell, and Aiken (1971), Flacks (1970), and McAdam (1989a) studies. Although the white activists' parents were no more affluent than the nonactivists' parents, they were somewhat better educated. According to the activists, their parents were also more active in politics, with a higher rate of both voter participation and activity in political organizations than the parents of nonactivists. As a group the white civil rights activists were more secular, but among the activists there was a contingent motivated by strong religious convictions. Few activists in the South were Jewish.

College orientation and experiences were significantly different for white activists and nonactivists. For the white activists the first basic goal in college was to change rather than fit into the system. They also wanted to delve into intellectual pursuits and to develop the necessary personal and social skills to function as adults. Nonactivists overwhelmingly (66 percent) chose preparing for an occupation as their first goal. The activists were much more likely than the nonactivists to major in the social sciences (57 percent versus 24 percent) and the arts and sciences (32 percent versus 21 percent). In their academic environment, they were more likely to discuss controversies over basic values, learn about social problems, and see in the outside world the relevance of what they learned in the classroom. Their average age of twenty-three was the same as that of the white volunteers who went to Mississippi in 1964 (McAdam 1989a), but they were somewhat younger than the nonactivists.[7]

## TALLAHASSEE: A LOCAL MOVEMENT CENTER

Detailed analysis of Tallahassee as a local social movement center provides the historical context for the baptism into politics. Over a period of eight years there were significant bus and economic boycotts, sit-ins, picketing, voter registration drives, and mass mobilization, all of which characterize a protest era. In this section the major events will be described and the relative success of the strategies and the protest in a hostile political environment will be examined.

On May 27, 1956, five months after the Montgomery bus boycott, the South's second major bus boycott was launched in Tallahassee. Students initially spearheaded the insurgency. Wilhelmina Jakes, an elementary education major at FAMU, and her roommate Carrie Patterson, a FAMU English major, boarded a crowded bus and sat down in the front row. The driver told them they could not sit there. Having ridden on desegregated buses in South Florida, Ms. Jakes asked, "Why?" Getting no answer, she said, "If I can't sit where I want to, then I'd like to have my money back, please" (Morris 1990). The driver refused to return the money, drove to a gas station, and called the police. The police arrested the young women. After teaching school for thirty-three years, Ms. Jakes, now Mrs. Street, returned to Tallahassee to celebrate Martin Luther King, Jr's, birthday. She described the event to a reporter:

"About this time I started to get real upset because of how they were treating us. Here they were treating us like criminals for paying to ride on a public city bus, I didn't know who they thought they were, I wasn't going to let them insult me. They were treating us like we weren't human beings and it really got to me." At the station, they were charged with inciting a riot. She was incensed. "I was astounded that they would say such a thing. We hadn't done a thing wrong. My guess is that they thought we were trying to make a statement here because of what was happening in Montgomery." (Morris 1990)[8]

Two important events occurred the next day. A cross burned in the yard of the two arrested students and FAMU students held a mass meeting led by Broadus Hartley, president of the Student Government Association. The students decided to boycott all buses and encourage all other blacks using buses to find other means of transportation. The chaplain at FAMU, the Reverend James Hudson, recalled, "Students were there in full numbers, it was a full auditorium, as many faculty as could get in—many of us were there. Well, the students decided that they would protest the action of the bus company and the police officers, and that they would withdraw student patronage of the bus company and that they would ask the community to join them in withdrawing patronage or boycott the bus company" (Killian 1984:773). C. K. Steele, a black minister who rose to prominence as a new black leader, stated in a 1978 interview, "Without the students, there would have been no protest, there would have been no movement. They are the militants. They are the soldiers" (Killian 1984:779).

Tallahassee had the local resources of black students and faculty at FAMU, an NAACP chapter, and a black ministerial alliance. The alliance took over the boycott almost immediately. One of the newest ministers in town, J. Metz Rollins, headed the first committee to talk to bus company officials. The ministers' leadership was crucial because as a group they were not as vulnerable as others to economic and political pressures and reprisals (Neyland 1989). The Reverend C. K. Steele was a key organizer and president of the local NAACP chapter. He was a relative newcomer to Tallahassee, having moved to the city just three years prior to the boycott. Martin Luther King, Jr., was his good friend, and later Steele became the first vice president of the SCLC.

Once the boycott was initiated, Steele started the Inter-Civic Council (ICC), modeled after the Montgomery Improvement Association. The NAACP was initially afraid to sponsor the boycott because of anticipated negative reactions from authorities, but later it did provide legal funds and advice. Numerous mass meetings were held at the black churches to encourage blacks not to ride the buses and to organize a successful boycott. Initially, two meetings a week were planned, but the leaders found it necessary to hold two or more meetings each evening at black churches during the mobilizing phase of the boycott. Attendance at these mass meetings was the baptism into protest for many Tallahassee citizens. An effective car pool was organized by Dan Speed, a black business owner whose store was an important meeting center for black leaders. As the chair of the Transportation Committee for the ICC, Speed was the "banker" of the movement, which could not have maintained a boycott without his able assistance (Killian 1984). The ICC made the identical demands as the Montgomery bus boycott, but they were rejected by the City Commission.

The boycott was so successful that the bus company quickly lost money. Most of its riders, 60 to 70 percent, were black. During the boycott 90 percent of the black passengers did not ride the bus (Smith and Killian 1958). When they stopped riding, the company was soon in financial trouble, and a fierce struggle ensued over the next nine months. The new militant black leadership of the ICC stuck to its position. It also expanded the bus boycott into a voter registration drive and an economic boycott of stores. The boycott lasted for eighteen months.

Tallahassee, although a state capital with two universities, was a small southern town with sentiments and values more akin to rural Georgia than to Miami. A survey completed shortly before the boycott revealed that the large majority of white residents opposed desegregation on principle and 75 to 80 percent specifically opposed bus desegregation (Smith and Killian 1958). City officials had a clear mandate to take a hard line against the bus boycott (White 1964).

The boycott's effect on the black community was the opposite. White (1964) argues that the boycott generated feelings in the black community that broke the social and psychological bonds of oppression. Smith and Killian (1958) reported almost universal black community support for the boycott. Zebedee Wright, elected FAMU student body president in 1956, credited the bus boycott with increasing the racial and political awareness of students (Hemmingway 1989). Rabby (1984:92), in her extensive historical analysis of the event, which uses many firsthand interviews, reports that, "blacks in Tallahassee were on the move. Feelings of self-esteem, of pride, and of accomplishment infused the black community and filled individual blacks with a new hope and belief in their future."

The charge has been made, however, that the Tallahassee bus boycott was a failure. Segregated seating returned after the protest stopped, and by 1957 the newly created ICC moved from a direct-action, protest organization to a planning and discussion group (White 1964). This critique does not fully take into account the harsh political environment. As the Student Nonviolent Coordinating Committee was to discover in other areas of the Deep South, Tallahassee was too tough to easily crack, particularly early in the black insurgency phase of the civil rights movement. The white power structure used every means available, outside of ordering the assassination of the boycott leaders, to stop the protest.[9]

Rabby (1984) describes most, if not all, of the threatening and repressive actions. These actions are worth reviewing to establish the environment of limited political opportunities and situational factors that affected strategic decisions. Governor LeRoy Collins, like other white authorities, used the old bromide of calling the bus boycott the work of outside agitators. He suspended all bus service after a critical test of the new federal court ruling which stated that segregated seating was unconstitutional. The Florida Supreme Court had judges whose racism influenced their decisions. One judge wrote the following in his opinion: "Segregation is not a new philosophy generated by the states that practice it. It is and has always been the unvarying law of the animal kingdom...When God created man he allocated each race to his own continent according to color. Europe to the white man, Asia to the yellow man, Africa to the black man, and America to the red man" (Neyland 1989:40–41). The judge neglected to explain why the white man dominated America.

In the summer of 1956 the legislature acted by convening a special session to resist desegregation, during which a committee was established to investigate the NAACP. Public employees, particularly FAMU faculty, were threatened with firing if they participated in the protest. On February 1, 1958, the legislative investigative committee, under the leadership of its chair, Senator Charley Johns, announced that it was going to investigate the extent of "Communist activities" in Florida. It targeted the NAACP and the Florida Council on Human Relations. This cold war, anti-Communist hysteria seems unusual until it is remembered that southern whites thought that the NAACP was a Jewish, Communist conspiracy hatched in Moscow.

The attorney general of the state, Richard Ervin, ruled that Speed's car pool was illegal and insisted that the Supreme Court ruling desegregating buses in Montgomery, Alabama, only applied to that case and must be specifically tested in Florida before segregation laws in Florida could be considered invalid. The governing body of the state universities, the Board of Control, (1) issued a strong warning to students to stay out of protests or accept strict disciplinary measures, (2) maintained a policy against black and white students fraternizing, and (3) put pressure on the two university presidents to control faculty and students with the accompanying threat of a loss of future funds. The president of FAMU, George W. Gore, warned faculty, staff, and students not to participate, and the president of FSU, Doak Campbell, expelled a white Ph.D. candidate. The student's "crime" was inviting three black foreign exchange students from FAMU to attend an FSU party for international students. At a meeting with a governor's commission, FSU's president also reported that he had been given profile reports on white students sympathetic to integration. In his estimation the students had erratic and unstable personalities.

The City Commission was the locus of much of the white resistance. On June 3, 1956, the commission denied the formal demands of the ICC for desegregating the buses and ordered the police to harass the organized car pool. C. K. Steele was the first to be arrested for speeding. The commission also planted a mole inside the ICC to gather information. It had all eleven leaders of the ICC and ten drivers arrested for operating a transit system without a license. The commission worked hand in hand with the Chamber of Commerce in refusing to negotiate with the protest organization. It pressured local judges to follow its mandates and interpretations of the law. In the meantime, the city shut down the financially ailing bus service. When the bus company wanted to restart the bus service in compliance with the federal ruling on Montgomery, the city arrested the bus company manager, Charles Carter, and nine drivers! It also tried to divide the black community by pressuring more conservative black leaders to criticize the boycott leaders and to offer compromises acceptable to whites.[10]

Another source of resistance was the local newspaper, which editorialized against the protest leaders. Elaborate and sanctimonious posturing was combined with criticisms of direct action. A white Presbyterian church which had provided some money to support the development of a segregated black Presbyterian church fired the black minister, the Reverend J. Metz Rollins, because of his leading role in the boycott. Leaders of the boycott found their auto and life insurance canceled. They had difficulty securing bank loans. The White Citizens Council urged white fraternities to mount a campaign against integrationists at FSU. The hooded KKK marched in front of C. K. Steele's home, paraded in front of the courthouse protesting the bus boycott, and held mass rallies (Rivers 1989). Vigilantes burned crosses in the yards of participants. Whites threw rocks at the cars of people attending ICC meetings and shouted threats over the phone and through church windows. Shotgun blasts were fired into C. K. Steele's home and into two black-owned businesses. Death threats were common. The heavy personal costs for these adult black leaders were so great they could not sustain direct-action protest through the remainder of the 1950s.

But although the battle to desegregate the buses may not have been a clear victory, the local civil rights movement was developing out of the challenge. A group of black FAMU and white FSU students began to meet secretly in 1957, drawn together by an existential commitment to change.[11] They were impatient with their elders and wanted to undermine university segregation. The students wanted to mobilize segments of the two student bodies to have a direct confrontation with segregated institutions. They felt a strong kinship with Martin Luther King, Jr., and the protest movement in Montgomery. To make themselves less controversial and vulnerable to harsh sanctions, they developed the facade of wanting to establish and broaden communication between the races (White 1964).

In addition, black students started an integrated Social Action Committee at FAMU. After learning about the organization, the FAMU administration stopped the meetings, but the students continued to build an organization base at FSU in semisecrecy. Their political action included participation in a national letter-writing campaign in support of a federal bill outlawing segregation in the armed forces. They also participated in the 1959 protest that erupted after the rape of a black FAMU coed by four white youths. In this incident, another black coed who escaped was able to quickly identify the rapists and they were arrested. The rape galvanized the FAMU student body into protest (Rabby 1984). In order to head off a planned mass march against the police department by angry, armed students, student government leaders held an all-day rally on FAMU's campus and classes were canceled. In Smith's (1961:225) words: "Again, the student body took action. They closed the University by refusing to attend classes, held mass meetings, and soon they were on national TV demanding justice." Events leading up to the rape trial were carefully monitored. The students and the NAACP demanded justice but not the death penalty, which they opposed because four young blacks were on Florida's death row for raping white women. National and international media covered the trial. The guilty verdict for whites raping a black woman was the first in the Deep South (Rabby 1984; White 1964).

## CORE AND THE SIT-INS

During the 1959 summer two FAMU students, Patricia Stephens and her sister Priscilla, were visiting relatives in Miami. Encouraged to attend an interracial workshop sponsored by CORE, they were reluctant until promised a dinner in Miami Beach after the workshop.[12] The Stephens sisters came from a politically active family. Their stepfather was a high school civics teacher and their mother was a Palm Beach County Democratic party committeewoman who participated in black voter registration drives (Rabby 1984). They were to be the next sparks kindling the fire of protest. CORE, a northern-based organization trying to establish itself in the South, was formed in the early 1940s to challenge segregation. Its constitution declared, "The purpose of the organization shall be to federate local interracial groups working to abolish the color line through direct non-violent action" (Meier and Rudwick 1973:18). In academic parlance, CORE would be considered a radically committed, single-issue organization. CORE developed an elaborate ideology and formulated strategies and tactics to challenge segregated institutions. The training program for potential members was extensive, requiring investigation before action and then nonviolent action. Yet it limped along for almost twenty years waiting for its time to come.

In 1959 CORE held its first southern interracial institute in Miami. Over six hundred people attended the first session on nonviolent direct action. CORE tested local lunch counters and theaters to document the extent of segregation. It launched sit-ins at a Miami lunch counter six months prior to the famous sit-ins in Greensboro. However, it succeeded only in closing the lunch counter, not in integrating the service. Patricia and Priscilla Stephens returned to Tallahassee primed to apply the lessons they had learned (Killian 1984; Rabby 1984).

Early in the fall semester they canvassed dorms at FAMU and met with C. K. Steele and other identified activists. The first organizational meeting was in October 1959 with thirty students, including the FSU white students who had been meeting secretly. Fifteen students joined. The national CORE office was impressed that this CORE chapter in the Deep South was interracial. Saturday training and indoctrination meetings were held at the NAACP-ICC office, and three strategies emerged: gathering information on intra- and inter-city bus segregation, exploring desegregation of the city-owned airport, and desegregating local lunch counters. On November 11, 1959, three CORE members sat down at a "white only" lunch counter in Tallahassee. They were refused service and asked to leave. This was three months before the famous Greensboro sit-ins (Killian 1984). Test teams of blacks and whites found they could ride the city buses with only occasional harassment. Blacks were able to purchase tickets at the "white only" counter at the Greyhound station but were refused at Trailways. CORE appealed for relief under the Interstate Commerce Clause, but received only recognition, not federal assistance. Long months were spent building a small organization, testing and following CORE policies, and attempting negotiations before direct action (White 1964).

Two weeks after the February 1, 1960, sit-ins in Greensboro, lunch counters were again targeted in Tallahassee. On February 13, CORE organized the first sit-in at Woolworth's lunch counter. James McCain, a field director of CORE, encouraged students to sit in as part of a regionally coordinated strategy. Supported by their deep humanitarian convictions that they would be able to win over the hearts and minds of white authorities, they had little idea there would be a bitter three-year struggle to desegregate lunch counters. Ten protestors—eight FAMU students and two high school students—sat in. They were refused service and left the store after two hours.

Patricia Stephens and Richard Haley, a FAMU music instructor, emerged as the two major leaders of the Tallahassee CORE chapter. They prepared CORE volunteers for the next sit-in on February 20. Seventeen sat in at Woolworth's. The mayor arrived and told them to leave or be arrested. Six left and eleven were arrested. The Stephens sisters, two sons of C. K. Steele, six other FAMU students, and an older woman who was a veteran of the bus boycott and an ICC member were marched to jail through an angry, jeering white crowd. The sit-ins around the country and the local arrests dramatized the need for action. Hundreds of FAMU students planned to attend the trial of the eleven protesters, but when authorities got wind of their plans it was postponed. Governor Collins denounced the sit-in demonstration and both he and the local newspaper defended the sanctity of private property over the rights of citizens to be served (Killian 1984; Rabby 1984; White 1964).

16  Ideal Citizens

*Student sit-in at Woolworth's lunch counter on March 12, 1960. The Police Chief and City Manager are observing the protesters before making arrests. (Florida State Museum Archives)*

On March 12, after three weeks of planning, CORE held its largest sit-in. Patricia Stephens mobilized two hundred FAMU students to march downtown. Part of the planning involved outmaneuvering the police who were waiting to prevent the sit-ins. Two activists, who were in ROTC, suggested a military diversion tactic. As explained by one activist, a large force distracted the police while those planning to sit-in took an alternate route along railroad tracks to the department store. Six whites and six blacks sat in at Woolworth's. They were quickly arrested and led off to jail. The day became confusing and tense. Another group of white CORE activists sat-in at another lunch counter, but the black CORE members failed to show up as planned because they had encountered an angry group of armed white men led by the local head of the White Citizens Council. The police retreated from the scene, exposing the students to imminent attack. A strategic decision was made to disengage and march back to campus, where 1,800

*FAMU students protesting outside Woolworth's, 1960. (Florida State Museum Archives)*

students were mobilized to march back to town. They were met by City Commissioner William Mayo and the police. Mayo ordered the students to disperse, and the police immediately began firing tear gas and pushing the students back toward campus (Rabby 1984).

Altogether thirty-five students were arrested that day, among them the editor and reporters for FSU's newspaper, the *Florida Flambeau*. Recorded comments reveal how ugly the situation was. Shouting at the white reporters, the police said, things like the following (Delevan 1960): "Your parents would be ashamed of you." "The niggers are better than you are." "You sons of bitches." "All those niggers live for is to produce bastards, and you want to help them." The police were not the only ones to overreact. The governor confined African American students to campus. The Chamber of Commerce demanded that strong disciplinary action be taken against faculty and students at both universities who were active in the protests. The City Commission stated that it would not tolerate "unlawful" demonstrations. The editors of the *Florida Flambeau* were told by university officials that the paper would be suspended unless coverage of the sit-ins was toned down. Enormous

*FAMU students about to be tear-gassed by the police. They were protesting the arrest of twenty-three students who sat-in at lunch counters. (Florida State Museum Archives)*

pressure was put on the universities' presidents.[13] Some students were disciplined and Haley's contract at FAMU was not renewed.

Again the cold war, anti-Communist hysteria rose from the slime. Governor Collins announced that the protests were following "a Communist script whether or not it is written from the Kremlin" (*Tallahassee Democrat*, March 15, 1960). A white student disrupted CORE by claiming that Carl Braden of the Southern Conference Education Committee, who came to Tallahassee to offer aid and financial assistance, was under a cloud of suspicion because of his testimony before the House Un-American Activities Committee (White 1964). Later, during the protesters' trial, Judge John Rudd told the students that their attorneys, Tobias Simon and Howard Dixon from the ACLU, were "closely affiliated with the Communist Party in the United States."

The trial of those arrested in the first sit-in received national attention. Eight of the eleven chose jail over bail and refused to pay their fines. They were the first students in the country to accept a jail sentence rather than be fined and go free (Rabby 1984). Patricia Stephens wrote CORE, "We could be out on appeal, but we strongly believe that Martin Luther King was right when he said, 'We've got to fill the jails in order to win our equal rights' " (Rabby 1984:137). The national publicity produced hundreds of sympathetic letters sent to the jail, including one from Martin Luther King, Jr., which stated, "As you suffer the inconvenience of remaining in jail, please remember that unearned suffering is redemptive. Going to jail for a righteous cause is a badge of honor and a symbol of dignity. I assure you that your valiant witness is one of the glowing epics of our time and you are bringing all of America nearer the threshold of the world's bright tomorrows" (Rabby 1984:140). The students, suffering under brutal conditions, composed freedom songs and defied their jailers. The political awakening of one activist, as explained in an interview, started in Dr. Haley's music theory course and fully blossomed during discussions while in jail. They were in jail for almost two months, and when freed went as minor celebrities on a nationwide speaking tour to raise funds for CORE.

Meanwhile, Governor Collins was undergoing a dramatic change of heart.[14] In a statewide television-radio address from Jacksonville on March 20, 1960, he pleaded for racial understanding and stated that if black patrons' business was accepted at a store, they had the moral right to be seated at the lunch counter. The speech caused an uproar in the Florida house and senate, where there were threats to convene a special session to address the sit-in issue. It also had a dramatic effect on black citizens. In an interview, one of the activists vividly recalled the speech. It was the first time a major southern official had recognized the legitimacy of the protest. In his later years as an elder civil rights statesman, Governor Collins took particular pride in the fact that he was successfully able to veto many bills patterned after the most radical segregationist actions taken in other southern states. Collins (1989:11) declared, "It is difficult to imagine what the world would be like without the work of nonviolent insurrectionists." He was referring to such people as Jesus Christ, Martin Luther King, Jr., Reverend C. K. Steele, and the students Wilhelmina Jakes and Carrie Patterson.

When the CORE-sponsored Freedom Riders came through Tallahassee, there were arrests at the Tallahassee Municipal Airport. During this period, it is clear that students were leading the way and reviving the local civil rights movement, as they were in many other areas (Branch 1988). In a statement by a coalition of black ministers pledging to continue the fight for freedom, they stated, "We are ashamed that it was not us who first led the struggle. We commend

20  Ideal Citizens

the young people for taking the leadership. They are far ahead of us but we are rushing to catch up" (*Tallahassee Democrat*, March 20, 1960). There were further sit-ins and arrests at department stores and other public accommodations.[15]

Boycott and picketing downtown Tallahassee stores because of lack of progress in desegregating the lunch counters at Neisner's, McCrory's, Woolworth's, Walgreen's, and Sears stores in December 1960. (Florida State Museum Archives)

The sit-ins in Tallahassee have received a mixed assessment. Rabby's (1984) assessment, although very positive, does state that the students were demoralized by the manifold forms of repression and that civil rights organizations did not have the monetary and legal resources to sustain the costly tactics of direct confrontation. It took three years of economic boycotts, protests, arrests, mass meetings, and other forms of direct action to get the lunch counters desegregated. White (1964) has a more comprehensive and critical assessment. He was a CORE insider, and as a militant activist committed to nonviolent direct action, he witnessed a number of internal and external problems. As CORE rapidly expanded, it was difficult to exercise discipline and maintain the high level of ideological commitment. His dissertation foreshadowed a number of problems that were to occur in the movement. When whites joined, they wanted to assume leadership roles and did not willingly accept the internal discipline that was necessary. There also was a conflict of generations. The adult black leadership of the bus boycott, although supportive, encouraged a "go slow" policy which delayed potential direct confrontations and slowed the movement's development. Commitment to organization building inhibited direct action. There were also internal jealousies over the attention the arrested CORE members received on their nationwide tour. External pressures forced CORE to compromise, delay, or postpone actions. Self-appointed white liberal leaders either interfered with CORE plans or encouraged delay because they did not want CORE actions to affect the governor's race or the selection of a new university president at FSU. As a white student, White witnessed how outside resources could, at best, be a mixed blessing for the local movement center.

## Desegregating the Movie Theaters

On the surface, desegregating movie theaters seems like a trivial pursuit of enjoying entertainment rather than seeking social and economic justice. However, the segregation practice mandating that blacks sit in the balcony was an insult to black students' dignity and a target for rising black militancy. After being absent for a year, Patricia Stephens-Due, married to fellow CORE member and law student John Due, had returned to Tallahassee to find renewed interest in direct action within the CORE chapter. On January 23, 1963, she and Julius Hamilton, another CORE member, were arrested at the Florida Theater after entering the lobby. The city eventually dropped the case, but Patricia filed a suit charging the city with practicing and supporting racial apartheid (Rabby 1984).

On the advice of C. K. Steele, Patricia agreed to drop the suit if the city would agree to desegregate the courtroom, and a "gentleman's

22  Ideal Citizens

*FAMU students protesting theater segregation in 1963. (Florida State Museum Archives)*

agreement" was reached between the judges and attorneys to immediately desegregate the courtroom. When they tested the changes the next day, however, four blacks were removed from the white side of the court by orders of Judge Rudd. Fed up with the total lack of good-faith bargaining by white authorities, CORE began to picket the two main movie theaters (Rabby 1984). Judge Ben Willis issued a restraining order, but hundreds of FAMU students defied it and continued to picket. Mayor Sam Teague felt he was losing control of the police and called all officers to a meeting, where, to prevent police violence and bad publicity, he told them to put their nightsticks and cattle prods away (Rabby 1984). Over two hundred students were arrested in front of the theater, and another thirty-seven were tear-gassed and arrested as they marched toward the jail. The city then changed legal tactics and amended the restraining order to allow a small number of students to march peacefully in front of the two theaters if they did not directly interfere with business. This tactic worked as the spring semester ended and student enthusiasm for continued picketing waned.

*FAMU students at their court hearing after being arrested for protesting segregated theaters in 1963. Women are in front and men in the back. (Florida State Museum Archives)*

During the summer of 1963, FAMU students attempted to use the city's "white" swimming pools. Priscilla Stephens was kicked in the stomach and arrested as she tried to enter the water (Rabby 1984). The city closed the pools, and Priscilla lodged a complaint of police brutality with the City Commission. The elected officials not only refused to hear the complaint, but they praised the splendid job of the police department in protecting the rights of all citizens. It took another struggle over a five-year period to get the pools reopened on a nonsegregated basis.

Inspired by the events in Birmingham that summer, students were primed to continue the protest in the fall. On September 14, 1963, Patricia Stephens-Due marched with hundreds of students to violate an injunction against public demonstrations and to test the restraint of hundreds of conservative white students shouting at the protesters. More than 248 were arrested when the protesters refused police orders to reduce their number to 18. The jails could not handle the number;

some students were kept in covered cattle bins at the Leon County Fair Grounds. The next night again witnessed confusion. Led by three black ministers, 450 black and white students marched to the jail. They were told they would all be arrested. The ministers pleaded with the students to return to campus, but the outraged students did not want to listen. Finally, Roosevelt Holloman, a student leader, convinced discontented protesters to return to campus. The next night, however, 100 students returned to the jail to be arrested, bringing the number arrested to at least 348 (Rabby 1984). In the next few weeks there was a mad scramble

*FAMU students during a tense, non-violent night demonstration in 1963. (Florida State Museum Archives)*

to relieve the crowded and unsanitary conditions at the jails, find legal representation, and get bonds reduced. Again FAMU university officials warned students to abide by the law. Stiff sentences and fines were assessed. The City Commission ordered a special grand jury investigation of the activities of university protesters. Patricia Due and another CORE leader were suspended from FAMU, and angry students demonstrated in front of the home of the FAMU president.[16] Rabby (1984:212) states, "The white power structure in Tallahassee had proven once again to be a formidable opponent in the legal, political, and economic struggle for black equality."

The picketing continued throughout the fall, with token white faculty and student support. Then an additional startling event mobilized larger numbers of white students and a few faculty to protest actively. The famed band leader, Count Basie, had been invited to play at FSU. When he and sociologist James Geschwender tried to eat at a restaurant adjoining the campus, they were refused service. In response a new wave of picketing, initiated by whites, started in front of restaurants that served the FSU community. The protesters were harassed when the campus police chief said he could not provide protection. Thus the appearance of white protesters and the snub of an internationally known musician brought significant attention to persistent patterns of racial inequality.

*Large demonstration in Tallahassee supporting the 1964 Civil Rights Bill. (Florida State Museum Archives)*

Demonstrations continued. One of the largest was a march by over one thousand blacks to the state capitol, demonstrating in favor of the pending 1964 Civil Rights Act. Shootings and mass incidents made

Tallahassee a tinderbox during the summer of 1964. A visitor to Tallahassee wrote the state Advisory Committee to the U. S. Commission on Civil Rights, "I spent four days recently in Tallahassee, which is truly sitting on a powder keg. The State, Leon County and the city ought to move rapidly to blow out the fuse and dampen the powder before there is a disastrous blow up" (Rabby 1984:204). Under tremendous pressures, originating in both the black and white communities, local law enforcement was stepped up to discourage vigilantism. Tallahassee began to adapt slowly to the new federal mandates. Leaders at the state and local levels began to realize that negative race relations were bad for business. Moderate white leaders were chosen and conciliatory decisions were reached. Blacks continued to mount protests on a number of fronts and to increase black voter registration. No dramatic victory parades occurred and the government did not fall. The community muddled through the slow process of abolishing segregation and recognizing African American political rights. The end results seem far more significant than each phase of the struggle, but the magnitude of change reflects the power and "magic" of political insurgency.

---

This chapter has reviewed the political baptism of the activists. Before they were old enough to vote, black students at FAMU and a small number of whites at FSU became political actors on the stage of protest politics. For most, their first participation in the political process was challenging the segregation practices of a uniform structure of white power. The white resistance took the form of carefully orchestrated threats and repression by white authorities and the vigilante tactics of white citizens. In retrospect it is amazing how wrong-headed public officials were.

The protests occurred in a local movement center in which the African American community provided the organizational resources and sustained leadership. The most critical element was a small group of black and white students who dared to challenge segregation. As Goethe once said, "Whatever you can do or dream you can begin. Boldness has genius, power and magic." The courageous students were backed by broad-based black community and student support. The local movement center created new leaders during the confrontations and forced old leaders to think and act in new ways.

One of the most interesting findings is the crucial role that women played in initiating protest action. A point that Rabby (1984) recognized in her dissertation. The bus boycott and the Tallahassee CORE chapter were initiated by women. Moreover, the one leader in the ICC who was also in the first group arrested during the sit-ins was Mary Gaines. This pattern was not uncommon during this period. Garrow (1987) comments on the crucial role Jo Ann Robinson played in the initiation of the Montgomery movement, and Branch (1988) demonstrates the critical part that Ella Baker played in keeping the SCLC operational and helping to found and guide SNCC.[17] Not burdened with local leadership roles in African American organizations that were trying to preserve and sustain limited gains, African American women were the sparks that ignited local protest. Another plausible reason for the importance of women as leaders is that African American families are less patriarchal than white families and thus provided more freedom for black women.

The movement drew small groups and occasionally hundreds into direct challenges of state and local authority. The local movement also benefited from the resources and talents from outside the community. National organizations committed to destroying segregation practices (CORE, the NAACP, and the ACLU) all contributed significantly. Proceeding in fits and starts, and often chaotic, the movement marched into the 1960s. The mobilized resistance in the white community almost successfully crushed the rebellion, and white liberals, however well intentioned, also frequently served as an impediment to the direct-action strategies of CORE. Although there were occasionally confusing strategies, group infighting, scarce resources, and tremendous risks, the impact on the black community was dramatic. Larger segments of the black community experienced liberation. Individuals became more militant and willing to protest.

The sustained period of student protest politics had a tremendous impact on all the young men and women who participated. In the black community it also influenced and educated those who had chosen not to get directly involved. If they had harbored naive ideas about how political institutions operated or how easy it might be to win over the hearts and minds of their white opponents, the struggle significantly altered their political education and involvement. They saw that moderate forms of state repression did not work, since increasing numbers of black and white students participated after each repressive act.[18] Compared with cohorts of less active college students, these students received a firsthand political education and gained not only a sense of self-worth but also new talents and skills. Thus to recount what happened is by no means to imply the story had ended. In a way it had just begun. As graduating classes were scattered after leaving the university, they took their political orientations and commitment to action to other communities inside and outside Florida. They had to find employment in those areas that needed their talents and were willing to hire African Americans. And they had personally acquired memories of what could be done and how to do it.

What did it all mean? What might follow in the remaining decade of political turbulence? Would the conservative 1980s finally change these no-longer-young radicals? Having set the stage by recounting the civil rights movement and the direct experiences of the activists' generation, the remainder of this book will explore the legacy of the important events and the lasting impact on the individuals who participated and, perhaps, the larger society.

# 2

## TRACKING THE CIVIL RIGHTS ACTIVISTS: HOW THE RESEARCH WAS DONE

Longitudinal studies are rare in the social sciences, for obvious reasons. It takes time to trace the same individuals or groups over extended periods. The sample of people originally selected for study deteriorates. People die or become incapacitated because of physical or mental health problems. Subjects move around seeking improved work opportunities or better environments. Women frequently change their last names when they marry, making it difficult to trace them. Despite these difficulties, longitudinal studies are the most rewarding. They alone provide answers to questions about changes and developments over the life cycle.

Identifying and tracing the former students were the first hurdles. Funding—the mother's milk of research—was in short supply. Funding sources were largely concentrated on discovering the antecedents, not the consequences, of student activism, and interest was in potential social control, not good citizenship. As a result, the first investigation of white activists was funded out of pocket.[1] In designing the research project, I knew it would be necessary to have control groups of nonactivists to compare with the activists. Therefore students were sampled along three points of a student political activism continuum. At one end was the politically noninvolved random sample of people who were not active in either student government or protest politics. At the other end were civil rights activists who had confronted segregated southern institutions to change racist practices during the 1960-63 period. In between these two groups were members of student government, whose political expression in the white community followed a consensual, cooperative model of institutional politics. Playing acceptable student political roles is good training for conventional political careers and four recent governors in Florida began in student politics. Although not actively opposed to the civil rights movement, these white student leaders, like their adult counterparts, felt that the civil rights movement was going too far, too fast.

I obtained addresses from a variety of sources: the alumni office, the registrar's office, university directories that provided information on home and campus addresses, and in a few cases faculty and students who knew the current addresses of activists and student government leaders. Questionnaires with stamped, self-addressed envelopes were sent and these were followed by a reminder postcard and a second wave of questionnaires. Ninety-five individuals, 63 percent, responded.[2]

Flushed with the initial success in gathering data on whites, I decided to do a similar study of African Americans who had attended Florida A&M University (FAMU). A small grant was secured from the National Institute of Education. Students who had attended FAMU during the massive demonstrations were sampled and two additional groups were sampled disproportionately. The first was student government leaders. In contrast to student government in white universities, student government on black campuses frequently played leadership roles in student protest (Matthews and Prothro 1966; Orum 1973; Searles and Williams 1962). Arrested students constituted the second group, whose names I found from city and county records. A composite measure tapped student activism, including the duration of involvement, commitment to the point of being arrested, and participation in protest marches.[3] The university alumni office and registrar's office provided the last known addresses of former students. Finally, questionnaires were mailed during the summer and fall of 1973. One hundred eighty-six, or 37 percent, returned completed questionnaires.[4] Most of the information was identical to that for the white study, but additional information on black nationalism and black identity was obtained.

A number of factors contributed to doing the twenty-five-year, second-wave follow-up studies. Individuals undergo significant changes during their lives, and they are likely to get more active in politics during their forties and fifties (Verba, Nie, and Kim 1971). When I completed the first research in the early 1970s, there was a significant residue from the 1960s. In the late 1960s black protest continued and black nationalism strengthened, while activism among whites shifted to a massive opposition to the Vietnam War. At the beginning of the 1970s there was a strong oppositional subculture reinforced by groups and organizations. The 1980s were a major contrast, an era of conservatism symbolized by the election of Ronald Reagan and the policies of his administration. A twenty-five-year longitudinal study provided an opportunity to investigate the broad contextual effects of a historically changing political environment and the development of aging activists in a distinctly different political atmosphere.

After securing a small grant from FSU, in 1986 I mailed a questionnaire to the whites who were surveyed in 1971. This was fifteen years after the first wave and twenty-five years after the whites' participation in political protest.[5] Six different sources were used to obtain current addresses: (1) the alumni office, (2) old addresses from 1971, (3) returned postcards sent to previous addresses either confirming or getting a new address, (4) phone directories from the twenty-five largest cities in the United States, phone directories from the area of the last known address, and all Florida directories, (5) the Florida Department of Motor Vehicles records of licensed drivers, and (6) local residents' knowledge of the subjects. Of the original 150 subjects, 101 were located and 88, or 87 percent, responded.

Again, the results from the white follow-up were encouraging. In 1988 a twenty-five-year follow-up of the black participants was undertaken. Plagued by a shortage of outside funds, the project moved doggedly forward while trying to find small amounts to cover research costs. It was necessary to cut back on the size of the project. The 186 black respondents from 1973 and another 190 from the original sample were randomly selected. Of those with correct addresses, 114, or 56 percent, returned questionnaires.[6] On both the twenty-five-year follow-ups the background characteristics were nearly identical to those of the first wave during the early 1970s.

Research designs in the social sciences have their trade-offs. The timing of the research and the selection of subjects make it possible to explore and test only a limited set of ideas. Moreover, social science research tends to rely on access to subjects, funds, human resources, and so forth. This study was no different; yet it had distinct advantages. When compared with other studies of civil rights activists, this was the only research that had systematic data on blacks and comparable data for both black and white activists. It also had two control groups that could provide baselines from which to compare the adult politics of activists. It was possible to explore more systematically the contours of adult politics and to test for the effects of specific factors that determine adult political attitudes and behavior.

## KEY QUESTIONS

A number of major questions prompted the research.

32   Ideal Citizens

- Did student activism affect other key life choices, like jobs, education, and participation in civic culture through voluntary organizations?
- Are there major differences between activists and nonactivists in their life choices and politics?
- Among the activists, are there major differences between black and white activists?
- Lastly, are there significant historical or period effects associated with the rambunctious period of insurgency and the conservative 1980s?

At the end of the 1960s the famous German radical, Rudi Dutschke, exhorted activists to "begin that long march through all the institutions of society." How would the long march affect important life choices about jobs, marriage, income, and organizational involvement? Are elective life choices related to the differences between activists and nonactivists? Are ex-activists pulling down good salaries and living in the suburbs like more conventional college graduates? Are they married with two kids like the media suggest? Although both groups faced similar pressures in their adult maturation, the politics and life-styles of the former activists should be different.

When this research was initiated in 1970 there was scant background on the long-range careers of the 1960s activists. The theoretical and empirical work tracing student activism into adulthood can roughly be broken down into three general research hypotheses: maturation, disillusionment, and the emergence of distinctive generational cohorts during periods of political and economic crises. The first hypothesis of aging goes back to Aristotle and is discussed in the writings of Weber (Lipset and Ladd 1972). This theory posits that as the young grow older they move away from extremes and become more moderate and mature in their judgments and behavior. Aristotle saw virtue in the moderate adult politics of men in their prime, which he identified as the period of the late forties. Weber (Gerth and Mills 1946) recognized the advantages of reasoned, mature judgment of men in midlife over the passions and extremes of youth. The hypothesis suggests that political activism during early adulthood will have no long-term effects. The important responsibilities of raising families, developing careers, and adjusting to new political realities force young adults to adapt and change. Thus, ex-radicals will be employed in the same type of occupations and belong to the same type of voluntary organizations as other college graduates. They will also be political moderates.

The disillusionment hypothesis receives less attention. Beginning with radical or reform ideologies, social movements are optimistic: "One must have hope in the sense that he must believe a better world is possible, and he must have faith in the sense that he believes that by joining together with others like himself he may develop sufficient collective power to bring about this better world" (Geschwender 1971:3). When activists do not see institutions changing as a result of their collective efforts and when they simultaneously experience various forms of repression, they can become disillusioned (Mauss 1971). If alternative life-styles are available, then ex-activists, licking their wounds, retreat to bohemia to experiment with various forms of accommodation to a hostile society? If this alternative were correct, ex-activists, when compared with other members of their generation, would neither be in the career mainstream nor participating in conventional or protest politics. Instead, they would be working in menial jobs and avoiding politics. There is a radical, literary version of this hypothesis. It argues that society is crazy and a few individuals are sane. The literary works of Ken Kesey (1962), Tom Robbins (1980), and Thomas Pynchon (1990) are fine examples. Their heroines and heroes are struggling against insane authoritarian bureaucrats, occasionally winning but mostly losing, while trying to maintain their sanity.

The third hypothesis is Mannheim's ([1928] 1972) idea of distinctive generational units forming out of intense youthful politics. Mannheim argues that generational differences are not a direct function of age or biology but are caused by major social events during young adulthood (eighteen to twenty-five), when political consciousness is formed. He contends that there can be different intragenerational units within the same age cohort, that is, subgroups within the same age group which work up the materials of their common experiences in different yet specific ways to constitute separate generational units. For example, Students for a Democratic Society (SDS) and the youth wing of the John Birch Society, the Young Americans for Freedom (YAF), emerged from the same age cohort but with different politics.

Mannheim explains that "personally acquired memories" are distinct from "appropriated memories." Appropriated memories are the accumulated knowledge and experience adopted from someone else. They may be shared by different generational units within the same age cohort. But personally acquired memories are those resulting from the direct process of human development. This type of knowledge is decisive for future political orientations.

If this theory were correct, the protesters should have been pursuing distinctive occupational careers which tolerated "unconventional" attitudes and behavior. Although this study did not expect to find absolute continuity, it expected that protesters would have progressive sentiments, be involved in a wide range of leftist political organizations, and be trying to change institutional structures. During the 1980s they would be confronted with the new conservative era and forced to adjust to, if not accommodate, the hostile political environment.[8]

The scarce research findings made it difficult to determine which hypothesis is correct (Alwin, Cohen, and Newcomb 1991; Blum 1970; Bell 1967; Carey 1968; Greene 1970; Lipset and Ladd 1972; Mankoff and Flacks 1972; Maidenberg and Meyer 1970; Newcomb et al. 1967; Sears and Funk 1990). During the 1970s and 1980s a small number of empirical studies (Braungart and Braungart 1988, 1991; Jennings and Niemi 1981; Jennings 1987; McAdam 1988; Marwell, Aiken, and Demerath 1987; Nassi and Abramowitz 1979; and Whalen and Flacks 1989) reported on the long-range consequences of white student activism. They generally confirmed Mannheim, particularly when there were good baselines or control groups.

## DIFFERENCES BETWEEN BLACKS AND WHITES

What about African American and white differences? Baptism into political struggles was different for black Americans. A larger percentage participated, and they had strong support from the adult African American community. The African American protesters were not rebels. They were advancing objectives that the larger community shared. Black students were also pursuing tangible goals that directly influenced their future opportunities and the quality of their lives. Thus the southern civil rights movement should have had a far greater and more diverse impact on African Americans than on whites.

The empirical research on the black activists' generation is limited to two studies of African American students (Jennings and Niemi 1981; Tripp 1987). Tripp's study consists of a small group of sixty-six black students who attended the University of Michigan during 1969. Virtually all of the students participated in campus protest. The research postdates the civil rights movement, so there is no information to determine whether Matthews and Prothro's prediction about the consequences for the movement participants is correct. Jennings and Niemi (1981) are astounded by the astronomically high levels of political participation among young black adults in voting, party politics and protests. The adjectives chosen by these eminent scholars are unusual. Possibly Jennings and Niemi did not fully understand or appreciate the significance of the civil rights movement for black citizens.

## PERIOD EFFECTS

Early 1960s activists matured as adults in two distinctive historical periods: the ten years after college during the extended period of political insurgency, and twenty-five years later, when Ronald Reagan was well into his second term. As pioneers in the struggle for political rights, the early wave of activists witnessed momentous challenges and turmoil between 1965 and the early 1970s. Did events confirm and reinforce, or modify earlier political commitments? For example, the student activists in the 1930s were pacifists, World Leaguers, and/or socialists sympathetic to the changes occurring in the Soviet Union. The 1940s brought revelations of Stalin's purges and a world war. Historical events tended to disconfirm fundamental beliefs for many of the 1930s generation of college students. Would the historical events following the 1960s civil rights movement have a similar or opposite effect? Remaining true to C. Wright Mills's dictum concerning the intersection of biography and history and Piven and Cloward's sound advice about the importance of the political and economic context in which maturation occurred a brief historical review will be presented.

### The Expansion of Protest Politics

By any standard the 1960s was an extraordinary decade. It began with a young president, John F. Kennedy, who inspired hope for significant changes in American institutions. It began with peaceful, mostly black, nonviolent civil rights demonstrations led by Martin Luther King, Jr. Before the decade was over King, Malcolm X, John Kennedy, and his brother Robert were assassinated. Chants from the African American protest movement changed from "Freedom now" to "Black power" and "Off the pigs." Early antiwar activists sang, "All we are saying is give peace a chance." Later waves shouted, "Fuck the war!" Activists enthusiastically supported President Johnson's election in 1964 because he, unlike Barry Goldwater, promised not to expand the war in Vietnam. Later they chanted, "Hey, Hey, LBJ, how many kids have you killed today?" By the 1970s people displayed bumper stickers on their cars that stated, "Would you trust a crooked dick?" and "Nixon's father should have withdrawn." The decade started with small groups of college students using the means of peaceful protest to achieve civil and democratic rights. It ended with 450 colleges shut down by student strikes after the killing of students at Kent State and Jackson State. In 1970, the National Guard was called out twenty-four times on twenty-one campuses in sixteen states (President's Commission on Campus Unrest 1971). As many as 60 percent of students took part in some form of protest activity between 1967 and 1970 (Wood 1974). By the end of the decade, public opinion polls declared that student unrest was the number one social problem in the United States.

My purpose is not to give a detailed history and interpretation of the 1960s. The more limited objective is to outline some of the most important events and forces that structured the political attitudes and behavior of college graduates, particularly activists. Dramatic changes occurred in the black protest movement after 1965. As young adults the activists' generation experienced a decade of political turmoil and racial strife. In contrast to the southern nonviolent movement of the previous ten years, the black protest movement entered a period of urban violence. Black militancy and black nationalism arose.

Black leaders and citizens initially thought the federal government would be an ally in their struggle. As they pushed forward and expanded their challenges to racial discrimination, they changed their orientation to white institutions. Early in the Montgomery movement, King (1964:90) stated the following:

> Feeling that our demands were moderate, I had assumed that they would be granted with little question; I had believed that the privileged would give up their privileges on request. This experience, however, taught me a lesson. I came to see that no one gives up his privileges without strong resistance. I saw further that the underlying purpose of segregation was to oppress and exploit the segregated, not simply to keep them apart.

Two weeks after the boycott victory, King (1957:32) commented as follows:

> We must face the appalling fact that we have been betrayed by both the Democratic and Republican parties. The Democrats have betrayed us by capitulating to the whims and caprices of the Southern Democrats. The Republicans have betrayed us by capitulating to the blatant hypocrisy of right-wing reactionary Northerners.

When confronted with a powerful challenging movement, government officials can try to downplay the significance of the challenge, help the development of the movement, or hinder the movement leaders and organization. As the protest movement developed a mixed strategy evolved.

During the 1960 presidential campaign the Kennedys played a minimal and reluctant role in trying to get Martin Luther King, Jr., released from prison (Branch 1988). The Kennedy administration largely ignored the significance of the movement in light of the pressing international problems. After John Kennedy's narrow election victory his advisors saw merit in encouraging private foundations to provide funds to the civil rights movement for voter registration drives. This strategy might have increased Kennedy's chances of reelection in 1964 (Branch 1988; Piven and Cloward 1979). Still, Kennedy was reluctant to sign an Executive Order that would have broadened federal enforcement and reduced discrimination. To placate southern Democrats, the Kennedy administration appointed known racists to the federal bench. The administration refused to use federal troops and was reluctant to use other federal resources to protect civil rights activists.

Being cold war warriors, the Kennedys came under the sway of the FBI director, J. Edgar Hoover, who had a visceral hatred for Martin Luther King, Jr. Hoover used the resources of his agency to discredit King and the movement (Garrow 1981; Marx 1979). At a White House meeting on June 22, 1963, King was warned first by Burke Marshall, then by Robert Kennedy, and finally by the president about the alleged Communists in his movement. King was dumbfounded by the treatment he received (Branch 1988). Later he ran into a buzzsaw of problems with the IRS and state-level officials conspiring against him (Branch 1988).[9]

The growing strength of the movement and the confrontations in Birmingham forced the federal government to take more positive action. Kennedy's support for civil rights always came as a result of the black movement's actions (Lemann 1991). Kennedy proposed the 1963 Civil Rights Act, which was passed in 1964. President Johnson used the words of the civil rights anthem "We Shall Overcome" in his first address to Congress. He pushed for the passage of the 1964 Civil Rights Act and supported the Voting Rights Act of 1965. Both laws were intended to restore order by getting African Americans off the street and into the courthouse (Flacks 1988). However, in 1964 the Democratic party refused to seat members of the Mississippi Freedom Democratic Party at the Democratic convention (McAdam 1988). By the time of the White House conference entitled "To Fulfill These Rights," convened in 1965, many black leaders were calling the federal government the enemy (Killian 1975). Johnson's assistant secretary of labor, Daniel Patrick Moynihan, released his controversial report, *The Negro Family:*

38   Ideal Citizens

*The Case For Action* (1965), which alleged that the lack of black achievements could be attributed to the tangle of pathologies in black families.[10] Like Kennedy before him, President Johnson also came under the spell of a more ominous source of political influence: J. Edgar Hoover. When the major black urban rebellions occurred, President Johnson was convinced that they were caused by outside agents and possibly foreign influences (Lemann 1991). Although somewhat reluctant, Johnson ordered federal troops into Detroit to quell that city's riot.

By the mid-1960s the protest movement's social composition had changed, and so had the nature of its political demands. The civil rights movement had begun with demands for equal access to public accommodations and for desegregated public education. By the early sixties much of the movement had passed into the hands of the newly mobilized students, who pressed for an expansion of the political rights to register and vote. Awareness of the deeper problems of inadequate jobs, housing, welfare, and health care intensified. Like the leaders of the SDS or the more recent liberation movements in Eastern Europe, the leaders of the civil rights movement found they could not keep up with demands or control the course of action taken by citizens demanding change.

The demonstrations in Birmingham had a strong impact on African Americans. Brink and Harris (1966) reported widespread support for the movement. In a national survey, 80 percent of black Americans believed that demonstrations achieved results, 46 percent felt obliged to get involved, and 48 percent were prepared to demonstrate even if it meant going to jail. In the North, however, there was not the same leadership structure and cohesiveness of local movement centers. The demands were different and more difficult to solve without altering the politics of distribution. Protests were not over public accommodations or voting rights but over adequate housing, jobs, and education. Another major grievance was police harassment and brutality (U.S. National Advisory Commission on Civil Disorders 1968).

Initially, northern urban blacks expressed their discontent by using the same nonviolent tactics as the southern movement. However, beginning in 1964 the type of protest that began to capture the nation's attention was the urban rebellion. A shooting incident triggered an uprising in New York City in 1964. Additional riots broke out in other cities in New York State, New Jersey, and Pennsylvania. In 1965 there was the major riot in Watts and riots in other cities like Chicago and San Diego. In 1966 two dozen cities had riots (Bloom 1987). The urban rebellions expanded in size and scope in 1967. In the 1967 Detroit rebellion forty-three people were killed, over one thousand injured, and seven thousand arrested; there was $50 million in property damage (U.S. National Advisory Commission on Civil Disorders 1968). President Johnson appointed a commission to study the problem and became furious when the commission did not confirm his conspiracy theory (Lemann 1991). There was ample evidence to document widespread community support for and involvement in the riots, which are a form of political protest (Bloom 1987; Feagin and Hahn 1973; U.S. National Advisory Commission on Civil Disorders 1968). More riots occurred after the assassination of Martin Luther King, Jr., on April 4, 1968.

Before King was assassinated, he was confronted with a black power and black nationalist movement. The movement was born out of the frustration of the slow pace of change and white resistance. King, like many other black leaders, believed that the black power movement was a blind alley that made it easier to isolate blacks and arouse white reactionaries. He tried to counter the trend by forming a new coalition and expanding the base of the movement. His organization, the Southern Christian Leadership Conference (SCLC), expanded its operations to Chicago in an attempt to address the grievances of northern blacks. King formed coalitions with organized labor and strongly backed efforts to organize black workers into public-sector unions. He spoke out against the expanding war in Vietnam, questioning its moral justification and the waste of governmental resources. Shortly before his death, he started the "Poor People's March on Washington" to present a multiracial challenge for more substantial economic changes and a reordering of governmental priorities in federal spending (Bloom 1987).

As the country grew fearful and impatient of black demands, white liberals became angry that King and other black leaders could not control black citizens. Cold war liberals were dismayed that King would dare to question the U.S. war to stop Communist aggression in Southeast Asia. Kevin Phillips (1969) writes that the dominant political force of the liberal Democrat/New Deal coalition broke apart because of the black revolution and the inability of liberal Democrats to cope with it. Killian (1975:108) comments:

> Despite the aid of the black vote in putting it in power, the moderate Democratic regime was still responsive to white political and economic power. It was still the government of a white man's society and was no more willing to preside over the liquidation of white power than Winston Churchill was to preside over the

liquidation of the British Empire. To this extent the federal government, like state and municipal government, did reveal itself as the enemy.

Alabama governor George Wallace demonstrated in his presidential campaigns that there was a significant minority of white voters susceptible to antigovernment and antiblack appeals (Carlson 1981). But even he was no match for the master of the politics of resentment, Richard Nixon. Nixon exploited the value of "symbolic racism" for his own purposes.[11] His key aide, John Ehrlichman, puts it politely: "There were subliminal racial messages in a lot of Nixon's campaigning" (Lemann 1991:203). Although federal assistance for achieving equal rights did not cease with the election of President Nixon, there were clear signs of retreat and new efforts to contain expressions of discontent. Moynihan survived the presidential transition and wrote the famous memo to Nixon that now is the time for "benign neglect." Top policymakers believed blacks rioted because the federal government promised too much, raising unrealistic expectations. The way to solve the problem was to promise nothing. A more threatening action was the Omnibus Safe Streets and Crime Control Act signed into law by President Nixon in 1969. The Nixon administration supported the repressive control recommendations, particularly the police's ability to respond to riots. During this same period J. Edgar Hoover believed that the Black Panthers were public enemy number one. In 1968–69 there were over thirty local police raids on headquarters of the Black Panthers in different cities. African Americans became angered, frustrated, and more militant and sympathetic to black nationalists' appeals.

*White Radicalization*

For white activists, one of the most important events was the development of the black power movement. White civil rights activists were invited to leave the civil rights struggle and organize their own communities. McAdam (1988) and Demerath, Marwell, and Aiken (1971) analyze the causes and consequences of this decision. The civil rights movement was changing its emphasis from civil rights to black power. Black power meant organizing a distinctive black community, leaving little room for whites. Both the hostile opposition to the movement by white authorities and internal racial tensions led to expelling whites. Emerging African American nationalist leaders believed that white supporters were paternalistic and insensitive. There was also resentment against whites because of the attention lavished on white civil rights activists (Lemann 1991). If a white was arrested, beaten, or killed, there was extensive media coverage. When the same things happened to a black activist, the media wimped out. It was almost as if an African American's life or work was unimportant.

The major impact the civil rights movement had on white volunteers was to radicalize them. The direct experience of being involved in a hostile struggle generated a radical reappraisal. Whites discovered the depths of federal, state, and white institutional complicity in maintaining a system of segregation. The timidity and reluctance to aggressively prosecute civil rights violations forced many to rethink their idealistic sentiments of how a democracy works. Early waves of white activists strongly identified with the heroic African Americans in the movement like Robert Moses.[12] McAdam (1988) notes that the most important legacy of white participation in the civil rights struggle is the "positive impulse to action." If one strongly believed that institutions must change, then it was necessary to commit oneself to a course of action to achieve political objectives. Maintaining a level of political sophistication or having a correct analysis was not enough. It was necessary to take action, sometimes risky action, to bring about change. McAdam (1988) documents how the white volunteers initiated and led other insurgent movements in white communities.

Political insurgency in the white community rapidly escalated after 1964. Universities, cities, and the federal government were confronted. Segments of the white community experienced a form of cognitive liberation similar to that in the African American community. It became legitimate to express pent-up grievances. On college campuses in 1967–68 there were 859 student protests. Students protested the quality of instruction, the lack of academic freedom for faculty and students, inadequate services, senseless university rules involving dress codes and other matters. Students were also protesting for civil rights freedoms and against the draft. There were demonstrations against on-campus recruiting by the military, the CIA, or corporations like Dow Chemical, which manufactured napalm. The Vietnam War and the existence of classified military research on campus were frequently the targets of protest (Peterson 1970). In many cases there was the delegitimation of authority and systems of domination. College administrators were found to be duplicitous frauds. On one level they warmly defended basic academic rights and freedoms, and at another level they made deals for classified research and cooperated with authorities to repress protest organizations and actions. Past practices or current actions could not be rationally defended. The marine lieutenant in Vietnam who said, "We must destroy the village in order to save it" was often quoted to illustrate the insanity of the war.

The direction and focus of the insurgency of white protest spun out of control and was often chaotic. One reason is that left-wing activists were not heavily sponsored, and thus controlled, by adult groups. Whereas local movement centers bolstered black protesters and wealthy conservatives financed the student right wing, the outside support for the student left was very thin. White leaders, like African Americans, found that they could neither direct nor control the intensity of the protest movement (Gitlin 1987; Hayden 1988; Miller 1987). Movement leaders lacked the ability or the desire to impose discipline and authority. Groups practiced "participatory democracy" and "doing their own thing." Internal disorganization befuddled strategic and tactical decisions. Although Vietnam became the overriding issue, there was a host of problems. Powerful liberal politicians remained cold war warriors and team players. Strong opposition caused a major rift between radicals and the old liberal-labor coalition. Vice President Hubert Humphrey supported Johnson's expanding war efforts and recruited labor leaders to join in their opposition to the antiwar movement. Cut off from institutional support and far ahead of American public opinion, the radical left developed a wide array of uncoordinated strategies to oppose the war. There were mass marches in Washington, D.C., draft resistance, numerous peaceful protests, direct confrontations with the war machine, and sympathetic contacts with the Viet Cong (Gitlin 1987). Movement leaders became convinced that mass mobilizations were difficult and expensive and had little impact. The movement was so disorganized that just when national public opinion was beginning to shift in their favor, demonstrations in the nation's Capital were abandoned.

Initially the federal response was to define the white insurgency as largely a local issue to be handled by local authorities. After massive demonstrations in Washington, D.C., particularly at the Pentagon, where it was estimated the antiwar demonstrators actually could have taken temporary control of segments of the building, the federal government decided to take more decisive repressive action. The FBI conducted a number of undercover operations. False information was spread to assassinate the character of leading activists. Undercover agents and agent provocateurs disrupted specific groups and actions (Marx 1979). The political intent was to marginalize the protesters. They were portrayed as deviant and unrepresentative, lacking in credible politics. The protesters' actions were trivialized or, occasionally, overdramatized as a revolutionary threat. At the local level, faculty members who were active in the movement were fired, students were suspended, and the student press was curtailed. There were political trials targeted against "political enemies" like antiwar Vietnam veterans in Florida, or, more notably, the Chicago Seven (Hayden 1988). The Chicago Seven were charged with illegal actions to disrupt the Democratic party's national convention in 1968, but those watching the convention were more impressed by the thuggish behavior of Mayor Daley's henchmen in Chicago, who beat up reporters on the floor of the convention. Observers also witnessed Chicago police rioting against antiwar protesters (Walker 1968). Although many of the mass actions of the insurgency movement were publicly ignored by Presidents Johnson and Nixon, the movement held both men captive in the White House and privately drove them to extremes.

Unlike the student activists of the 1930s, who were peace activists and supporters of the Soviet revolution, the 1960s civil rights activists did not have their radical political orientation disconfirmed by subsequent events. The domestic and foreign policies of the 1960s reinforced the radical critique of U.S. policy. As the decade unfolded, the civil rights activists could tell their friends and relatives, "I told you so." The escalation of the volume of insurgency also provided opportunities to continue to engage in protest politics. The need to take action was frequently reinforced during this period.

The white nonactivists were not deeply touched by the civil rights protests while attending college. If anything, they mildly disapproved of the militant tactics of the civil rights movement.[13] As the militant insurgency escalated in the late 1960s over the Vietnam War and other highly divisive issues, the nonactivists were open to opposing views. The strongest influences were indirect. They had no personally acquired memories from the protest era, so their knowledge of the movement's goals and tactics was gained from the media and public officials. In general, the mass media were much less sympathetic to the antiwar movement than to the southern civil rights struggle (Gitlin 1980; Parenti 1986). Tactics and leaders were often ridiculed or condemned. Thus the nonactivists would be inclined to accept the harsh pronouncements of authorities against challengers of domestic and foreign policy. They were also susceptible to the Republican party's drive to form a new conservative majority by gaining support of white southerners (Phillips 1969). A strong negative reaction to the political insurgence is captured in an open-ended response volunteered by one of the nonactivists in 1971:

> As to political party, by heritage I am a Democrat. But, I am offended with the theatrics and posturing of the PR conscious, pseudo-personalities who clamor for headlines as Democrats. So, if I voted today, I'd be more likely to vote Republican. I would also observe that, now to vote Democrat is a subtle encouragement for the revolution...I frankly fear a tyranny of a mob much more than I fear dictatorship. The most tragic, unproductive eras in history have been at times when the tyranny of the masses was sovereign.

In terms of careers and personal life-styles, the nonactivists could be expected to grow into what they were supposed to do and be. As rule followers rather than rule challengers, they were willing conformers to middle-class life-styles and middle-class goals. Their life-styles during a period of economic prosperity and upward mobility were rather conventional. As they "matured" the nonactivists were prone to develop a visceral dislike for highly publicized antiwar activists like Jane Fonda and Tom Hayden.

### The Transformation of American Politics: The Counterrevolution

Although there is no question that the 1980s witnessed the resurgence of a conservative era, how this resurgence occurred is fiercely debated. Edsall (1984) traces the rise of the new conservatism to the declining fortunes of the Democratic party and the rise in the resources of the business-dominated Republican party. Both he and Vogel (1989) acknowledge that fundamental problems in the political economy contributed to the rise of conservatism. But the roots go deeper. The situation in the United States is analogous to the rise of "Thatcherism" in Great Britain. When the socialist-oriented Labor party in Great Britain dominated the House of Commons during the late 1960s and early 1970s, they expanded the social welfare state and threatened eventually to nationalize the banking industry. The peril to profits and control over the economy was significant, and dominant conservative forces launched a counteroffensive against Labor, putting Margaret Thatcher in office, privatizing the economy, and destroying the power of the labor unions which supported the Labor party (Useem 1984). In the United States Reaganism was a counteroffensive against the threats and accomplishments of the insurgent movements.

Beginning with the civil rights movement, the politics of insurgency during the 1960s mushroomed into a political agenda to expand

and complete the programs begun during Roosevelt's New Deal. Between 1964 and 1974 there were major reforms in four different areas: civil and democratic rights, social welfare and the social wage, increased regulation of the business and financial community, and limitations on what politicians could do in foreign and domestic policy. In the area of civil and democratic rights there was not only the 1964 Civil Rights Act, the 1965 Voting Rights Act, and the 1968 Fair Housing Act but also legislation affecting the legal rights of the poor, special consideration for small minority-owned businesses, and the outlawing of credit discrimination against women. Social welfare benefits and the social wage were expanded through the growth of the food stamps program; eligibility for Aid to Families with Dependent Children (AFDC) and the growth of public housing; significant increases in Social Security; the creation of Medicare and Medicaid and Supplemental Security Income, the Occupational Safety and Health Administration, the Mine Safety and Health Administration, and the Employee Retirement Security Act; expanded unemployment and disability coverage; and extension in minimum wage coverage. The period of insurgency spawned the environmental and consumer movements that created the Environmental Protection Agency, the Consumer Product Safety Commission, and the National Traffic Safety Commission. Domestically politicians were somewhat limited by campaign reform laws and changes in the Securities and Exchange Commission which attempted to limit corporate influence over political decisions. In foreign policy there were limits placed on the president through the War Powers Act and limited controls over the cloak-and-dagger activities of the CIA. The draft was also abolished.

The late 1960s and early 1970s were heady times. It was almost as if the broad-based political objectives articulated in SDS's Port Huron Statement (Miller 1987) had been implemented. There may not have been a major shift in the basis of class power in the United States, but economic and political elites were faced with a growing regulatory state. However, Domhoff (1990:276) wisely cautions, "People won, but the power structure did not lose." Indeed, for Domhoff the major task is not to explain the return of conservatism, but to decipher how a basically conservative, business-dominated country, without strong unions or a social democratic party, could generate liberal legislation and social wage increases during this period. The two-party system, winner-take-all elections, and the southern Democratic and Republican party coalition dominated U.S. politics. The combined strength of this conservative compact assured dominant business interests that their needs would be the first to be met at the congressional bargaining table. The conservative coalition had the power to enact legislation or veto bills proposed by a liberal president and a minority in Congress. The interests and concerns of ordinary people or public interest groups were rarely considered because these segments normally lack power.

The insurgent movements of the 1960s altered the power of the dominant conservative coalition. A minority of ordinary citizens developed the power to disrupt the hegemony of the ruling coalition. Piven and Cloward (1971) demonstrate that governments do not respond to the needs of citizens until there is the actuality or threat of serious political disruption. The politics of turmoil loosened the bounds and conventions of everyday life, created an atmosphere of a legitimation crisis, and threatened the accumulation of profits.[14] A number of studies confirm the power of the politics of disruption (Alford and Friedland 1975; Gamson 1975; Isaac and Kelly 1981; Swank and Hicks 1984) in winning new additional benefits. Insurgent politics was transformed into electoral politics when citizens voted the bums out. Some elected officials, like the mythical leopard, changed their spots.

By the early 1970s political insurgency rapidly diminished. The reasons for the decline are numerous. People had to get on with their lives, to take advantage of new opportunities and limited gains (Flacks 1988). Women went to law school, college-educated African Americans sought new openings into American society, and activists completed degrees or found work. The repressive tactics of the government reduced the effectiveness of movement organizations. For example, the SCLC saw its financial contributions drop after the FBI discredited the organization (Garrow 1981; McAdam 1982). Other movement organizations self-destructed because of internal dissension and a poor choice of tactics and strategies (Gitlin 1987; Orcutt and Fendrich 1980). Issues changed, concessions were made, and the targets of opposition for challenging groups became more elusive.

The decline in the U.S. economy had the biggest impact in shaping public policy and the future of race relations during the 1980s (Fendrich 1983; Jaynes and Williams 1989). By 1973 the early signs of the reversal of postwar prosperity were evident. Nixon was forced to float the dollar in the international currency market. The Arab-Israeli war, which led to the formation of OPEC and the rapid increase in oil prices, caused strong inflationary pressures. U.S. corporations were going global, seeking higher prices and cheaper labor (Barnett and Muller, 1974). Fierce international competition from Europe and Japan was influencing economic development (Burnstein 1988). The profit rates of U.S.

corporations began to fall dramatically, creating a crisis environment in which the business community wanted special favors from the government (Bowles and Gintis 1982; Harrison and Bluestone 1988).

The economic decline and the harsh reality of stagflation created a political environment ensuring the success of Reagan's candidacy for president. Significant tax increases in the form of bracket creep were paying for liberal welfare programs, but the increases were exceedingly unpopular with voters (Edsall 1984). Although the Watergate scandal temporarily slowed the counteroffensive, the ruling conservative coalition gradually gained the upper hand (Edsall 1984). In order to win back popular support, it was necessary to commission conservative scholars working for think tanks to develop new policy rationales to attack the welfare state. They dutifully reported that government regulation was too expensive and anti-inflationary measures were justified. Conservatives also learned an important lesson when President Ford lost his reelection bid. Ford's loss to a born-again Christian, Jimmy Carter, made it necessary to forge a coalition with the radical right on single-issue, social questions and to develop a thinly veiled attack on racial minorities and feminists to gain white working-class support. The U.S. Chamber of Commerce and other political arms of the business community were strengthened with an infusion of money, new ideals, and modern technology which enhanced lobbying and political campaigns.

The power elite as defined by Mills (1956) and Domhoff (1990) marched back into power with the election of Ronald Reagan. Reagan got the support of the business community by endorsing radical economic proposals emerging from conservative think tanks. The proposals included lowering taxes for wealthy individuals and corporations, dismantling the welfare state, and decreasing federal regulations that cost corporations profit. Most of the hated regulations involved environmental and worker safety issues. However, one of the "worst" twenty business regulations was affirmative action. The legal and administrative cost to businesses to comply with affirmative action made this federal regulation particularly onerous; it was targeted for deregulation.

Reagan also needed popular voter support. Borrowing from the earlier success of George Wallace, he ran an antigovernment campaign that was also antiblack. Reagan announced his campaign in Philadelphia, Mississippi, where three civil rights workers had been murdered seventeen years earlier. He talked about states' rights, making a direct appeal to white voters in the South. As the campaign continued, Reagan sharpened racial lines with campaign rhetoric about "welfare queens" who drove their Cadillacs to pick up their welfare checks and "wasteful federal programs," suggesting that African Americans profited from poverty.

As president, Reagan dismantled the war on poverty in a single year (Piven and Cloward 1985). He eliminated the Comprehensive Employment Training Act, slashed $1.5 billion from child nutrition programs, and cut four hundred thousand families from welfare benefits. The budgets for federal enforcement of civil rights legislation were slashed (Fendrich 1983).

The Reagan administration's attitude on race relations was clearly evident in its effects on the federal judiciary. The retreat from civil rights became the litmus test for appointing federal judges (Ripley 1990). The Justice Department, ironically, became the locus of assault on minority Americans.[15] The Leadership Conference on Civil Rights (1982) released a blistering attack. It accused the Justice Department of repudiating the Supreme Court's definitive interpretation of the Constitution, abruptly switching sides on civil rights cases before the courts, reaching into other agencies to curb civil rights policies, and corrupting the legal process by making decisions based not on law but on political favors that were owed to big financial supporters.

The economic success of the African American middle class and the political success of black elected officials, whose numbers increased from a few hundred in the early 1960s to over 6,800 by 1988 (Jaynes and Williams 1989), were ironically used by Reagan officials as justifications for the demobilization of civil rights enforcement. The 1981 tax cuts, military expansion, and the reduction of social welfare programs sealed the end of the social contract created by the New Deal. The 1980s, with its borrow-and-spend ideology, became a roaring decade making greed a virtue and the conservative political ideology popular (Phillips 1990).

How was the African American activists' generation going to respond to this concerted attack on the legacy of the civil rights movement? Would it buy into a conservative, laissez-faire, individualist ideology that coincided with its economic success, or would it serve as an oppositional group that remained committed to achieving collective gains for the African American community?

How would the white cohort of the 1960s respond? The activists, although they contributed to many earlier political victories, were faced with the crushing defeats generated by the new conservative era. Were they demobilized and disillusioned politically, or were they digging in

Tracking Civil Rights Activists 49

for the long haul? The demographics of the nonactivists from the same cohort, that is, their education, jobs, and money, made them ideal recruits for the Reagan counterrevolution. Where did they stand politically in the 1980s, and what active role did they play in politics? Chapters 3 and 4 will report the major life choices and politics of black and white activists, comparing them with their nonactive counterparts.

# 3

# THE BLACK PROTEST GENERATION IN THE 1970S AND 1980S

This chapter will explore the consequences of the protest movement by examining the politics of the black protest generation in 1973 and 1988: ten and twenty-five years later. When the students left college, they were politically efficacious and highly distrustful of government officials. The combination of the feeling that it is possible to make changes through personal and collective action and distrust of or alienation from established political authorities is an explosive mixture (Gutterbock and London 1983). For example, one female activist who left Florida A&M University (FAMU) before graduation said in a 1991 interview that she became a black nationalist because she was disgusted with the level of white hostility toward the movement. Yet the activists were demobilized as a political force. When they left Tallahassee, they no longer had the important resources of the local movement center. Moreover, they faced the challenges of adulthood: making life choices concerning their careers, further professional education, and families. Before studying the specifics of their political orientations and behavior, it is necessary to examine the college students' career and educational trajectories. How many chose to advance their careers by graduate education and training? What types of jobs did they seek? What kinds of jobs did they find? What types of family commitments were made? These are important life choices that can influence adult politics.

## THE ACTIVISTS' ASPIRATIONS AND ACHIEVEMENTS IN 1973

In their analysis of African American college students between 1964 and 1970, Gurin and Epps (1975) found very high aspirations, expectations, and competencies. Black college students aspired to high grades, graduate and professional training, good jobs, marriage, and families. Their ambitions were consistent with realistic expectations of achieving their goals. The students were both academically self-confident and self-assured that they had the skills for a desired job. Activists and nonactivists did not differ in these characteristics. The research forecasted extraordinary upward mobility.

A comparison of the educational, occupational, and income levels of former FAMU students with their fathers' or principal guardians' indicates major achievements across one generation. They moved from the striving working class of their parents' generation to solid middle-class positions. On average, the parents of the FAMU graduates completed ten years of schooling, whereas the majority of the FAMU graduates (53.2 percent) had some graduate education. On the Nam and Powers Occupational Status Index (Nam 1963; Nam and Terrie 1981), the fathers or guardians had an average score of 40.5.[1] They were working in relatively low-status, low-paying jobs as roofers, tailors, parking attendants, truck drivers, laundry workers, janitors, hospital attendants, and soda fountain workers. For example, the father of one activist was a migrant worker who moved to Long Island, New York, to work on a potato farm and eventually found a semiskilled industrial job. His activist daughter worked as a social worker for eighteen years for New York City and nine years for the Florida Department of Labor. Another activist, raised by his sister, rose to the rank of colonel in the army and eventually became the director of student affairs at FAMU. The FAMU graduates had an average occupational score of 86.6. They worked as teachers, social workers, managers in retail trade, public administrators, and as holders of other high-status jobs. As would be expected, the incomes of the FAMU graduates were substantially higher than their parents' incomes. In 1973 their average earnings were $10,440, compared with the family income of their parents during their top earning years, of $7,904. Less than ten years out of college, the former students were earning about $2,500 more than their parents did during their peak earning years.

Both the talent and ambition of the black college graduates and the federal enforcement and expansion of affirmative action programs contributed to this upward mobility (Landry 1987; Wilson 1978). Three factors, however, limited the achievements of FAMU graduates. First, as Gurin and Epps (1975) found, black college students from the poorest backgrounds had lower levels of aspiration because of the hard realities of the lack of family resources. The analysis of family resources for

FAMU graduates indicates that those former students who came from better-off families were more likely to go to graduate school and eventually earn higher incomes. The relatively affluent and resourceful parents were able to transfer their advantages into increased opportunities and rewards for their children.

The second factor operated mainly on women. Gurin and Epps (1975) found that during the early 1960s black college women, like their white counterparts, had lower educational and occupational aspirations than the men. Women sought occupations in female-dominated professions. Experiences in college during the early 1960s attenuated these differences; that is, the differences in the aspirations and expectations between men and women increased while in college. The women in this study were selecting their careers prior to the women's liberation movement. Black women, like white women, were socialized into sex-role segregation and reduced opportunities. FAMU women were about as likely to go on to graduate or professional school as men; however, they held traditional female public-sector jobs like teacher and social worker and earned significantly lower incomes than black males. As they attempted to advance up career ladders, they encountered the "good ol' boy" network. One former activist was angry about training males who were soon promoted above her (1991 interview). In 1973 the average working woman earned more than $2,000 less than the men: women earned on average $9,060 and men $11,260.

The third factor was fewer opportunities in private-sector employment. During this period there was less discrimination against African Americans in the public sector.[2] The Great Society program generated two million new government jobs, and many were filled by blacks (Lemann 1991). Seventy-four percent, or almost three-fourths of the women, were in the education profession, and only 7 percent were in the private sector in 1973. The comparable figures for men were 37 percent in education and 28 percent in the private sector. Both men and women were concentrated in the public sector. Seventy-two percent of the men and 93 percent of the women held public-sector jobs.[3]

Gurin and Epps (1975) did not find any significant differences in aspirations and expectations when they compared protesters with nonactivists, but this pattern did not hold for FAMU activists. When the level of student activism was introduced, the more active protesters were significantly more successful on measures of education and income than their nonactivist contemporaries.[4] There was an extraordinarily high level of educational attainment. Out of the 186 respondents, 99, or 53 percent, had attended graduate or professional schools.[5] Thirty had done graduate work without completing a degree, 65 had earned a master's degree, 3 had earned a Ph.D. degree, 1 was a lawyer, and 3 were medical doctors. The activists were more likely to receive advanced training than the black students who did not participate. Among the activists, 58 percent pursued advanced training, compared with 45 percent for the nonactivists. Moreover, they were more likely to have completed degrees, earning all the Ph.D., law, and medical degrees. There is no clear evidence that the activists were the academically brightest students. The correlation between grade point average and activism was negative, $-.09$, but not significant.[6] The subsequent success of the activists compared with the nonactivists reflects their drive and ambition as much as their academic talent.[7]

In 1973 the former FAMU activists were making almost $2,000 more than the nonactivists. The activists earned $11,100 and the nonactivists earned $9,340. A heightened awareness of the persistence of discrimination, blocked opportunities, a stronger motivation to explore new opportunities, and challenging discriminatory practices account for these differences. Activists believed they were more in control of their fate, were more aware of discrimination, particularly in the private sector, realized the need to work for collective goals, and were personally committed to gaining equal rights (Gurin and Epps 1975; Tripp 1987). Being activists contributed to their success. Using their talents and initiative, they aggressively challenged existing barriers to success. One of the former activists stated:

> Although I am quite liberal in some of my views, I am somewhat conservative in others. I don't feel that any black should sit back and expect anyone to give him anything. I am all for the cause of equal opportunity in jobs, etc. I am against a man using his color, be it black, white, green or yellow, to gain the upper hand on anyone else. I feel that a man should be allowed to and be given every chance to advance according to his own abilities. He should also be given every chance conceivable to develop his abilities regardless of his color.[8]

Another activist who had been arrested stated, "Blacks must first emerge as self-respecting and financially powerful in their own right before being absorbed into the mainstream."[9] In general, the findings confirm the analyses of Boston (1988), Blackwell (1975), and Landry (1987), who report the contributions of the civil rights movement to upward mobility for a well-prepared segment of the black community.

Getting married and raising a family is another area in which FAMU students achieved their aspirations. By 1973, 39 were still single, 20 were married without children, 102 were married with children, and 25 were divorced. There was no difference between activists and nonactivists. For example, 54 percent of the nonactivists were married and had children, compared to 56 percent of the former activists. Three variables did affect marital status: age, occupational status, and income. These were typically associated with young adults' marital status. Older and more successful FAMU graduates were more likely to be married and have children.[10] In contrast to studies of white activists, the African American sample in 1973 showed that marital and family obligations were not influenced by previous political experiences.[11]

## VARIATIONS IN ADULT POLITICS IN 1973

There are three major dimensions of the adult politics of the African American activists' generation. The first is the extent to which they were influenced by black nationalism. The second is their formation of political attitudes as adults, and the third is their level and type of political participation. Both black nationalist sentiments and political attitudes need to be interpreted cautiously. Attitudes and sentiments, by themselves, are not necessarily good predictors of political behavior. What people do, in contrast to what they feel, is constrained by their structured environment or facilitated by organizations that are mobilizing to take action. Individuals, whatever their personal histories, act within a structured context that offers limited opportunities to express true feelings. Political attitudes can, however, reveal deeply held sentiments and preferences. Attitude shifts can also be important early warning signs of potential changes and trends in politics.

Two important factors influence the interpretation of black nationalist sentiments and political attitudes. First, nationalism is not a cohesive, unitary body of thought or action (Jaynes and Williams 1989). Black nationalism is multidimensional. The majority of the African American population may share sentiments of racial pride and black control over black community affairs, but the majority may differ widely in the extent to which it favors complete cultural and physical separation from the larger white society. For example, Smith (1982) found that at the peak of nationalism in the late 1960s only 7 percent of the black population favored a separate black state. Black nationalist intensity varies over time by region and class (Cole 1976; Marx 1967). Nonseparatist forms of positive black sentiments reflect a favorable ethnic identity which expanded significantly during the civil rights era (Jaynes and Williams 1989; Lemann 1991).

Second, as a group black Americans do not fit along the conventional left-right ideological continuum that is used to measure white political attitudes. On certain social issues they are more conservative than whites, for example, on abortion and the role of women in politics. On economic issues, African Americans are more progressive than whites. They believe the government should guarantee a basic level of support to all citizens and protect people from calamities beyond their control. They hold that progress is the result of progressive federal policy (Gurin, Hatchett, and Jackson 1988).

African Americans are very pragmatic, more concerned with attainable goals than with ideology (Hamilton 1981; Jaynes 1986). Political ideology, tactics, and strategy are determined by direct experience. Moreover, black priorities are related to the possibilities that exist within the spectrum of the larger political debates and struggles in the society (Jaynes and Williams 1989). The key debating points within the African American community are not conservative versus liberal, but integration versus separatism, accommodation versus self-determination, and class versus race (Carmichael and Hamilton 1967; Cruse 1967; Walters 1988; Wilson 1978).

*Black Nationalism*

Patricia Gurin and Edgar Epps (1975) documented the shifting black nationalist ideology during the 1960s. They studied black college students in 1964, 1968, and 1970. The first study occurred at the end of the sit-ins, voter registration drives, and campaigns to desegregate public accommodations. This is the same period during which African American students were protesting and demanding integration into the larger society. They demonstrated prior to the major race riots, the assassinations of Martin Luther King, Jr., and Malcolm X, and the development of black power and black nationalism. In 1964 Gurin and Epps found that students wanted an integrated society, were optimistic about positive changes, and believed that reform methods could bring about change. The second study in 1968 reported significant shifts. The targets of political action changed and the scope of student protest broadened. Protest activity shifted from community civil rights to confrontations, and attitudes shifted from reformist to revolutionary positions. By 1970 further evidence of a trend was available. Students were more aware of the patterns of institutional racism and became angry, bitter, and cynical. The students were evolving toward revolutionary-collectivist and black nationalist theories of social change.

In the study described in the present volume, the influence of black nationalism and separatism was measured in two different ways by using a simple single item and a multidimensional scale. In 1973 the members of the activists' generation were asked if they were integrationist, racial pluralist, nationalist, or separatist. Despite the high levels of African American distrust and anger over an emerging white backlash (Killian 1975; McAdam 1982), the college-educated protest generation did not strongly identify itself as black nationalist or separatist. The majority, 57 percent, called itself integrationist, and another thirty-seven, or 20 percent, considered themselves racial pluralists. Only thirty-two, or 17 percent, labeled themselves nationalists, and eleven, or 6 percent, said they were separatists.

Racial ideology was also measured by twenty-six questions about black nationalism and separatism. Five distinct dimensions emerged: (1) support for black nationalist leaders and organizations, (2) black community control and separation, (3) black pessimism, (4) distrust in public officials, and (5) support for CORE (Congress of Racial Equality) and SNCC (Student Nonviolent Coordinating Committee). The fifth dimension was somewhat unique for this sample because the FAMU student protests were coordinated by a CORE chapter and FAMU students were part of the student-dominated phase of the black movement.[12]

Table 3.1 reports the responses to the five factors of black nationalism for 1973. In general, there was a good range of responses to all the items except to measures for support for CORE and SNCC, which received overwhelming approval.[13] On the items measuring black nationalist leaders and organizations, only one person received majority approval. The majority (52 percent) approved of Malcolm X, who for African Americans epitomized distrust of the larger white racist society. The second highest approval rating was accorded to Stokely Carmichael (38 percent), who is credited with launching the black power slogan and movement during the 1960s. H. Rap Brown, who became nationally known for his declaration that "violence is as American as cherry pie," only had a 24 percent approval rating. The Black Panthers and the Black Muslims received the strongest disapproval ratings of 49 percent and 40 percent, respectively.

Although not strong supporters of black nationalist leaders or organizations, the activists were very tolerant of black groups and organizations. The in-group solidarity was evident in open-ended unsolicited comments. One person stated, "I feel that every political and social black leader and organization listed had a positive effect and only different means are used to achieve equality." An activist gave the following unsolicited response:

> I feel that black oriented organizations serve some purpose even if I disagree with some of their methods. As far as politics are concerned *most* politicians are not truly concerned with the problems of black people, but simply respond to pressure, both violent and nonviolent. Race relations between blacks and whites will probably improve to the extent where we *tolerate* each other, but we will never achieve a utopia.

On the items measuring black community control and separation there was generally stronger agreement. For example, 81 percent agreed that African history should be part of the curriculum for black children. One person said that African American history should be taught to all children. Sixty-seven percent asserted that they identified first as a black person and second as an American. One former activist, who was against regulations, insisted on having an Afro hairstyle while serving as a medical doctor in the Army (1991 interview). There was also strong agreement on blacks controlling their schools and preferential hiring for blacks. The one item that stated, "Blacks should work outside the two major political parties to gain political power," was exceptional. Only 20 percent agreed with this item; 63 percent disagreed. This response pattern suggests a pragmatic approach to politics.

The black pessimism questions revealed strong disagreement on the first three items. The respondents disagreed (58 percent) that race relations were going to get much worse, they disagreed (76 percent) that blacks and whites could never live peacefully together, and they disagreed (77 percent) that violence was the only way for blacks to obtain their rights. The respondents were more evenly split on whether a major race riot could occur in their communities in 1973. The last two items reflected a lack of faith in publicly espoused values. Sixty-three percent agreed that people were more concerned with law and order than with justice, and 67 percent agreed that the concept of equal opportunity is only a myth in the United States.

Ambivalence about trusting public officials was quite common, with large minorities unwilling to express an opinion of either trust or distrust. Better than 50 percent of the respondents trusted a member of a civil rights commission. Only 23 percent trusted the police, 16 percent trusted a labor leader, 28 percent trusted a political party leader, 17 percent trusted a local elected official, and 15 percent trusted a member of Congress. In general, the activists' generation did not appear to be as strongly nationalistic or militant as Gurin and Epps's (1975) survey of black college students in 1970 suggested, but it did appear to be more distrustful than earlier national surveys of African Americans by Brink and Harris (1966) indicated. Even though the political agenda of black separation was unrealistic, a strong positive ethnic identity emerged during the turbulent era.

TABLE 3.1
African American Attitudes in 1973

| Attitudes | Percentage | |
|---|---|---|
| *Black Nationalism* | *Approve* | *Disapprove* |
| 1. Stokely Carmichael | 38 | 26 |
| 2. H. Rap Brown | 24 | 37 |
| 3. Malcolm X | 52 | 16 |
| 4. Deacons for Defense and Justice | 25 | 17 |
| 5. Black Muslims | 28 | 40 |
| 6. Black Panthers | 26 | 49 |
| *Black Community Control and Separation* | *Agree* | *Disagree* |
| 1. Black people should run the schools in their neighborhood. | 41 | 34 |
| 2. African history should be part of the curriculum for black children. | 81 | 9 |
| 3. If I owned a black business, I would prefer to hire a black man over a white man. | 36 | 34 |
| 4. Blacks should work together as a separate group outside of the two major political parties in order to gain more political power. | 20 | 63 |
| 5. Black leaders should only try to peacefully persuade white leaders to change their politics on race relations. | 53 | 19 |
| 6. I think of myself first as a black man and second as an American. | 67 | 27 |

*(continued)*

60    Ideal Citizens

TABLE 3.1 continued

| Attitudes | Percentage | |
|---|---|---|
| *Pessimism* | *Agree* | *Disagree* |
| 1. Black-white relations are going to get much worse before they get better. | 15 | 58 |
| 2. Blacks and whites could never live peacefully together. | 8 | 76 |
| 3. It is becoming clear that violence is the only way for blacks to obtain their rights. | 9 | 77 |
| 4. A major race riot could easily break out in this town in the near future. | 31 | 35 |
| 5. People today are more concerned with law and order than with justice. | 63 | 17 |
| 6. In the U.S., the concept of equal opportunity is only a myth. | 67 | 21 |
| *Distrust in Public Officials* | *Distrust* | *Trust* |
| 1. Police officer | 43 | 23 |
| 2. Labor leader | 29 | 16 |
| 3. Political party leader | 18 | 28 |
| 4. City or county commissioner | 25 | 17 |
| 5. Member of Congress | 40 | 15 |
| 6. Member of civil rights commission | 5 | 54 |
| *Support for CORE and SNCC* | *Approve* | *Disapprove* |
| 1. Congress of Racial Equality | 72 | 2 |
| 2. Student Nonviolent Coordinating Committee | 67 | 9 |

*Political Attitudes*

This study used both simple and sophisticated ways of examining political sentiments and attitudes. The first was an item measuring political self-identification.[14] In contrast to other studies of white 1960s activists (Jennings 1987; McAdam 1988; Whalen and Flacks 1989), this study found that the black activists' generation was not concentrated on the progressive end of the continuum. Altogether 15 percent were conservatives, 45 percent were moderates, 35 percent were liberals, and 5 percent were leftists. Those historic events that radicalized whites during the late 1960s and early 1970s did not have the same type of radicalizing effect on blacks. Consistent with research on comparable groups of black college graduates during the same era (Jennings and Niemi 1981; Tripp 1987), the respondents were either highly identified with the Democratic party (70 percent) or were independent (17 percent). Only 3 percent identified themselves as conservative, moderate, or liberal Republicans.

On another measure of political attitudes, the activists' generation had a high level of personal efficacy. This generation believed that it understood government, that it had a voice and could make things happen.[15] This feeling was much stronger in this sample than in national samples of African Americans in 1972 and 1974 (Abramson 1977): about 60 percent of the respondents felt highly efficacious. However, this contrasted sharply with their level of alienation from the government (the third measure): 79 percent felt highly alienated. They believed the government served the interest of a few, wasn't concerned about their needs, and was hopelessly incapable of dealing with the crucial problems facing the country.[16] The activists' generation shared the same level of political distrust as a national sample studied during this same period (Abramson 1977).

The activists felt efficacious because of positive results stemming from protest action within the black protest movement. They remained alienated, however, from the government because they believed that government officials were either doing too little to advance legitimate black interests or were actively opposing black gains. A good example of feelings of personal efficacy as well as alienation was given by an activist who spent two months in jail. In a 1991 interview, he said he was commissioned in ROTC and served two tours in Vietnam, rising to the rank of colonel in an intelligence unit. He took advantage of opportunities the army provided; however, he remained alienated. At his base in Vietnam he saw African American troops disproportionately disciplined, punished, and discharged. He wrote his superiors to protest the discriminatory treatment. Although he was successful, he was alienated from the military. He was awarded for achieving assigned military objectives, but these objectives were not consistent with his personal standards of success, which included advancing African Americans collectively. After twenty years he retired and found work in a university setting more consistent with his personal objectives.

The fourth measure of political attitudes was a radicalism-conservatism scale developed by Nettler and Huffman (1957). The Nettler and Huffman scale is the best one available to measure political attitudes beyond the liberal dimension. The scale juxtaposes positions that would favor either a capitalist or a socialist political economy, using items such as the following: "Profits of the great industries should be rigidly controlled by the federal government," "The right to inherit wealth is a sound principle which provides a strong incentive for creative work," and "In a socialist system the worker maintains his dignity and self-respect, while under capitalism he is just a tool or instrument to be exploited."[17] Using the mid-point of the scale as a dividing line, the study found that the activists' generation was more conservative than radical. Sixty-seven percent held conservative views; 33 percent were radical. In general, however, FAMU graduates clustered around the middle of the scale, being neither highly radical nor highly conservative in their political attitudes.

The final measure is political behavior. The analysis of the extent and type of political participation of African Americans is not well developed in the social sciences. Jaynes and Williams (1989) state that the frequent definitions of political participation such as voting, campaigning, and lobbying elected officials do not generally apply to black politics because African American participation in the political arena is so recent. I disagree. The analysis of African American political participation is essential for understanding the dynamic changes occurring within the community and their potential effect on national politics. Without detailed analysis, it is possible both to be surprised by what is actually occurring and to draw incorrect conclusions.

Five measures of political behavior were used; these determined the extent to which respondents (1) followed political events in the media, (2) voted in elections, (3) worked in political campaigns, (4) participated in demonstrations, and (5) participated in any form of illegal political activity during the previous two years.[18] The findings are consistent with findings from Jennings and Niemi's (1981) and Tripp's (1987) studies of the black activists' generation. Almost 100 percent followed political events in the media. In a nation where barely 50 percent of the citizens voted in national elections, only 3 percent of the graduates said they did not vote. Sixty percent took an active part at some level in political campaigns—a high level of participation in institutional politics. The opportunities for noninstitutional or protest politics were not normally provided by political institutions and therefore were less frequent. Nevertheless, 40 percent stated they had participated in some form of public demonstration within the two previous years. Eight percent said they had participated in some form of illegal political activity, such as an unlawful demonstration or a riot. Despite, or maybe even because of, the repressive activities of government agents, the black activists' generation remained highly active in politics as adults.

The first analytical question about politics asked who within the activists' generation was most affected by the black power and black separatist movements. A detailed analysis is provided in the Appendix, where the technical details are outlined. Here I am only concerned with those formative experiences and sentiments that had the strongest relationship to adult politics. Who most identified as a separatist or a nationalist? A partial answer is, those former students who were the most active as student protesters. As hardened veterans of a civil rights struggle who faced harsh white opposition, the most politically active students were the most likely to identify as nationalist or separatist. This pattern fits with the development of nationalist, separatist, or black power sentiments after what was viewed as the Democratic party's betrayal at the 1964 Democratic convention and the urban rebellions and government response in the late 1960s. In an interview, one activist said that while working as a social worker in New York City, she took course work with Ron Karinga in New Jersey, attended events featuring nationalist speakers like Stokely Carmichael, and was a member of a nationalist organization. Another college experience that accounted for a separatist self-identification was majoring in the social sciences or liberal arts. These disciplines train students to develop a more critical understanding of the larger society and its major institutions. This type of educational exposure is "successful" in the sense that these majors are most likely to view the larger society as one characterized by an oppressive internal colonialism (Blauner 1972) rather than as one that is being color-blind, open, and democratic. The experiences after college are more difficult to explain. The members of the activists' generation who had achieved the highest-status jobs, who valued extrinsic rewards like money, status, and security, and who felt they had advanced the least since college were more likely to identify on the single item measuring nationalists or separatists. A profile emerges of a hard-driving, dissatisfied, but ambitious segment of the activists' generation being affected by the black power movement.

A similar profile emerges for those who expressed favorable black nationalist sentiments on the multidimensional scale. Appendix Table A.1 reports the analytical factors that influenced the level of black nationalism. Both the level of student activism and achieving an advanced degree were significantly related to black nationalism. Those in the activists' generation who became most involved in the protest movement supported black nationalist leaders and organizations, wanted black community control, were distrustful of public officials, and were pessimistic about the future of race relations. Having been political leaders as students, they were the most influenced by the political trends during this historical period and supported the black power movement. Those African Americans who did go on to graduate and professional training were also more nationalistic, much like whites during this era. The most radical white students during the protest era were frequently graduate students. One can conclude that graduate education and prolonged exposure to campus unrest contributed to the development of a critical racial ideology.

Sex, age, a desire to work in the private sector of the economy, higher occupational status, and higher incomes were related to black nationalism. Younger males agreed more positively with black nationalist sentiments. They were more open to a more radical ideology that could explain both the resistance of the larger white society and how it needed to be confronted or changed. On the way up the social ladder of success, young, bright, and talented African Americans were discovering flaws in the American Dream. Their college idealism and self-confidence did not prepare them for artificial job ceilings, discriminatory practices in the private sector, and a government willing to use a big stick to quell black demands.

Appendix Table A.2 reports the factors that influenced political self-identification, political efficacy, alienation, and radical or conservative attitudes. What influenced a political self-identification along a political spectrum from right to left? Although there was a healthy amount of variation in the political identification of the African Americans, only a small but significant part of the variation can be explained. The members of the activists' generation who were further to the left were younger, social science and liberal arts majors with higher overall grade point averages. Bright, younger members of the activists' generation exposed to a more critical education identified themselves as leftist. In this respect the leftists were similar to many whites of the same generation. Postcollege experiences, or even the level of student activism, did not affect political identification. The activists' generation's political self-identification stands largely by itself. It cannot be easily explained, nor did it affect other political sentiments or behavior.

Who were politically efficacious? Who felt that her or his voice and actions had some impact on the political process? Here the results were much stronger, accounting for about three and a half times the amount of variation in political efficacy than could be explained in political self-identification. The most efficacious African Americans had higher personal incomes, were more involved in political organizations, and formerly majored in the social sciences and liberal arts. The economically successful, those most active collectively in political groups, and those trained in critical disciplines believed that their voice and actions made a difference. Less significant influences on efficacy were sex, student activism, career choice, private-sector preference, and valuing money, status, and security in one's job. The younger, male former activists, those who worked in the public sector but wanted to work in the private sector, and those who valued the material rewards from a job felt they were more efficacious.

The explanation for political alienation is different. Black nationalists were the most alienated or estranged from government institutions. They had the least confidence that the government was capable of doing right. The levels of student activism had no impact on the levels of alienation. The degree of alienation reflected racial ideology rather than past patterns of political involvement. The more alienated also remained isolated from the African American political community.

As a group, the African Americans were neither highly radical nor highly conservative in their beliefs about the political economy. They neither praised nor strongly condemned capitalism. There were, however, four sets of factors that explained a significant amount of the variation in radicalism. First, those African Americans experiencing blocked opportunities were more radical. Both black women as a group and blacks with lower incomes were significantly more supportive of a regulated, socialist-oriented political economy. So were those who were the least satisfied about what they had been able to achieve since leaving college. Second, the African Americans who expressed black nationalist sentiments had the strongest preference for a socialist-oriented political economy. These findings are very consistent with the Gurin and Epps (1975) research on growing nationalist sentiments during the late 1960s. There was a merging of black nationalist and anti-capitalist sentiments. Third, African Americans in public-sector jobs and those who did not place a strong value on money, status, and security in their jobs were also more radical politically. Working in the public sector and placing a low value on acquisitive occupational rewards contributed significantly to supporting a more socialist-oriented political economy. This segment of the activists' generation was not exclusively oriented to pursuing individual economic success in the private sector and preferred a strong government interventionist role in the political economy. Finally, those with prolonged educational exposure in graduate and professional education were also more radical politically.

*Political Behavior*

Richard Flacks (1988) offers his analysis of why citizens are not active politically and why democratic institutions are failing. The way society is structured creates a situation in which the everyday work and family life experiences of most Americans are alienating and constricting. Most citizens must carefully husband their meager resources to survive on a day-by-day basis. Many Americans are not registered to vote, and those who are are passive, doing little else politically. They are making a living and do not have the luxury of "making history." Making history means influencing the conditions and terms of everyday life in a collectivity. This sounds suspiciously like being a good citizen, yet it is a relatively rare pattern of political behavior for adults.

The African American activists' generation is an exception. In 1973 these activists were trying to make history by fully exercising their citizenship rights. There were two distinct dimensions of this attempt to make history. First, activists stayed involved in institutional politics by keeping up with events in the media, voting regularly, and being active in party politics and political campaigns. Second, they participated in demonstrations or politically illegal activities. Although the two types of political behavior are moderately interrelated,[19] the analytic factors related to each type of political participation are different.

Appendix Table A.3 reports the factors that influenced attempts to make history. Those ex-students who were the most active as student protesters were very active in institutional politics. Those most committed to active adult politics also were younger, had achieved high-status occupations, favored a more socialist political economy, identified themselves as liberals or progressives, were highly active in both political and other organizations, felt a sense of personal efficacy, and were somewhat dissatisfied with their level of success to date. This is a powerful combination of youthful energy, talent, organization experience and resources, achievement, and political ideology. Those most active in making political history were following in the tradition of Jeffersonian Democrats.

Black nationalism was not related to participation in institutional politics: it neither inhibited nor facilitated such participation. However, black nationalism was the driving force for African Americans' involvement in protest politics. Those most likely to engage in protest politics held the strongest black nationalist sentiments. By 1973 African Americans did not have to rely exclusively on the extraordinary means of protest politics to make history: they could use the existing institutional means of getting something done. Yet in a pluralist but unequal society there was good reason to protest. Forty percent of the activists' generation was so motivated by the ideology of black nationalism they used the means of political protest to influence public policy. A second factor significantly related to protest politics was fewer family obligations. Those who were single or married without children were more likely to continue to protest ten years out of college. Free from obligations, single men and women can take more risks. One highly active black nationalist delayed marriage until thirty-six (interview). A third factor was belonging to political organizations, which facilitated rather than inhibited protest politics. Other factors that contributed to a lesser extent to protest behavior were graduate education, a sense of personal efficacy, and black organizational involvement. The level of student activism contributed both directly and indirectly to the level of protest politics. Although the direct effect was modest, student activism affected protest politics through graduate education, occupational achievement, income achievement, membership in political organizations, and personal efficacy.

The high levels of participation in both institutional and protest politics were the most significant findings. The rise of black nationalism and the emerging negative responses of the federal government to black demands did not discourage this generation. The findings verify the much-discussed transition to electoral politics (Piven and Cloward 1979; Rustin 1965). Those who were the most active as student protesters were, ten years later, the most active in institutional politics. Such highly active forms of citizenship were similar to those found by Jennings and Niemi (1981) during the same period.

The type of college experiences and upward mobility or success contributed to explaining the participation rates. As many other studies have demonstrated, the more privileged, because of discretionary resources, were more likely to be active citizens (Marger 1987). Yet protest politics continued to be an essential part of the political repertoire of the activists' generation. Forty percent continued to protest and demonstrate. The willingness to use the means of protest to achieve political ends was motivated primarily by a sense of racial identity, or ethnicity, that emerged during the racial turmoil that followed the decade of peaceful protest. The government's mixed strategy of responding to black demands may have successfully blunted revolutionary movements like the Black Panthers (Marx 1979), but it certainly did not lessen black anger and mistrust. On the other hand, the partial measures to improve opportunities for racial minorities were not sufficient in scope to dampen the demands of the black movement.

## Ten Years Later: A Summary

Many of the questions about the future of the black activists' generation have been clarified. Ten years out of college, the young adults were achieving success. As a group their upward mobility was substantial: they were moving from the striving working class of their parents into solid middle-class positions and incomes. Some traditional barriers of restricted job opportunities, gender, and the lack of family resources placed limits on what some members of the generation could achieve. The level of student activism, however, contributed to upward mobility, with the most active gaining the most education and having better jobs and higher incomes. Although they were not better students, their aggressive pursuit of individual and collective goals helped them take advantage of opportunities opened by new federal laws and enforcement of civil rights.

The political and movement environment changed while these young adults were starting their families, careers, and orientations to adult politics. During the insurgency period of the late 1960s and the early 1970s, there was a growing sense of black militancy and nationalism. Urban rebellions occurred in many cities. The leaders of the civil rights movement could neither contain and channel the demands nor force the government to make more far-reaching structural changes. The federal government's carrot-and-stick response to black demands created expanding opportunities for qualified blacks and, at the same time, vigorously repressed movement leaders, organizations, and the urban rebellions. These emerging events generated black power and black nationalist sentiments.

Yet, as successful, middle-class Americans, FAMU graduates shared the beliefs of Martin Luther King, Jr. The black power movement in its most extreme form was considered a blind alley and was viewed as a potential threat to the collective interests of black citizens. The activists' generation had a mixed or ambivalent response to the different measures of black nationalism. Former student activists and the respondents with the most education were the strongest supporters of various dimensions of black nationalism. They rejected violence but were becoming cynical about the myths of racial equality and opportunity. Thus although they rejected violence, they supported militant critiques and challenges to a racist society. They wanted better opportunities and more black community control. Rather than believing in a complete separation from white society, they preferred some form of political pluralism, a desired state yet to be achieved.

The analysis brings into sharper focus the politics of the activist generation as young adults. The level of political participation was very high in both institutional and noninstitutional politics. Participation should be considered the proper legacy of black student protest in local black movement centers. It is estimated that 70 percent of the black student population participated in the protest movement during the 1960s. They had overwhelming support from the black community. The experience of organizing groups and challenging authorities, the witnessing of positive results in the protest community, and the perception of tangible gains launched the students into active citizenship. In this sense the earlier predictions of Matthews and Prothro (1966) about this group becoming a leadership class were correct.

Activism did not strongly affect radical beliefs about the political economy. Radical beliefs were the consequence of blocked opportunities for some members of the activists' generation and a consequence of the black nationalist movement and militancy during the late 1960s. As will become apparent in later chapters on the ideological contrast between white activists and nonactivists, the black activists were not radicalized in a leftist direction. Collectively, they can best be described as militant reformers, not black radical revolutionaries. Although willing to employ a wide variety of tactics and strategies to bring about change, they wanted to fundamentally improve institutions and not radically restructure them. This political orientation was the product of the success of the movement and the continuing challenges faced by African Americans.

Black student activism had both a direct and indirect impact on adult political participation. Student activism contributed to individual success, which was related to organization involvement and political participation. Activists were more likely to be joiners in interest groups and protest organizations, and they sustained their high level of commitment in group settings that influenced political participation. Former activists also were more supportive of black nationalist leaders and organizations. This limited form of black militancy was in turn related to political participation in noninstitutional politics. By 1973 the activists wanted to experience the American Dream of being good citizens in an open and pluralistic society. Yet they continued to be confronted by a white-dominated society with its own rules and agenda which limited what African Americans could achieve individually and collectively. By the early 1970s, the activists' generation glass was partially filled but remained more than half empty.

## AFRICAN AMERICAN POLITICS IN THE 1980s

One of the first questions explored when analyzing the activists' generation in 1988 was whether it was comparable to the 1973 group.[20] Some characteristics could vary over time, and others were expected to be similar or identical to 1973. Fifteen years after the first survey, the respondents were fifteen years older. The occupational status of their fathers while they were in college, their major in college, their undergraduate grade point average, and the level of student activism were almost identical. For example, in 1973, 37 percent of the respondents reported that they did not participate in the student protest. The percentage was identical in 1988. The same percentages were identical (18 percent) for those who reported the highest level of protest, that is marching or demonstrating, being arrested, and being active in a civil rights group six months or longer. The mean levels of student activism and the standard deviations were almost identical: 2.37 and 2.27, respectively, in 1973, and 2.54 and 2.30 in 1988. Because tracing women who change their last names is more difficult over time, there was a higher proportion of males in the 1988 sample, but the difference was not significant.[21]

Certain expected changes occurred over time. More blacks attended graduate or professional schools. Sixty-three percent had some education beyond an undergraduate degree, and more advanced degrees were completed in the interim. There were more family obligations. In 1973, 54 percent were married and had children. By 1988 the percentage had increased to 65. There were sharp differences between men and women in current marital status. Only 40 percent of the women were living with spouses, compared with 75 percent of the men. In a 1991 interview one activist commented that she knew ten female activists who were currently divorced. When questioned further, she stated that women like herself wanted more independence, but their former husbands, holding "traditional" male values, were unwilling to change. The common complaint was, "He didn't grow."

Children posed different challenges. One of the common concerns expressed by parents was that they may have "overprotected" their children within comfortable middle-class environments. Protection from negative racial experiences is a long-standing custom; however, the protection provided by a middle-class cocoon seemed to have dulled children's awareness of the importance of the civil rights struggle. Parents were concerned that their children lacked an understanding of the historical period.[22]

The incomes were also substantially higher. The average income for the individual respondents in 1988 was $34,998. However, neither the occupational status nor the occupational sector of employment changed. The average occupational status in 1988 was 86.55, compared with 86.63 in 1973. This finding confirms the work of Landry (1987), Diprete and Grusky (1990), and Hout (1984), who reported that the major occupational gains for African Americans occurred in the late 1960s and early 1970s and leveled off afterwards. Only 25 percent of the graduates worked in the private sector, and were divided between private-practice professionals and private firms. Twenty percent worked for some level of government, 46 percent were in education, and 9 percent were in social work or other helping professions.

In 1988, among the activists' generation, women were more likely than men to have majored in education, were less involved in the protest movement, advanced less far in their graduate education, were more concentrated in public-sector jobs, and had significantly lower incomes. The average personal income for women was $29,699 compared with $37,758 for men. Overall the incomes were substantial for these respondents, who were reaching the height of their earning years.

Five factors contributed to income differences among the activists' generation, explaining 27 percent of the variance in income: degree of graduate education, economic sector, age, occupational status, and level of student activism. Those who completed advanced degrees, who worked in the private sector, who had prestigious occupations, who were older, and who participated actively in the student protest movement had higher incomes in 1988. Sex differences were not significant when other factors were controlled. Except for the levels of student activism, all of these factors were normally associated with income differences. The drive, ambition, and talents of those former students who played an active role in the black protest movement still continued to have a strong effect on their economic success twenty-five years later.

In revisiting the politics of the activists' generation in 1988, I made some changes and improvements to the testing measures. Three were dropped: political efficacy, alienation, and a single item measuring a separatist identity. Five comparable measures—black nationalism, political identification, radicalism-conservatism, participation in institutional politics, and participation in protest politics—were used. The new political information addressed included the following: a history of political involvement since college, support for presidential candidates during the 1980s, support for mainline African American leaders and organizations, expanded measures of organizational involvement, the level of approval of the Reagan administration, and a more comprehensive measure of the level and type of political behavior. The additional information provides an opportunity to examine in more detail the participants' political sentiments and behavior twenty-five years after the student protest period. The continuity or changes in comparable measures of black nationalism, political attitudes, and behavior will be examined before discussing the new measures.

*Black Nationalism in 1988*

Three of the five dimensions of black nationalism remained remarkably stable over the fifteen-year period, with very slight declines on some of the individual items. Table 3.2 reports the comparable results. The level of support for the former student organizations—CORE and SNCC—remained strong, with over two-thirds giving approval and less than 10 percent disapproving. The emphasis on black community control and a positive racial identity remained stable. In both 1973 and 1988, 81 percent agreed that African history should be part of the curriculum for black children. In 1973, 36 percent stated a preference for hiring a black man over a white man; the percentage in 1988 was 40. In 1973, 67 percent identified as a black person first and an American second; by 1988 the figure had dropped slightly, to 61 percent. There was some change on the measure of black pessimism about the future of race relations in a peaceful society and the viability of American ideals about racial equality. Prospects of interracial violence declined. However, in both 1973 and in 1988 about two-thirds believed that American ideals about justice and equal opportunity remained more a myth than a reality.

Two dimensions of black nationalism changed significantly. The level of distrust in public officials declined in every case except for a member of a civil rights commission. The levels of distrust in police officers and members of Congress fell by two-thirds since 1973. Changes in other items were less dramatic.[23] The well-publicized stacking of the U.S. Commission on Civil Rights with conservative Reagan appointments and the policy shifts at the Equal Employment Opportunity Commission under Clarence Thomas explain increased distrust of members of a civil rights commission. There was also a significant loss of support for identified black nationalist leaders and organizations. Approval for the teachings of Malcolm X fell from 52 to 40 percent. Stokely Carmichael's approval fell from 38 to 22 percent. Support for the Black Muslims declined by 10 percent, and support for the Black Panthers by 15 percent, down to 11 percent approval. These declines were not caused by the particular leaders being historically dated or outmoded. In 1988 an additional question was included on the level of support for the highly visible black nationalist leader Louis Farrakan. Only 17 percent approved of Farrakan; 46 percent disapproved.

TABLE 3.2
African American Attitudes in 1988

| Attitudes | Percentage | |
|---|---|---|
| *Black Nationalism* | Approve | Disapprove |
| 1. Stokely Carmichael | 22 | 37 |
| 2. Malcolm X | 40 | 29 |
| 3. Black Muslims | 18 | 43 |
| 4. Black Panthers | 11 | 56 |
| 5. Louis Farrakan | 17 | 46 |
| *Black Community Control and Separation* | Agree | Disagree |
| 1. Black people should run the schools in their neighborhood. | 40 | 38 |
| 2. African history should be part of the curriculum for black children. | 81 | 15 |
| 3. If I owned a black business, I would prefer to hire a black man over a white man. | 40 | 32 |
| 4. Blacks should work together as a separate group outside of the two major political parties in order to gain more political power. | 22 | 60 |
| 5. Black leaders should only try to peacefully persuade white leaders to change their politics on race relations. | 45 | 36 |
| 6. I think of myself first as a black man and second as an American. | 61 | 34 |
| *Pessimism* | Agree | Disagree |
| 1. Black white relations are going to get much worse before they get better. | 28 | 67 |
| 2. Blacks and whites could never live peacefully together. | 6 | 80 |
| 3. It is becoming clear that violence is the only way for blacks to obtain their rights. | 4 | 84 |
| 4. A major race riot could easily break out in this town in the near future. | 30 | 44 |

*(continued)*

74    Ideal Citizens

TABLE 3.2 continued

| Attitudes | Percentage | |
|---|---|---|
| *Pessimism (continued)* | *Agree* | *Disagree* |
| 5. People today are more concerned with law and order than with justice. | 65 | 21 |
| 6. In the U.S., the concept of equal opportunity is only a myth. | 63 | 26 |
| *Distrust in Public Officials* | *Distrust* | *Trust* |
| 1. Police officer | 12 | 51 |
| 2. Labor leader | 24 | 31 |
| 3. Political party leader | 19 | 29 |
| 4. City or county commissioner | 15 | 40 |
| 5. Member of Congress | 16 | 38 |
| 6. Member of civil rights commission | 16 | 42 |
| *Support for CORE and SNCC* | *Approve* | *Disapprove* |
| 1. Congress of Racial Equality | 70 | 3 |
| 2. Student Nonviolent Coordinating Committee | 69 | 5 |

I used a second method for comparing the level of support for a separatist ideology with support for black leaders and organizations that supported a pluralist racial and political ideology. In 1988 members of the activists' generation were asked about their approval of mainline leaders and organizations. There was strong support for Martin Luther King, Jr. (95 percent), Jesse Jackson (94 percent), and Andrew Young (85 percent). The level of support for pluralist or mainline black organizations was equally high. Ninety percent approved of the Southern Christian Leadership Conference, 93 percent approved of the NAACP, and 85 percent approved of the Urban League.[24]

*A New Profile*

A new composite picture of the racial ideology emerged in 1988. In 1973, after a decade of racial turmoil, the activists' generation was sympathetic to, if not strongly supportive of, a black nationalist ideology. In the ensuing years the more extreme components of a nationalist and separatist ideology declined. The racial ideology of the activists' generation represented a positive, pluralist ideology. These findings support Lemann's (1991) detailed descriptions of the emerging positive ethnic identity, particularly among the middle class. There was support for leaders and organizations that advocated pressure-group tactics and continued black protest, but support for leaders and groups advocating revolutionary rhetoric and cultural separatism was much lower. The activists wanted control over resources in their communities, were proud of being African American, and remained somewhat distrustful of public officials in a white-dominated society. Since college this generation may have lost the romantic idealism of creating an integrated society. However, it had not given up hope for the future by withdrawing into cultural and political separatism. By the late 1980s the components of ethnic identity were more similar to those of Jews, Italians, and Irish Americans than to those of the Black Muslims.[25]

One former activist went out of his way to emphasize that he had no feelings of personal hatred toward whites. The movement had taken him beyond hate and provided hope and a deeper understanding of race relations. When asked if he had recently experienced discrimination, he said, "not personally," but added, "I avoid situations where I know I'm not wanted." He also reported what he considered to be the racial insensitivity of a white friend who was a judge. The judge asked him how he felt about Nelson Mandela in light of the fact that Mandela and the African National Congress had been supported by Communists. Although tempted, the activist refrained from asking the judge who supported South African apartheid (1991 interview). Another activist maintained a strong African appearance in clothes, jewelry, and hairstyle. She also actively promoted an African American dance troupe and planned a visit to Africa. She stated in an interview that her strong emphasis on her African heritage was occasionally met with opposition from her white bosses, African Americans who were not as nationalist as she, and the African student subculture in her university hometown.

Another new measure tapped the centrality of political involvement over the life cycle. Each person was asked to recall how important politics was to his or her life during the presidential administrations of Johnson, Nixon, Ford, Carter, and Reagan. The importance was measured by asking if political activities were the most important part of one's life, central to one's life, occasionally important, only rarely important, or something to be avoided. The trend over time was for African Americans to be more active during Democratic presidencies; however, they were more politically involved during the Reagan presidency than during the Nixon presidency. Those who became the most politically involved after college majored in the social sciences, supported mainline civil rights organizations, and held high-status jobs, but they did not value extrinsic rewards. Staying involved politically depended on having a preparation in the social sciences, which provided more information for active citizens, and having the resources

76   Ideal Citizens

that come with a prestigious occupation. It also involved less commitment to acquisitive values and stronger commitment to those organizations and leaders that were perceived to be advancing the collective interests of African Americans. One activist, a medical doctor, established himself in an interview as a successful legislative lobbyist. One measure of his success was the fact that white doctors retained him to lobby for them.

*Political Attitudes and Behavior*

The political self-identification of the activists' generation had remained very stable since 1973. The percentage of conservatives (15 percent in 1973, 17 percent in 1988), moderates (45 percent in 1973, 46 percent in 1988), liberals (35 percent in 1973, 32 percent in 1988), and radicals (5 percent in 1973, 6 percent in 1988) had not substantially changed. The two factors most strongly related to a liberal or left political self-identity were having been active in the protest movement as a student and wanting black control over black community resources.[26] As the activists' generation matured, it did not move significantly in the conservative or liberal direction, but sorted itself out according to the previous political experiences and political objectives it wanted to achieve.

Identification with the Democratic party increased from 70 percent in 1973 to 80 percent in 1988. Fewer were self-professed independents; the percentage dropped from 17 percent to 8 percent over the fifteen years. The percentage of those identifying as Republicans increased from 3 to 4 percent. Party identification increased with age, but the Democratic party reaped the gains in the upwardly mobile activists' generation. Over the three presidential elections in the 1980s there was overwhelming Democratic support. Ninety-two percent voted for Carter in 1980, 83 percent voted for Mondale in 1984, and 86 percent intended to vote for the Democratic candidate in 1988, with Jesse Jackson as their overwhelming first choice among Democrats.

There was a significant shift in support of a more capitalist-oriented political economy. In order to score at the radical end of the radicalism-conservatism scale, a respondent had to express support for a more socialist-oriented political economy. In 1973, 33 percent favored a socialist political economy; this had dropped to 24 percent by 1988. Conversely, those favoring a capitalist political economy increased from 67 to 76 percent. As in 1973, opinions were not extreme, with most scoring around the middle of the scale. Nevertheless, there was a statistically significant move in the conservative direction. This shift was due to the combined forces of declining socialism in Eastern Europe and the almost universal praise for a capitalist political economy in the United States.[27] In a later chapter, when the scores of white nonactivists are reported, it will be evident that the African American activists' generation sings the praises of capitalism far less enthusiastically.

Consistent with the research on aging, the level of political behavior increased for the activists' generation. Activists universally voted and kept informed about politics. Only 20 percent reported they had not been active in political party politics or political campaigns during the previous two years. Only 37 percent said they had not participated in some form of political protest, such as a march or demonstration. Protest participation actually increased since 1973. One activist recently protested against cuts in municipal funding caused by the Reagan administration and another was active in the protest politics of his teachers' union (interviews). A substantial minority even reported it engaged in some form of political behavior that could lead to an arrest. The average scores on the five items for political behavior increased from 11.17 to 13.06, which is a statistically significant change. One can conclude that over time the political involvement of the activists' generation increased.

*New Measures of Political Attitudes and Behavior*

The new era of conservatism, as exemplified by the Reagan administration's policies and programs, changed dramatically what the government was willing to do in solving domestic problems. Conceivably the economic success of this generation could have moved it into the group defined as the backbone of support for Reaganism (Phillips 1990). This group of African Americans was the first secure generation of the black middle class. Phillips implies that this segment of the larger black population could have become conservatives, being in the upper two income quintiles that strongly supported conservative Republicans. There is, however, a strong counterargument. The black middle class was committed to collective goals for the African American community (Jaynes and Williams 1989). The group was more liberal and critical of government than less affluent blacks and strongly believed that the primary obligation of government is to help the less fortunate (Gurin, Hatchett, and Jackson 1988). Given its level of political sophistication and history of political involvement, the activists' generation should have been very critical of the Reagan administration's attempts to dismantle the welfare state and redistribute wealth upward.

The Reagan administration was evaluated on six policy issues. The activists' generation was asked to evaluate Reagan's handling of policies on nuclear arms control, protection of the environment, balancing of the national budget, enforcement of civil rights, support for social welfare programs, and tax cuts for wealthy individuals and corporations. It disapproved of the Reagan administration's policies on all six issues. Twenty-four percent agreed, and 49 percent disagreed with Reagan's handling of nuclear arms control. Only 16 percent agreed with Reagan's commitment to environmental protection, compared with 59 percent who disagreed. On balancing the national budget, only 4 percent agreed with the Reagan administration; 86 percent disagreed. In the area of civil rights enforcement, only 2 percent agreed that Reagan was doing a good job, and a whopping 92 percent disagreed. A similar pattern held for Reagan's programs on social welfare. Only 4 percent agreed and 86 percent disagreed. When it came to tax cuts for wealthy individuals and corporations, 7 percent agreed, and 77 percent disagreed with the Reagan administration. Although there was some variation depending on the issue, the evidence is clear that the African American activists' generation was strongly opposed to Reagan's policies in the new conservative era. Ten variables related to attitudes toward the Reagan administration at the bivariate level: major in college, membership in civil rights organizations, membership in liberal organizations, the four major dimensions of black nationalism, amount of graduate education, history of political involvement since college, and student activism. Together they explained 16 percent of the variance. The two variables that had the strongest direct effect were the history of political involvement and distrust of public officials. The findings clearly suggest that the past political experience of the activists' generation, their current organizational involvement, and a healthy distrust of public officials were important components of an oppositional culture within the African American community.

*Good Citizenship*

Were the activists ideal citizens in 1988? Were they trying to make history by keeping informed about politics and informing others? Did they work in political campaigns and political party activities between elections? Were they active in local politics? Did they continue to use the means of protest politics to air their political grievances? To answer these questions, I expanded the measures of political behavior to include five distinct dimensions of political behavior. The first was a passive form of political participation that involved voting and exhibiting some form of patriotic expression. The remaining four dimensions—political communication, party and campaign work, local political activism, and protest—were active forms of participation.[28]

Table 3.3 reports the extent of participation for each item on the five different dimensions. The activists universally voted and did have a strong feeling of love for the country. Almost three-fourths demonstrated their loyalty through patriotic acts. The remaining four dimensions are presented in the order of the threshold of difficulty, that is, by how much individual effort was needed and how easy it was to perform the political tasks. The large majority of American citizens never engages in these activities, but that was not true for the black activists' generation. Table 3.3 reveals that better than three-fourths were involved in a high level of political communication in 1988. Ninety-nine percent kept informed about politics, 98 percent engaged in political discussions, 77 percent sent messages to politicians, 93 percent tried to inform others, and 74 percent tried to persuade others how to vote.

The activists' generation was active in party and campaign work. Ninety-one percent joined and supported a political party. Eighty percent took an active part in political campaigns, and 73 percent participated in political party activities between elections. These actions would involve serving on local party committees, raising funds, attending meetings and conventions, and helping with voter registration drives. The Democratic party was the beneficiary of almost all the political participation on this dimension.

Almost two-thirds participated at every level of local politics except being a candidate for office or going with a group in protest to a local official. Eighty-seven percent worked with others on a local problem. Sixty-five percent helped to form a group to work on a local problem; 65 percent contacted a local official on a social problem. The activists' generation was less likely to complain about a personal problem than it was to work within a group context. Only a minority, 23 percent, sought public office.[29] Two served in the Florida and Georgia legislatures. Sixty percent had gone with a local group to protest to an official. And there was plenty to protest. Citizens complained about streets, lighting, drugs, and safety in their communities. They protested about the lack of resources in predominantly black schools and the poor administration of justice in black communities. The protests frequently involved inadequate political representation for the African American community. During the 1980s there was a sustained drive by the NAACP in the South to enforce U.S. Supreme Court rulings on "one person,

TABLE 3.3
African American Political Participation in 1988

|  | Regularly percent | Occasionally percent | Seldom percent | Never percent |
|---|---|---|---|---|
| *Voting and Patriotism* | | | | |
| Vote in elections | 93 | 5 | 1 | 1 |
| Have a feeling of love for my country | 61 | 30 | 6 | 3 |
| Show patriotism by flying the flag or in some other way | 25 | 30 | 18 | 27 |
| *Political Communication* | | | | |
| Keep informed about politics | 82 | 14 | 3 | 1 |
| Engage in political discussions | 47 | 40 | 11 | 2 |
| Send a message to a political leader | 20 | 38 | 19 | 23 |
| Inform others in the community about politics | 29 | 43 | 21 | 7 |
| Try to persuade others how to vote | 28 | 30 | 17 | 24 |
| *Party and Campaign Work* | | | | |
| Join and support a political party | 49 | 20 | 22 | 9 |
| Take an active part in a campaign | 31 | 30 | 19 | 20 |
| Participate in a political party between elections as well as at election time | 28 | 30 | 15 | 27 |
| *Local Political Activism* | | | | |
| Be a candidate for office | 4 | 7 | 12 | 77 |
| Work with others on a local problem | 30 | 40 | 17 | 13 |
| Form a group to work on a local problem | 18 | 29 | 18 | 35 |
| Contact local officials on social issues | 21 | 35 | 20 | 31 |
| Contact a local, state or federal official about a particular personal problem | 10 | 35 | 24 | 31 |
| Go with a group to protest to a public official | 8 | 27 | 25 | 40 |
| *Protest* | | | | |
| Join in protest march | 6 | 26 | 31 | 37 |
| Attend a protest meeting | 11 | 30 | 31 | 28 |
| Participate in any form of political activity that could lead to arrest | 4 | 13 | 25 | 58 |

one vote." City and county at-large elections changed to give blacks representation on local governing bodies and a positive incentive to remain highly involved.

On the separate protest dimension, which measured participation in noninstitutional politics, almost two-thirds reported they had participated in a protest march. When local officials were unresponsive to grievances from the black community, small-scale protests were mounted to gain press coverage and pressure local officials. The percentage of the activists' generation engaged in protest politics actually increased from 1973. This finding reflects the trend reported by Jaynes and Williams (1989). Local protests sponsored by African American community organizations were on the increase. Although the intensity of protest politics may have declined, using protest as a means of expressing good citizenship had increasingly become part of the repertoire of adults in leadership roles in the African American community.

Advocates of classical democratic theory (Dahl 1989; Milbrath and Goel 1977) frequently point to the ancient Greek city-states or older New England town meetings as models of good citizenship. Identifiable groups that fully exercise the range of citizenship opportunities in the contemporary United States are more difficult to find. Jewish Americans are one group frequently mentioned as highly active citizens. The activists' generation from the civil rights era needs to be included in any discussion of who ideal, or highly active, citizens are. They were the complete activists, or ideal citizens, of the 1980s.

The activists' level of citizenship was compared to a national sample from the General Social Survey (Davis and Smith 1987). Six items of political behavior or citizenship are comparable. The activists' generation had a significantly higher level of political participation than a national sample of black Americans who were the same age and had the same level of education.[30] Unfortunately, the national data from the General Social Survey contained few African Americans with college educations. The number of females was overrepresented and incomes were significantly lower. Therefore, a precise comparison is not possible.

A better comparison is with the Gurin, Hatchett, and Jackson (1988) study of a larger national sample of African Americans. Although precise item-by-item comparisons are not possible, there are a number of similarities. African Americans were strongly committed to full political participation and were generally more active than white citizens. As citizens, they favored a strong, activist national government and were heavily opposed to the policies of the Reagan administration.

African Americans had a strong social infrastructure, parallel to white organizations, that sustained and encouraged a high level of citizen participation. This infrastructure supported protest politics as well as other types of active involvement in institutional politics. It also reinforced a strong sense of community and solidarity. Despite the historical and contemporary betrayals by established white politicians, African Americans were willing to and capable of practicing ethnic group politics.

Variations in levels of good citizenship can be explained. Appendix Table A.4 reports the analysis of those background factors and adult experiences that are related to good citizenship. Seven factors stand out as having strong direct effects. The history of political involvement since college and the degree of organizational involvement in both civil rights organizations and political organizations contributed significantly to being a complete activist.[31] Active citizens were more likely to trust local public officials. The complete activists, however, were highly critical of the Reagan administration's policies. Those who were older and wanted to be agents of social change were also better citizens. The variables in the equation accounted for 69 percent of the variance in citizenship.

Inspection of Appendix Table A.4 reveals that student activism had only a weak direct effect on full citizen participation. It would be incorrect, however, to conclude that the level of student protest participation was not highly important in shaping adult political behavior. As in McAdam's (1988) study, the influence of student activism was pervasive: it strongly determined distrust in public officials, nonsupport for the Reagan administration, and the level of involvement in civil rights and political organizations. The level of student protest guided adult life choices and a political orientation to the larger white society. Thus student activism affected adult participation indirectly through the intervening factors.

The causal dynamics of full citizenship are similar to McAdam's (1989a) findings for former white civil rights activists. The effects of high-risk activism were both personal and structural. African Americans from the civil rights era emerged from their experience more committed than ever and formed a personal orientation to politics that laid the foundation for ongoing involvement. They maintained an aggressive, ethnic oppositional orientation and were highly involved in civil rights and political organizations. The two key elements for sustaining the politics of these black political gladiators were the aggressive ethnic stance toward the white-dominated society and the level and type of organizational involvement.

## CONCLUSIONS

Tracing the African American activists' generation reveals both continuity and change. Compared with their parents, this generation had a much higher level of education, occupational status, and income. Thé cohort took advantage of the opportunities provided by the civil rights movement and federal enforcement of equal opportunity. Their gains were somewhat limited to opportunities in the public sector and benefited men more than women, and the economic gains leveled off after the early 1970s. Although the civil rights movement produced benefits and changes for the entire generation, the specific level of activism within this generation continued to have long-term effects. The former student activists, because of their high levels of drive and ambition, were the most successful as adults.

The mixed strategies by the federal government, the white backlash, and the emergence of a black power and black nationalist movement temporarily influenced the development of African American political orientation. As black nationalism faded, positive African American ethnic identity emerged. African Americans in the 1980s were proud of what the civil rights movement had achieved. As a distinctive, organized ethnic group, they wanted to fully participate in an open pluralist society (Jaynes and Williams 1989). As a leadership group within the African American community, the activists' generation continued to demand its fair share of scarce resources and opportunities. The major means of achieving collective goals was the full range of political opportunities and participation.

The activists' generation made ideal citizens. They kept informed and informed others about political developments. They participated in political party activities and campaigns. The opportunities for and necessity of being active locally were thoroughly utilized. In moving into electoral politics, the activists' generation did not abandon the effective means of noninstitutional protest politics. When the need arose, they publicly redressed their grievances by using protest politics, which remained part of their political repertoire. Over time they demonstrated an adaptive continuity in their attempts to make history.

In a pluralist but unequal society the activists' generation served as an oppositional force to the conservative era of the 1980s. They were strongly opposed to the Reagan administration's budgetary policy, cutbacks in civil rights enforcement, slashes in social welfare spending for the poor, and the redistribution of wealth upward. Even with their high levels of personal success, they did not adopt the popular

84  Ideal Citizens

conservative ideology of "I've got mine, now you get yours." They continued to work for broad collective or communal goals. They were an effective leadership group for the black working class and underclass, in part because the black middle class frequently used the professional services of whites. Black professionals served the less fortunate, who kept them abreast of the chronic needs and problems the majority of blacks face.

The factors that sustain ideal citizenship are readily apparent from the analysis. The civil rights movement radically transformed pluralist ethnic politics. Those former students who had been the most intensely involved in the movement continued to be the most politically active as adults. The consequences of student activism were pervasive. The protesters even influenced those in their cohort who had not been directly involved in the movement. The civil rights movement opened opportunities and modified the political orientation of the entire generation. Yet youthful politics, by itself, cannot account for effective citizenship. That has taken the achievements of the movement in opening opportunities in electoral politics, particularly within the Democratic party, and the strengthening of black civic organizations. Continued participation in viable civil rights and political organizations is necessary to sustain earlier political commitments. Finally, having the discretionary resources that come with the rewards of professional middle-class occupations provides the material base to offset the normally negative costs of exercising citizenship.

# 4

# THE DIVERGENT POLITICS OF THE WHITE GENERATION

This chapter will explore the consequences of the protest movement for the white cohort. Activists were compared with two other groups of white students: student government leaders and a random sample of noninvolved students. Their subsequent careers and politics were examined in 1971 and 1986. The two historical periods—insurgency during the late 1960s and conservatism in the 1980s—should have had strong and differential effects on the distinctive generational units. Unlike the African American activists' generation, the white cohort should have had a wider variety of life-styles and adult politics. They were more heterogenous, varying from radicalized activists, to ambiguous student government leaders to conventional college males seeking their fortunes in business. Therefore social mobility, careers, occupational values, marital status, and education will be examined before the adult political attitudes and behavior are reported. Many of these factors should be related to the different orientations of young adults. In the second phase of the research additional factors were added to explore the effects of the growing political conservatism during the 1980s. The primary concern is explaining variations in the level and types of citizenship over time and across groups.

## MOBILITY AND LIFE-STYLES OF THE WHITE COHORT IN 1971

Compared with the mobility of the African American activists' generation, the upward mobility of whites, although substantial, was not exceptional. The African Americans were from striving working-class families, whereas the white college students were from the lower middle class. The father or principal guardian worked as a manager or owner of a small business, or as a foreman or supervisor. On the Nam and Powers Occupational Status Index (Nam 1963; Nam and Terrie

1981) the fathers or heads of household have an average occupational status score of 64.8. The average score for white graduates was 86.6, the same as for the African American activists' generation. The upward mobility for white graduates was from the lower middle class to the upper middle class. The average level of education the fathers completed was a little beyond high school. For the 1960s white cohort, 55 percent had some graduate training beyond college. In 1971 the average income of the graduates was $13,074, whereas the family income of their parents while they attended college was $9,010. The upward mobility for the white cohort was substantial by contemporary standards.[1] Their individual incomes also compared favorably to the African American activists' generation, whose average personal income was $10,440 in 1973.

Among the white cohort there was no significant difference between the civil rights activists and the other graduates in terms of their parents' occupational status or income. The parents of activists, however, were better educated than the parents of the nonactivists. Fifty-seven percent of the parents of activists had some education beyond high school, compared with 28 percent of the parents of nonactivists. Other studies of civil rights activists during this period (Demerath, Marwell, and Aiken 1971; Flacks 1971) report higher levels of parental education. This family characteristic is one of the distinctive contributing factors of student activism. Not infrequently it was the mothers of activists who had unusually higher education levels and deeper political commitments.[2]

In contrast to the African Americans, those white students who were active in the civil rights protest were not more upwardly mobile in terms of occupation and income. In 1971 there was no significant difference in the occupational prestige or income of activists when compared with the nonactivists. However, the white activists did have significantly more postcollege education. Eighty-nine percent of the activists, compared with 40 percent of the nonactivists had some graduate education. The activists, moreover, were more likely to complete Ph.D. degrees. The differences reflect the activists' stronger commitment to intellectual pursuits (Baird 1970; Flacks 1971).[3] Part of the difference in advanced education was also due to the college major chosen: activists were more likely to major in the social sciences and needed advanced degrees for professional jobs.

Civil rights activists chose distinctive careers and life-styles. When asked about the ideal requirements for a job or profession, the activists ranked the extrinsic rewards of money, prestige, and a stable, secure future as relatively unimportant. Sixty-eight percent of the student government leaders ranked money the highest, compared with 44 percent of the noninvolved and 21 percent of the activists. Prestige was ranked the highest by 23 percent of the student government leaders, compared with 11 percent for the activists and 6 percent for the noninvolved. The noninvolved ranked a stable, secure future the highest (53 percent), compared with 39 percent for the student government leaders and 14 percent for the activists. The differences in the value placed on these extrinsic rewards were significant.[4] Whatever motivated activists in their career pursuits, it was not money, status, or security.

When given different choices about the ideal organization to work in, the activists selected the public sector, and the nonactivists selected the private sector. Sixty-one percent of the activists preferred working for a government agency, educational institution, nonprofit organization, or social agency. These public-sector jobs could provide greater latitudes of personal and political freedom (Wiltfang and McAdam 1991), and protest politics, although not necessarily approved, was less likely to be negatively sanctioned. Only 22 percent of the nonactivists chose the public sector, and when they did, their choices were different. The nonactivists expressed an interest in a military career, whereas none of the activists did. In an interview one of the activists stated that while in graduate school he had a security clearance and worked in a navy laboratory. He liked the intellectual challenge of research but stated that his major reason was avoiding the draft. After the Vietnam War he used his expertise in physics and worked in the antinuclear movement. The major choices for the nonactivists were working in their own business or professional office, working in a family business, or working for a large corporation.

Occupational preference was related to where the graduates actually worked. Only 11 percent of the activists worked in the private sector. This finding is almost identical to the finding of another study of white civil rights activists (McAdam 1988). Activists concentrated in educational institutions and a variety of social agencies. Fifty-four percent worked in educational institutions, some as college professors in the social sciences.[5] Twenty-seven percent worked for nonprofit organizations, whereas only one nonactivist worked in that capacity. One of the unusual public-sector jobs chosen by an activist was working for AID in Vietnam. As insurgency grew over the war, he wanted a firsthand, nonmilitary view of developments. Later he completed advanced training in social work and became a highly placed state official administering welfare programs for poor families. Another activist's first job after graduate school was with the Internal Revenue Service. As he indicated in an interview, later he went on to university teaching and, as an ex-marine, was effective in the antiwar movement. In contrast, 71 percent of the former student government leaders and 78 percent of the noninvolved worked in the private sector of the economy. A substantial minority followed their father's footsteps in a family-owned business. The occupations of the few activists who did work in the private sector were somewhat unusual. One former activist waited tables in New York while trying to become a successful writer. Another worked as a self-employed photographer to put bread on the table but spent most of his time working on political causes.

Other studies of white radicals (McAdam 1988; Whalen and Flacks 1989) report different career paths because of commitments to political struggles. Similar pressures existed for the early wave of white activists during the period of insurgency. Frequent and intense political protest delays career development and success (Kupers 1990). There are additional reasons for the different career paths. At the cultural level this generation of activists was exposed to the antibureaucratic critique found in David Riesman's *The Lonely Crowd* (1950) and William Whyte's *The Organization Man* (1956). Many of the activists wanted to avoid the twin plagues of conformity and acquisitiveness. Becoming an organization man in a gray flannel suit was unattractive (Gitlin 1987). A psychotherapist (Kupers 1990) who has ex-activists as clients observed that a large number were and still are committed to the struggle to put political principles into everyday practice. For activists there is a grand refusal to be like the men who are most successful in society, those so ruthlessly concerned about getting ahead that they are incapable of caring about others.

The civil rights activists differed strongly from their counterparts in marital status. Early in their adult lives only 25 percent were married and had children. This contrasted with 61 percent for the student government leaders and 86 percent for the random sample. Thirty-nine percent of the activists, 29 percent of the student government leaders, and 6 percent of the noninvolved were married without children. The activists made up the bulk of those who were single or divorced. These findings are similar to those of other studies of the white activists' generation (McAdam 1989a; Whalen and Flacks 1989).

McAdam characterizes the unusual marital status of the activists as part of the personal costs of keeping the faith. Continued involvement in radical politics with an uncertain future works against normal courtship and marriage plans. Unusual and deep political commitments also reduce the pool of eligible spouses. With less than 10 percent of their generation sharing their political commitments (Astin 1970), it could have been difficult for activists to find compatible mates.[6] One white activist married an African American activist, but they could not sustain their marriage in a hostile environment both in and outside the civil rights movement. Another reason for the lower rates of nuclear families was the extensive postcollege graduate and professional training. Marriage and children were delayed while both activists and student government leaders furthered their professional training. A third reason was the experimental sexual revolution, which was revealed in interviews. One activist had a steady mate whom he eventually married. However, he and his activist friends explored a number of relationships. Free, open sex and experimenting with peyote caused the early divorce of another. A fourth reason may have been the emerging women's movement. As one activist indicated in an interview, activists encouraged their wives to become involved, but marriages could frequently not absorb the change.

As young adults, the activists participated more frequently in political organizations. Fifty-four percent belonged to at least one political organization, and 18 percent belonged to two or more. In contrast, 19 percent of the student government leaders and 14 percent of the random sample belonged to a political organization. The activists' political organizations were left wing and antiwar. After being encouraged to leave the movement, only two remained active in civil rights groups, but there was almost universal involvement in the antiwar movement through organizations or protest activities. Membership overlapped slightly in political party organizations and environmental groups, but even here the activists supported more progressive candidates and groups. When working for the Clamshell Alliance, one former activist anticipated a long jail sentence and put his finances in order (related in an interview). If active in the Democratic party, activists supported the candidacy of Eugene McCarthy or Robert Kennedy in 1968 and George McGovern in 1972. Participation in nonpolitical organizations was also different. The cohort members were joiners, with 86 percent of the activists in organizations, compared with 77 percent of the student government leaders and 72 percent of the random sample. The activists were in professional, educational, and service organizations, whereas the nonactivists joined athletic, social, cultural, and religious organizations. The nonactivists were most involved in groups related to their career or business, such as the Chamber of Commerce or the American Bar Association.

The descriptive portrait of the aspirations and achievements of the white generation reveals a greater diversity among the white graduates than was apparent among the African American activists' generation. The civil rights movement had a strong and almost universal impact on African Americans. Their occupations, values, and political commitments were structured by what the movement accomplished. In contrast, the civil rights movement affected only those whites who played an active role in the movement.

The white activists had the distinctive life-styles, values, commitments, and organizational involvements that were common among members of the "New Left" during this period (Flacks 1971; Miller 1987). Most remained active in a variety of movements and causes. An atypical example was a civil rights activist who was recruited by a seductive radical woman and went on to become a leader of the sexual freedom movement (related in an interview). In contrast, the student body leaders on the white campus, unlike their black counterparts, did not participate in movements during the early 1960s; eventually they pursued careers consistent with their high levels of ambition. One former student government president was a successful attorney and very active in electoral politics. The random sample representing the large majority of students pursued the normal paths of conventional careers and life-styles. They, like the student government leaders, welcomed the opportunity to wear the gray flannel suit.

These findings are similar to those of the excellent qualitative studies by McAdam (1988) and Whalen and Flacks (1989). Radicalized students lived unconventional life-styles. Over time nonactivists attending the same universities during this period of political turmoil developed very conventional life-styles of nuclear families and career success in the private sector. Their long-term goals were to make money, move up the corporate hierarchy, or become economic entrepreneurs and maximize their individual talents in the business world. As a generational unit the activists were nonacquisitive compared with other members of the cohort. As academically oriented, relatively unattached, and organizationally active adults their political characteristics should be different.

## Variations in Adult Political Attitudes in 1971

One of the first questions asked about the adult political orientations was how power is distributed in society. Three choices were provided. The first was the pluralist view that no one group really runs the government. From this perspective important decisions about national policy are made by many different groups: labor, business, religious, and educational. These groups influence both political parties, but no single one can dictate to the others and each one is strong enough to protect its own interest. The second was the power elite view developed by C. Wright Mills (1956). This view argues that a small circle of men at the top really run the government. The heads of the biggest corporations, the highest officers in the military, and a few important members of Congress and federal officials are the top policymakers. These interests dominate the Republican and Democratic parties. The third was the class or Marxist perspective. Big business really runs government. The heads of large corporations dominate both the Republican and Democratic parties. Major domestic and foreign polices in Washington go the way big business wants.

The nonactivists believed in pluralist politics. The student government leaders (74 percent) and the noninvolved (75 percent) believed that power is widely distributed. Only 32 percent of the activists accepted this view. The majority of the activists but only 22 percent of nonactivists believed there is a power elite which runs the country. Only 14 percent of the activists, however, believed in a class or Marxist theory of political power, and almost no nonactivists accepted this view. These results confirm the emergence of a "New Left" politics among the activists. The New Left cut their teeth intellectually on the writings of C. Wright Mills (Miller 1987). Contrary to Collier and Horowitz (1989), this early wave of protesting students did not become revolutionary Marxists.

Revealing patterns emerge from the levels of political efficacy and alienation among the three groups.[7] The former student government leaders felt the most efficacious. As political moderates who had a history of involvement and a strong interest in institutional politics, they believed they understood government, had a voice, and could make things happen. The young adults in the random sample, having the least political experience, felt the least efficacious. The former activists varied; their average score fell between those of the other two groups. The activists believed they understood government but felt more powerless about developing a voice and making solid changes. In general, these college-educated respondents were more efficacious and less alienated than a national sample of white adults at that time (Abramson 1977). Within the white cohort the activists were the most alienated. After the Johnson presidency and the early excesses of the

Nixon administration, it is easy to understand why they would be alienated from the government. While working in a federal agency, one of the activists received criticism concerning his earlier arrest and believed he and others were being observed by undercover agents (related in an interview). The former student government leaders who were grooming themselves for traditional political careers in the established political community were the least alienated. The noninvolved had scores in the middle range, being neither highly alienated nor supportive of government.

The difference in political identification is a robust confirmation of the distinctive politics of the activists. During the insurgency period activists maintained a leftist, liberal identity. None of them were political conservatives. Fifty-four percent were self-identified leftists, 25 percent were liberals, and 21 percent were moderates. One activist who was arrested in a protest demonstration vividly recalled in an interview the outrageous behavior of a judge. He came from a middle-class family and expected judges to have some respect for the law. The raw power used by the judge to squash the movement radicalized this liberal reformer. In contrast, there were no leftists among the student government leaders or the random sample. Of student government leaders, 19 percent were conservatives, 71 percent were moderates, and 10 percent were liberals. Among those former students who were not active in student or protest politics, 36 percent were conservatives, 50 percent moderates, and 14 percent liberals.

Party identification differed significantly. During the Nixon presidency no activist became a Republican, whereas 45 percent of the student government leaders were Republicans, as were 44 percent of the noninvolved. Only 29 percent of the activists identified with the Democratic party, compared with 35 percent for the student government leaders and 31 percent for the noninvolved. These figures reflect the difficulties of the Democratic party. The radicalized ex-activists did not trust Democrats because most Democrats supported the Vietnam War and were too entangled in the system to change it. The nonactivists were the targets of the Republican party's new southern strategy (Phillips 1969). Many distrusted the Democratic party for being too oriented toward social welfare. As one white nonactivist volunteered, "Please be aware that my major political disappointment centers on 'liberals' trying to control private property for their ends, e.g., conserving the environment." If members of these three groups ever met at an alumni event, they would have little in common.

Little overlap existed in ideological beliefs about the political economy. The absolute mid-point or neutral stance favoring neither a socialist nor capitalist political economy, was a good dividing point to compare the activists with the nonactivists. Seventy-one percent of the activists favored a socialist political economy; only 3 percent of the nonactivists did. An activist volunteered the following in an open-ended response, "What this country could use is a big group of folks committed to democratic socialism." Conversely, 97 percent of the nonactivists favored capitalism, compared with 29 percent of the activists. Among the activists a socialist ideology was emerging during the period of insurgency. The Vietnam War was viewed either as a giant blunder of the elite national security state or a war fought for the long-range interests of international capitalism. The repressive actions by government agencies against activists and minorities, the sharp lines drawn in fights over domestic welfare legislation, and the adamant resistance to the antiwar movement by political figures like Governor Ronald Reagan of California and Vice President Spirow Agnew (Gitlin 1987; Hayden 1988) tended to further radicalize activists, ideologically if not behaviorally.

## ANALYTICAL RESULTS

Appendix Table A.5 provides the analytic results of the factors that influenced evaluations on how power is distributed, political efficacy, alienation, political self-identification, and radicalism or conservatism. Two variables—age and marital status—significantly influenced beliefs on how power is distributed. The older members of the generation, possibly because of their more extensive political experience, saw power as concentrated among elites or in the hands of the capitalist class. Those who were single, divorced, or married without children also believed that power is more concentrated. There were additional moderate influences on the perception of how it is distributed. Because those from lower socioeconomic origins did not see their parents represented by powerful special interest groups, they believed that power is more concentrated. Student activism had a moderate direct effect and also affected perceptions of power via marital status, public-sector employment, and involvement in political organizations. Among activists, those most likely to believe that power is highly concentrated were those living outside nuclear families, those working in educational or social welfare occupations, and those remaining highly active in political organizations. Lastly those who had lower incomes saw power as more concentrated. They did not feel they had a voice in a pluralist political system.

Ten years out of college, those who felt they were most politically efficacious were younger, were majors in the social sciences or the liberal arts, and were members of political organizations. They felt they understood the political system and that their voice and actions made a difference. Two other sources of efficacy were student activism and not valuing extrinsic occupational rewards. Activism not only had a direct effect but also influenced efficacy through marital status and extrinsic rewards. Those former activists who were outside nuclear families and were not pursuing money and status felt they were the most efficacious. Not valuing material rewards from one's work frees up time to pursue broader political objectives and contributes to a stronger sense of political efficacy.

In the multivariate analysis only one variable was significantly related to the level of alienation. Those college graduates who were not organizationally involved were the most alienated from their government. They suffered from a sense of isolation and experienced powerlessness. At the bivariate level student activism, marital status, and not valuing extrinsic occupational rewards were significantly correlated with the levels of alienation, but their contribution diminished in the more inclusive analysis. The college and postcollege experiences that affected perceptions of concentrated political power also contributed slightly to a sense of alienation from the government.

The major differences among the three groups in political self-identification can be explained more effectively for whites than for African Americans. The white cohort's politics were more ideologically polarized. The two major determinants of a leftist self-identification were activism and lower incomes. The early wave of student protesters were radicalized by their college experience (McAdam 1989a; Whalen and Flacks 1989) and strongly influenced by the direction and intensity of insurgent movements. Student activism also had a strong indirect effect via marital status, occupational sector and occupational preference, keeping active in political organizations, and not valuing extrinsic rewards. The furthest to the left were the former activists who remained outside of nuclear families; enjoyed working in the public sector; did not care about big bucks, job status, and security; and maintained their political commitments in radical or progressive political organizations.

The relationship between lower incomes and a leftist identification reflected leftist involvement in political struggles. Even if they were not full-time political activists, activists expended a great deal of time and energy in pursuing political objectives through movement politics.[8] Activists holding high-status positions such as college professor were, nevertheless, devoting significant energy to political objectives. They were not concentrating solely on those tasks and achievements likely to bring material rewards. One activist teaching at a major university was involved in numerous antiwar protests both on and off campus. Another, although not active in movement politics, devoted his research career to studying the doubly oppressed, such as black women and black adolescents. His official position was at a southern medical school. He was strongly opposed to the location and practice of population control clinics which sterilized thousands of black women after they gave birth, calling it a form of genocide. His outspokenness had negative career consequences and he moved to another university (interview). Thus the narrow objective of career success either was delayed (McAdam 1988; Whalen and Flacks 1989) or never became the sole objective which consumed the activists' creative energy and talent. Incomes, although comfortable, were not likely to increase at the same rate as incomes for those least committed to political struggles.

Who were most likely to support a socialist view of the political economy in 1971? The analytical results are not surprising. Student activism had a very strong direct influence on a leftist ideology and strongly affected leftist beliefs indirectly via marital status, occupational sector, extrinsic rewards, and membership in political organizations. Activism by itself accounted for a significant proportion of the 54 percent of the variance in radicalism that can be explained. Moreover, activists who made the life choices of delaying a nuclear family, working in the public sector, declining the pursuit of material occupational rewards, and choosing to remain active in political organizations were particularly likely to favor a socialist over a capitalist political economy. Younger respondents, more open and adaptable in the formation of a political ideology, also were more radical. Those who came from lower-income families and those earning lower incomes believed in the benefits of socialism.

## POLITICAL BEHAVIOR IN 1971

Given different camps of political ideology, who were the active citizens in institutional politics? Who were informed citizens, active voters, and participants in political campaigns? Are the harsh assess-

96  Ideal Citizens

ments by neoconservatives like Collier and Horowitz (1989) correct? Did the radicals of 1960s want to destroy democracy because of their totalitarian sentiments? Looking first at participation in institutional politics, the results clearly indicate that the activists were highly involved. Like the former student government leaders, they were very active as citizens when compared with the random sample. The average score of participation in institutional politics was identical for the activists and student government leaders (9.61) and higher than for the noninvolved (8.83). The differences were not significant. The activists were slightly less likely to vote at every opportunity, possibly because of the choices available, but they remained highly informed about politics and participated in political campaigns of their choosing. Sixty-eight percent of the activists participated in political campaigns, compared with 61 percent of the student government leaders and 44 percent of the random sample. If active in the 1972 presidential campaigns, the activists supported McGovern and the nonactivists supported Nixon.

The comparisons for protest politics are different. When it came to exercising political options by participating in protest demonstrations or engaging in political activities that could lead to arrest, the activists stood separately from the other two groups. This was the period of heightened political insurgency. In 1971, 75 percent of the activists had participated in protest activities in the previous two years, compared with 13 percent of the student government leaders and 19 percent of those who were uninvolved during college.[9] Thirty-nine percent of the activists had engaged in political behavior that could lead to arrest, whereas only 1 percent of the nonactivists had done so. The white activists remained more involved in protest politics than the black activists. On the dimension of protest behavior the differences were highly significant and provided little evidence to support theories of moderation or disillusionment.[10]

At the descriptive level the results are clear. The activists were full citizens ten years after college. They fit the appropriate label of Milbrath and Goel (1977) of being political "gladiators." They used every means available to make their voices heard. The student government leaders also were highly active citizens but confined their political behavior to institutional forms of politics. Although not completely passive citizens, those in the random sample played a smaller role in either institutional or protest politics.

Appendix Table A.6 reports the analytical results for the two dimensions of political behavior. The two strongest determinants of participation in institutional politics were a high level of political efficacy and involvement in political organizations. Two other factors commonly associated with high levels of institutional political participation—higher incomes and a prestigious occupation—were also related to being active. Those better off had more time and discretionary resources to participate. In addition, their precollege, college, and postcollege experiences contributed to being active citizens. Those former students who came from more economically privileged backgrounds, who majored in the social sciences, who were student activists in institutional or protest politics, who were not married and living with their children, and who worked in the public sector were more active citizens in institutional politics.

By far the most significant experience accounting for differences in protest participation was being an activist. That experience also led to choosing a nonmaterialistic, publicly regarding, political life-style which significantly contributed to participating in protest politics after college. Those graduates who reported that their parents were active in politics were also likely to protest. Both lower income and leftist ideology contributed significantly to protest participation. Over 50 percent of the variance in protest behavior can be explained.

Like the African American generation from the 1960s, the white civil rights activists were ideal citizens. Given the historical context of political turmoil, government repression, and the intense insurgent movement against the Vietnam War, it is a wonder that the activists were not withdrawn and cynical. Ideologically, they were far to the left of the electorate and the leaders of the two major parties. Why would they continue to struggle? First, the activists' baptism into politics was intense. It was a radicalizing experience to work for a just cause and to confront fierce official and unofficial resistance. Once established, strong political commitments are not easy to extinguish. Second, they did not struggle alone. The African American community initially welcomed their support and worked closely with them, and later there were antiwar and reform groups who provided support and reinforcement. In the United States there were wide-ranging movements, from developing unions in the public sector to nuclear disarmament movements. Overseas, insurgency spread across Western Europe, demanding reforms and frequently taking inspiration from the civil rights and antiwar movements in the United States. Third, the activists' distinctive life-styles kept them active and in touch with other activists. They selected progressive causes and joined left-wing organizations that provided mutual support, a social network for expanding political participation, and a larger movement community ready to challenge established authorities. Indeed, those with the strongest organizational links remained the most active (McAdam 1988). One of the activists described in an interview the different types of links to the movement. He kept in contact with previous activists, he was active in a progressive local community organization, he was an active member of Klan Watch, and he was involved in three research projects helping the disadvantaged. Fourth, in their long march to change social institutions, the activists were gradually picking up support and winning small victories. America's Berlin Wall of resistance to reform was beginning to show some cracks. Public opinion against the Vietnam War was moving in their direction. Major reforms in domestic programs were being pushed through Congress. In the long push to restructure American politics, high-risk activism was not without its personal and collective rewards. Whatever minor career costs there were could be absorbed by those committed to an existential, progressive politics.

The student government leaders also became ideal citizens. The risks to them did not exist. Involvement in institutional politics fit with their long-range career plans. Although the links between student and adult political institutions were not as developed in the United States as in many other countries (Weinberg and Walker 1969), they did exist. Political parties and established political organizations readily welcomed these "responsible" young adults into their ranks. The only possible cost was conformity; however, this was negligible because their political ideology was consistent with the business-oriented groups within the two parties. Those who believed that Democrats were going too far were welcomed into the Republicans' embrace. For other active citizens maintaining a moderate ideology, the emerging environmental movement provided a middle-class, safe haven for those unwilling to get involved in more controversial causes.

The sharpest contrast was between the activists and the random sample. The noninvolved were the least active in institutional and protest politics, and their attitudes were at the opposite end of the political spectrum. They were very similar to the acquisitive non-activists in the Whalen and Flacks (1989) study and were likely to become strongly opposed to racial minorities and welfare spending and strongly supportive of individual rights and a "free enterprise" system.

## THE 1980s DEMOGRAPHICS AND LIFE-STYLES OF THE 1960s COHORT

Before the white cohort during the 1980s was analyzed, two comparisons were made. The respondents in 1986 were first compared to those respondents in 1971. The full number of respondents in 1986 were then compared to those who responded to both surveys. The results indicated that the larger number of respondents (eighty-eight instead of seventy-one) was the appropriate group for the analysis. The respondents were identical on those characteristics that should not change.[11]

Demographic changes did occur, but the full and reduced samples shared the same changes. In the 1980s the white cohort was significantly more educated, with additional numbers having completed graduate and professional education. They were more likely to be married and living with children and made significantly higher incomes. They did differ in one important respect from the African American activists' generation: African Americans did not experience any additional upward mobility after 1973.[12] The white cohort continued to be upwardly mobile. In 1971 their average occupational prestige score on a scale from 1 to 100 was 86.65, and this increased to 90.67 by 1986. The difference is significant. There were also some significant differences in political attitudes and behavior. Attitudes became more conservative during the 1980s, and political participation increased. There were no significant differences between the full and reduced samples on these characteristics.

All three groups increased their graduate and professional education, but the earlier differences persisted. Eighty-three percent of the activists had some education beyond college, with over 50 percent going beyond a master's degree. Sixty percent of the student government leaders and 41 percent of the noninvolved had some training after college. The activists pursued master's and Ph.D. degrees, and the student government leaders pursued law. The differences in the level of higher education were highly significant and are partially explained by the majors of the three groups: work in social science fields requires advanced degrees. Seventy-five percent of the activists majored in the social sciences, compared with 40 percent of the student government leaders and 18 percent of the noninvolved.

One of the reasons for doing a two-wave longitudinal study was to see if earlier differences persisted. One major difference from the early 1970s was marital status. In 1971, the activists were much more likely to be single, divorced, or married without children, but by the 1980s the activists were just as likely as the other two groups to be married and living with their children. In general, family sizes were small, averaging less than two children per family. Activists had fewer children, but the difference is not significant. The one characteristic that explains the difference in family size is coming from less affluent families. Those from lower socioeconomic backgrounds were more likely to concentrate the advantages of middle-class status by having smaller families: fewer children means that more family resources can be devoted to each one. The insurgent politics of the 1960s and the heavy investments in graduate and professional training delayed normal family life for the activists. However, once they reached their mid-forties, their family life was similar to that of the nonactivists. Being single and unattached was not a preferred life choice. In an interview one activist stated that his greatest joys were his wife and three children. His wife had been an extremely hard-core leftist earlier in their marriage and remained active in the feminist movement while working as a successful attorney in state government.

Striking differences remained in occupational location and occupational values. Whereas 70 percent of the student government leaders and 62 percent of the noninvolved worked in the private sector, only 17 percent of the activists did. Activists remained concentrated in the educational and helping professions: 62 percent of the activists, 17 percent of the student government leaders, and 12 percent of the random sample were in these professions. Only one nonactivist, compared with 21 percent of the activists, worked in the helping professions. In other types of government jobs the percentages were similar but the work was different. Activists worked primarily in policy areas dealing with the human services. The nonactivists were more likely to be military officers, supervisors in the criminal justice system, or workers in those areas where the governmental and private sector interact, such as departments of commerce and transportation.

The activists' choice of careers reflected their distinctive values and commitments to fostering the public good. They were much less committed to making money and having a secure high-status job. They also were strongly committed to being agents of social change. In their jobs they wanted to redistribute wealth, reduce social inequalities, and improve democratic institutions and procedures. The long-range consequences of the 1960s student protest movement were not limited to adult politics and behavior. Activism significantly affected the type of values associated with careers as well as the particular careers chosen.

Two other characteristics related to the occupational sector of employment were coming from less affluent homes and parents being better educated. The parents of many activists were also public-sector employees in jobs requiring a high level of education with only modest pay.

In the early 1970s the activists earned lower incomes than the other groups, but the differences were not great; by 1986, however, the differences were dramatic. The average individual income for the entire white cohort was a substantial $37,770. The average for the activists was only $32,502, compared with $44,800 for the student government leaders and $37,412 for the noninvolved. Major in college was unrelated to these differences. The single most important factor was student activism. Curiously, the sharp differences in income declined significantly when family instead of individual income was compared. Inspection of the data reveals that activists were more likely to be married to professional women who worked full time. Activism also affected the choices of getting a graduate education, working in the public sector, and holding nonacquisitive values. Occupational prestige had an independent effect on the group's income, but the most important influence was having engaged in protest politics.

The activists certainly did not take a vow of poverty, and in the 1980s they were living comfortably as they pursued broader-based career and political goals. But they were committed to a collectivist dream of transforming society by improving the quality of life for all. By contrast, the acquisitiveness of the nonactivists is consistent with the qualitative findings of Whalen and Flacks (1989). The nonactivists were committed to making money and expanding their economic power by garnering greater control over economic resources and economic independence. Their version of the American Dream was achieving individually oriented economic success.

Another major difference in the life-styles of the three groups was their voluntary organization membership. By the time they reached their late forties, just about everyone belonged to one or more organizations. However, the activists belonged to more organizations and were more active in the organizations they supported.[13] The biggest difference was the type of organization the three groups supported. For example, no activist participated in the Republican party, but 47 percent of the student government leaders and 29 percent of the random sample did. Seventy-five percent of the activists participated in the Democratic party, compared with 33 percent of the student government leaders and 35 percent of the random sample.[14] Since the early 1970s, activists had been becoming more active in the Democratic party. No nonactivists were members in the Rainbow Coalition, feminist groups, or human aid groups such as Amnesty International. Under 5 percent of the nonactivists supported civil rights groups, liberal political action, prochoice, antinuclear, or peace groups. In contrast, the activists were involved in a broad spectrum of liberal and progressive organizations. One helped organize an antiapartheid rally at a private southern university (related in interview). Twelve percent of the males even participated in feminist groups like the National Organization for Women. One very successful activist said in an interview that he hedged his bets. He was active in the prochoice movement and Amnesty International, but because of his high government position he joined and financially contributed to the conservative Democratic Leadership Council. Since this council just might have won a Democratic party internal power struggle, he wanted to be in its good graces. There was some overlap in business and professional organizations that had a political agenda. In business groups the activists were the least involved (21 percent), compared with student government leaders (47 percent) and the noninvolved (23 percent). In professional groups the activists (62 percent) were about as likely to be members as were student government leaders (73 percent), and about twice as likely as the random sample (35 percent).

The organizations can be classified into three groups according to type of participation.[15] The first involved low-risk liberal activism in the Democratic party and in civil rights, humanitarian, and prochoice groups. Although the commitment ran deeper than "checkbook" liberalism, these groups were well established and attempted to reach their political objectives through electoral politics, public information, lobbying, and fund-raising. They were in liberal political organizations. The second kind of participation involved conservative political organizations, including the Republican party as well as conservative political action funds, business associations, religious political action groups like the Moral Majority, and antiabortion groups. The third was a more action-oriented progressive cluster of the Rainbow Coalition, antinuclear, peace, and feminist groups. These progressive political organizations were similar to liberal groups, but their political repertoire also included mass rallies, demonstrations, and protests. Progressive groups combined the normal means of achieving political objectives with more innovative and noninstitutional approaches. Involvement could entail high-risk and high-cost activism requiring ongoing interaction with other activists (McAdam 1989a).[16] The activists were highly involved in liberal and progressive organizations, whereas the student government leaders stood out by their high level of involvement in conservative groups. The random sample was the least involved in liberal groups and moderately involved in conservative groups. No student government leaders belonged to progressive groups, and the noninvolved had only token participation. Comparisons of the activists, student government leaders, and the random sample on the three types of groups were all highly significant.[17]

## POLITICAL ATTITUDES AND BEHAVIOR IN 1986

Changes and improvements were made in the analysis of the white contingent's political characteristics. Attitudinal measures—estimates of how power is distributed, political efficacy, and alienation—were dropped. Political involvement over the life cycle, the level of approval of the Reagan administration, and a more comprehensive measure of the level and type of political behavior were added. The comparable measures with the 1971 study will be presented before the new measures. The three comparative characteristics were political self-identification, the radicalism-conservatism scale, and five items measuring participation in institutional and noninstitutional politics.

Results indicated that there was a significant period effect on political attitudes. Since 1971, the three groups had moved in a conservative direction. The trend toward conservative beliefs, however, did not reflect maturation toward moderate political views because all three groups responded to the new era of conservatism but remained different from each other. Political self-identification shifted. In 1971, 54 percent of the activists were self-identified radicals, 25 percent were liberals, and 21 percent were moderates. By 1986, 29 percent were radicals, 33 percent were liberals, 29 percent were moderates, and 8 percent were conservatives. The degree of change among the student government leaders was even more pronounced: in 1971, they were 19 percent conservative, 71 percent moderate, and 10 percent liberal, and in 1986 the conservative percentage was 57, the moderate percentage was 40, and the liberal percentage was 3. Although not as dramatic, the random sample also shifted toward conservatism. In 1971, 36 percent were conservatives, 50 percent were moderates, and 14 percent were liberals; by 1986, 47 percent were conservatives, 47 percent were moderates, and 6 percent were liberals. The drift in the conservative direction was only statistically significant for the former student government leaders. As moderates in the early 1970s, they waited and observed political trends. By the mid-1980s they had moved to the far right. The differences between the activists and the two groups of nonactivists remained statistically significant.[18]

The random sample was very similar to samples of other white males of the same education and age. In one sense this is not surprising. The demographic characteristics of the student body at Florida State University were very similar to national profiles of college students in terms of majors, gender ratios, parental social status, urban and rural background, and other measures. Indeed, the student body had been used as a test market for new products designed for college students.[19] The political self-identification of the random sample of noninvolved students was comparable to that of a national sample of white males who had the identical average age (47.64 versus 47.28) and had at least a college degree (Davis and Smith 1987). National data in 1987 revealed that 52 percent were conservatives, 25 percent were moderates, and 23 percent were liberals. The strong conservative sentiments among middle-age, white male college graduates reflected this cohort's propensity to conservatism. They were a core group among voters who voted for conservatives. The comparison also demonstrates how the former civil rights activists stood in sharp contrast to other white males in their age and education fraternity. White male activists had more in common with African Americans, women, and segments of the working class.

Appendix Table A.7 reports the details of the regression analysis on political attitudes. The variables having the strongest direct effect on maintaining a leftist political identity were majoring in the social sciences, having been a student activist, wanting to be an agent of social change in one's work, earning lower incomes, and belonging to liberal organizations while avoiding conservative organizations. The influence of student activism was pervasive and had a strong indirect effect on a leftist identification through the different life choices of careers, values, and organizational membership, and the intensity of political involvement over the life cycle. Being less acquisitive and more oriented toward collective goals helps explain how low incomes were associated with leftism. In contrast, nonactivists who chose to emphasize economic success and held acquisitive values defined themselves as conservatives. Thus the radicalized protest generation chose broad-based political careers and life-styles and had sustained political involvements in liberal and progressive organizations.

Political views about the economy also shifted. During the 1980s world leaders like Reagan and Thatcher proclaimed that socialism was dead. Many citizens in Eastern bloc countries shared those views, and even left-wing scholars like Heilbroner (1990) agreed that a socialist ideology was declining and procapitalist sentiments were getting stronger. In 1971, 71 percent of the activists favored a socialist-oriented political economy. By 1986, the percentage had dropped to 58, but this is still extraordinarily high in a capitalist society. The nonactivists supported capitalism in 1971 and did so even more strongly during the Reagan years. This is further evidence for a period effect rather than a maturation effect. Thus all three groups shifted in a conservative direction, but all three groups remained distinctly different. The former civil rights activists were the most progressive and the former student government leaders the most conservative, followed closely by the random sample (Fendrich and Turner 1989).

The second column in the regression analysis in Appendix Table A.7 reports a similar array of influences on favoring a socialist over a capitalist political economy. A leftist political identity was highly correlated with prosocialist sentiments ($r = .81$). Those holding the most radical attitudes worked in the public sector, wanted to be agents of social change, earned significantly lower incomes, and belonged to progressive organizations willing to engage in high-risk, high-cost activism. They also came from less privileged backgrounds; their parents had lower levels of education and earnings. Student activism did not have a strong direct effect. Its influence, however, can be traced through the life-styles and choices that activists had made over the past twenty-five years. The few activists who became political dropouts after college did not hold the same political beliefs, the organizational memberships, the public-sector occupations as those who remained active. They were, however, the exceptions within their generational unit. Moreover, some of them retained their former feelings. I had a long phone conversation with one former activist who had changed politically. He was in the real estate business and had voted for Reagan. I caught him during a cocktail party. Slightly loose, he began to recall the vivid memories of being in a small white minority and facing hostile opposition because of his civil rights activism. The strong personally acquired memories were still part of his life and he was proud of his civil rights activism.

A different pattern emerges on the comparable five items measuring political behavior. As young adults grow older they generally become more involved in politics as they reach their forties and fifties.

This trend is referred to as "political maturation" and is particularly likely for college graduates who, because of their work, see the merits of, or necessity for, getting politically involved. The nonactivists—the student government leaders and the random sample—did become significantly more active in institutional politics. They were reaching the level of political maturity the activists had attained in 1971. In contrast the activists' level of political activism did not change but continued to be significantly higher when compared with the nonactivists' (Fendrich and Turner 1989).

The most massive protest rallies in the United States occurred during the early 1980s. The nuclear freeze rally in New York turned out between eight hundred thousand and one million participants. Over five hundred thousand came out for the labor Solidarity demonstration in Washington, D.C. The twentieth anniversary of Martin Luther King, Jr.'s speech drew a larger demonstration in 1983 than in 1963. There were also numerous opportunities at the local level to protest over policies involving Contra aid, civil rights, the environment, and feminist issues. What remains strikingly different among the activists is their persistent participation in protest politics. They continued to demonstrate and engage in political activities that could lead to arrest. In 1971, 75 percent of the activists continued to protest. In 1986, the percentage was identical. This finding is the strongest evidence for Mannheim's thesis of generational unit continuity.

## NEW MEASURES OF POLITICAL ATTITUDES AND BEHAVIOR IN 1986

During the 1980s the activists held different political attitudes about the Reagan administration's foreign and domestic policies. Their orientation was very similar to that of the African Americans, in that they disagreed on all six policy issues, and were very dissimilar to the student government leaders and random sample. Eighty-five percent of the random sample and 70 percent of the student government agreed with Reagan's handling of the nuclear arms race, whereas only 20 percent of the activists agreed. While refusing to be enthusiastic, 50 percent of the student government leaders and 32 percent of the random sample concurred with environmental policies, compared with 17 percent of the activists. Although there was concern about balancing the national budget, 40 percent of the student government leaders and 44 percent of the random sample agreed with Reagan's attempts to balance the budget, compared with 13 percent of the activists. On domestic issues, Reagan received strong support from the nonactivists. Seventy-four percent of the random sample and 70 percent of the student government leaders agreed with Reagan's civil rights policies, compared with 25 percent of the activists. The nonactivists were also convinced that affirmative action went too far, and this issue continues to be an important Republican party vote-getting issue. In the 1988 and 1990 political campaigns (Blumenthal 1990) the Republican party used the issue of race to its advantage. Similarly, 68 percent of the random sample and 57 percent of the student government leaders approved of the cuts in social welfare programs, compared with 17 percent of the activists. One former activist who is now a highly placed social welfare administrator was so discouraged by the lack of funding that he was considering taking a major salary cut and working for a United Nations–sponsored relief agency (1991 interview). In 1986, there was not a full awareness of the enormous redistribution of income that would result from the 1981 tax cuts for wealthy individuals and corporations (Phillips 1990). The student government leaders were the best off financially and were, therefore, most likely to agree with the tax cuts—57 percent. Only 41 percent of the random sample and 17 percent of the activists agreed. One financially secure activist commented that before the Reagan tax cuts he had to go to a credit union every spring to borrow money to cover taxes. Now he was seeing his savings grow, but he nevertheless opposed the redistribution of wealth upward. The average level of agreement was significantly different for the three groups, with the activists strongly disagreeing with the Reagan administration's policies and the student government leaders strongly supporting Reagan; the random sample was a close second.[20] The counterrevolution of the Reagan era was clearly reflected in the different response patterns.

Appendix Table A.7 reports the regression analysis on attitudes toward the Reagan administration. The causal dynamics were precisely opposite that of a leftist political identification and support for a socialist political economy. Support for Reagan not only correlated negatively with student activism ($r = -.499$) but also had a strong negative relationship to a leftist political identification ($r = -.773$) and radicalism ($r = -.731$). The strongest determinants of support for Reagan were having majored in more vocational-oriented programs, not wanting to be an agent of social change in one's work, being married with children, and belonging to conservative organizations. Those who came from higher occupational-status families also were more pro-Reagan.

108  Ideal Citizens

Another new measure tapped the centrality of political involvement over the life cycle. Each person was asked to recall how important politics was to his or her life during the presidential administrations of Johnson, Nixon, Ford, Carter, and Reagan. The importance was measured by asking if political activities were: the most important part of one's life, central to one's life, occasionally important, only rarely important, or something to be avoided. There was a linear relationship among the three groups. Activists considered national politics more central to their daily lives during each presidency than did the student government leaders, who in turn considered politics more central than the random sample.[21] However, the centrality of national politics declined for activists over time. For example, during the Johnson and Nixon years, 71 percent and 54 percent, respectively, considered politics the most important part of or central to their lives, whereas 33 percent of the activists during the Carter years and 38 percent of them in the Reagan era considered national politics as central. The results should be interpreted carefully. There is no significant decline in good citizenship or political participation: political involvement remained high. Only 16 percent of the activists either rarely participated or avoided politics during the Carter and Reagan presidencies, compared with the random sample: 44 percent (Carter) and 38 percent (Reagan). What the cohort was expressing is the importance of involvement in national as opposed to local issues. During the Johnson and Nixon presidencies, there was a high level of political insurgency and participation because of the Vietnam War and the political crimes and malfeasance uncovered by Watergate. As a result, the passionate intensity of politics during the mobilization of massive insurgency declined, but political commitments and participation did not.

## GOOD CITIZENSHIP IN 1986

Given the greater diversity in the white cohort, the level of politics on the five different types of political participation will be reported for each group. Table 4.1 reports the level of political participation, beginning with the passive form of voting and patriotic acts and continuing with the hierarchical levels of active citizenship based on the threshold of difficulty. The percentages in the table are for those who said they regularly or occasionally participated, except for the protest dimension which also included seldom participate.

On the first dimension, voting and patriotism, the activists were as likely to vote as others but were much less likely to demonstrate patriotism by expressing a feeling of love for the country or flying the flag, whereas this last type of patriotism was very strong among the two groups of nonactivists. The activists were significantly different.[22] Passive political participation was highly correlated with support for Ronald Reagan, both in terms of the scale measuring agreement with the Reagan administration's policies ($r = .643$) and in terms of open-ended comments. When asked what was their major reward, or positive political benefit, a number of the passive citizens volunteered the election and presidency of Ronald Reagan as the answer. Expressions of voting and patriotism were also unrelated to any of the other levels of active political participation. Among the nonactivists there were a number of what Blumenthal (1990) calls "sunshine patriots." These are adults who love to hear strong nationalistic appeals and idolize a strong leader, but do little else politically. As Blumenthal states, "Reagan's leadership did not engage the citizenry but was an attempt to disengage and soothe them" (p.20).

The next level of political participation was active political communication. The cohort was active in keeping informed about politics and engaging in political discussions. When using the full range of scores, instead of percentages, the activists were more likely to send messages to a political leader, inform others about politics, and try to persuade others how to vote. They were followed closely by student government with the random sample bringing up the rear. The next level of participation, being active in a political party, takes more effort than communicating about politics. On the three measures of party participation—joining and supporting a political party, taking an active part in the party, and participating in party activities between elections—the activists were either more active than or as active as student government and more active than the random sample.

The number of persons who remained fairly active in local community politics begins to fall off because such work takes more time and effort. Running for office, forming a group to work on a local problem, and going with a group to protest or lobby a public official are activities associated with the highly committed. Activists and student government leaders had about the same average level of involvement, and both groups were about twice as active as the random sample. Local political involvement was strongly related to issues, and it would not be unusual to find members of this age cohort on opposing sides of the same issue. The average levels of political participation in local politics for the activists, student government, and the random sample were 12.88, 12.22, and 9.79. The differences were significant.[23]

TABLE 4.1
White Political Participation in 1986

| Type of Participation | Activists Percent | Student Government Percent | Random Sample Percent |
|---|---|---|---|
| *Voting and Patriotism* | | | |
| Vote in elections | 96 | 100 | 97 |
| Have a feeling of love for my country | 75 | 97 | 100 |
| Show patriotism by flying the flag or in some other way | 38 | 90 | 77 |
| *Political Communication* | | | |
| Keep informed about politics | 92 | 100 | 88 |
| Engage in political discussions | 96 | 87 | 74 |
| Send a message to a political leader when he or she is doing well or poorly | 71 | 63 | 32 |
| Inform others in my community about politics | 83 | 63 | 32 |
| Try to persuade others how to vote | 71 | 73 | 41 |
| *Party and Campaign Work* | | | |
| Join and support a political party | 67 | 67 | 50 |
| Take an active part in a political party | 58 | 67 | 41 |
| Participate in a political party between elections as well as at election time | 38 | 33 | 21 |
| *Local Political Participation* | | | |
| Be a candidate for office | 8 | 13 | 6 |
| Work with others on a local problem | 58 | 70 | 35 |
| Form a group to work on a local problem | 29 | 37 | 15 |
| Contact local officials on social issues | 54 | 43 | 18 |
| Contact a local, state, or federal official about a personal problem | 25 | 40 | 27 |
| Go with a group to protest to a public official | 17 | 17 | 9 |
| *Protest* | | | |
| Join in a protest march | 62 | 7 | 9 |
| Attend a protest meeting | 75 | 37 | 23 |
| Participate in any form of political activity that could lead to arrest | 62 | 7 | 9 |

The highest level of political participation is exercising one's constitutional rights by airing one's grievances through protest activities. This behavior automatically involves group effort and interaction, and it is frequently risky because it may alienate or anger friends, work associates, or bosses. The activists of the 1960s had much higher levels of participation, with protest politics being part of their normal repertoire. The nonactivists rarely attended a protest march or engaged in political activities that could lead to arrest. A minority of the nonactivists did go with a group to protest to a public official; however, this was not the politics of the streets but the more orderly confrontation and bargaining politics involved in disputed community affairs. The differences among the three groups on the four active dimensions of political behavior were all significant.[24]

The four active dimensions were combined into a complete political activism scale. The scores ranged from 17 to 68. The average scores for the activists, student government, and the random sample were, respectively, 42.96, 39.50, and 32.74. The differences were significant.[25] Twenty-five years after their student protests, the activists were still the complete activists, or political gladiators. In this respect they continued to march to a different drummer and more closely resembled the African American activists' generation than they did their own cohort of white college graduates.[26] For activists, being a citizen was more than dutifully voting and waving the flag on the Fourth of July. When full citizenship or patriotism was defined as being active citizens but not engaging in protest, the activists still had the highest total scores. They were the "true patriots" or ideal citizens, in contrast to the sunshine patriots. Many of the student leaders and some of the random sample were also active citizens. Given that their political and economic interests were often embodied within, or protected by, elected officials, they had less need to use noninstitutional politics.

It is possible to compare the citizenship of the three groups with a national sample from the General Social Survey (Davis and Smith 1987) on six items of political participation. Three active dimensions of citizenship (local politics, party participation, and political persuasion) and voting were addressed in the national survey.[27] White male college graduates in their forties and fifties were compared, and they turned out to be very similar to the random sample on a number of characteristics. The two groups were the same age, had fathers with the same level of education, earned similar incomes, and had similar proportions of Democrats and Republicans.[28] The levels of political participation or citizenship were almost identical for the random sample and the national survey. Both the activists and the former student government leaders were significantly more active as citizens than their counterparts in the national sample of the population.[29]

Appendix Table A.8 reports the regression analysis for complete activism. The strongest determinants of full citizenship were being younger, wanting to be an agent of social change, having a history of political involvement over the life cycle, and belonging to liberal political organizations. Those who were younger, that is, those in their early forties instead of late fifties, still had the energy and health to maintain a high level of citizenship involvement. Student activism had a weak direct effect. The long-term consequences were diffuse. Activism influenced the level of citizenship through the life choices, values, lifestyles, and organizational involvements that set the activists' generational unit apart. Factors that had weaker effects on full citizenship were the advantages that came from advanced education and prestigious occupations, a left-liberal political identification, and lower incomes.

The analysis of complete citizenship was extended to take into consideration the proportion of student activists, student government leaders, and the random sample in the college population. Each group was assigned a proportional weight, and the regression analysis was recomputed.[30] Appendix Table A.9 reports the results. The model for citizenship improved in that the amount of variation explained increased to almost two-thirds, or 62 percent.[31]

The model for citizenship using proportional weights makes good intuitive sense. Those college graduates who came from more privileged backgrounds in terms of having better-educated parents in prestigious jobs earning higher incomes were more likely to exercise full citizenship as adults. The advantages of higher social status and political participation were passed on to the next generation. College experiences also contributed to full citizenship. Those who were active in either protest or student government politics were more active as adults, and students who majored in the social sciences were more active citizens. Lower college grades were also associated with being politically active as adults. This is because lower grade point averages are considered a social indicator of being more well rounded and more involved in group activities which can lead to greater citizenship participation. Valuable time spent studying and earning higher grades can deter students from participating in group activities that foster active citizenship.

Postcollege experiences contributed significantly to explaining full citizenship. The two strongest determinants were the centrality of political involvement over the life course and commitment to a set of change-oriented occupational values. Those who sought work that improved the quality of life for all participated more as citizens. Curiously, advanced graduate education worked against full citizenship. It demanded an intense period of professional socialization, which normally required a reduction in political commitments and political participation. These early demands as well as those associated with success in a profession no doubt diminished the amount of time and energy that could be devoted to political participation. Lower incomes were also associated with full citizenship: higher incomes reflected the high value, or importance, of acquisitiveness. Those who devoted their lives to making money and gaining economic power and resources did not have the time or inclination to fully participate as citizens. Also, the younger members of the white cohort had the energy and health to participate more actively.

Lastly, group involvement was crucial in reinforcing the values of democratic citizenship. Liberal organizations promoted and reinforced full participation, whereas both conservative and progressive organizations discouraged some types of participation. Those who were highly active in conservative organizations were likely to delegate some forms of political participation to their leaders and not participate in noninstitutional or protest politics, whereas those committed to progressive organizations were involved in protest politics but were less active in party and local politics.[32] This particular model of full citizenship may accurately reflect what causes variation in the citizenship participation of middle-aged, white, male college graduates.

## Conclusions

The stormy 1960s left its mark on the white college graduates. The activists did not start the decade as radical leftists. If anything, they were from the "radical center" and unlike the red diaper babies of radicals from the thirties who led demonstrations at Berkeley and other elite universities.[33] The earliest white activist wave was motivated by liberal idealism and religiously based humanitarian commitments (Demerath, Marwell, and Aiken 1971; McAdam 1988). The movement was the beginning of their radicalization. As the decade advanced, the activists' radical beliefs were developed and reinforced, and they became the New Left of American politics. When new movements sprang up and the antiwar movement intensified, there were plenty of chances to continue to engage in protest politics. Seventy-five percent of the former activists took advantage of those opportunities and continued to protest. What McAdam (1988) identifies as the strongest legacy of the civil rights movement—the impulse to action—is evident in the distinctive careers, occupational values, and life-styles the activists chose. Their choices provided both the opportunities for and reinforcement of the commitment to an action-oriented, politically motivated advancement into adulthood.

One of the major differences between groups was the activists' relative lack of acquisitive values. For them money, status, and job security were unimportant. In the second follow-up it was clear that the activists wanted their work lives to contribute to social change. The contrast of the activists working in the public sector and the nonactivists working in the private sector is consistent with these different commitments and choices. When the activists and nonactivists overlapped in the same sector, their jobs were dissimilar, with the activists concentrated in educationally oriented and human service jobs and the nonactivists concentrated in social control or more political- and business-oriented public-sector jobs. For the few activists in the private sector, their means of livelihood were incidental to their preferred work activities.

During the height of political insurgence, the liberal wing of the Democratic party floundered on the twin rocks of the African American and antiwar protest movements. In the early 1970s, the activists distrusted the leadership of the Democratic party because of the persistent domination by cold war warriors and the willingness of the liberal-labor coalition to compromise on important domestic legislation. With no viable third party and the rejection by the Democratic party, crazy politics ensued, as exemplified by the Yippies. The wounds from these battles on the left have yet to fully heal (Blumenthal 1990). The nonactivists saw the Democratic party as going "too far" in social welfare legislation and shared the beliefs of conservative Democrats that the party was being taken over by "kooks" (Edsall 1984). The Republicans' strategy of developing a new conservative majority (Phillips 1969) was designed to capture the nonactivists, and the strategy was successful. Nonactivists turned to the Republican party or became "Democrats" for Reagan.

As the counterrevolution gained a full head of steam, the nonactivists were eager passengers. How politics changed! The spin doctors of the new conservative ideology popularized the myth of a new oppressed class. Because of excessive regulation, they said, the new victims in society were the rich and powerful. If the government got off their backs, they could stimulate economic development that would lead to a full recovery.[34] Another major development during the 1980s was the decline of state-centered socialist economies. This new historical period of conservatism was reflected in a conservative shift for both the activists and nonactivists.

But the activists did not mature politically and become nondistinct. There was instead a period effect, with the activists and nonactivists maintaining their relative positions in a new political environment. The activists moved from the far left to left of center, and the nonactivists moved from moderate conservative to the far right in terms of political self-identification and beliefs about the political economy. As Kupers (1990) states, "The compelling common denominator of sixties activists is that early adulthood was played out on a stage of social upheaval while at midlife the environment seems downright hostile to those who would put progressive ideas into practice" (p.89).

The emergence of distinctive generational units from the same age cohort is clear. The advantage of having two control groups is to see not only how the activists were different, but also how the student government leaders differed from the typical student. The student government leaders were very active in institutional politics and highly efficacious. They were the promising recruits for the two parties. After college they participated in political campaigns and established interest-group politics. They may have been dismayed at McGovern's capture of the Democratic party's nomination in 1972, but there were still opportunities to work with the business-oriented segment of the Democratic party and an open invitation to join the Republican ranks. They were living conventional life-styles and developing conventional political orientations.

For those who did not participate in college, politics was less central to their personal life choices and career development. They were less involved organizationally and politically. Being college graduates, they had more information, resources, and opportunities than most U.S. citizens, but they were only marginally active in politics and did not fit the definition of ideal citizens. Representing the bulk of college graduates from this era, they shared a distaste for the extremes of the insurgent movements.

Comparisons between the two periods are possible. The strongest confirmation of Mannheim's thesis that distinctive generational units emerge during certain historical periods is that the activists continued their commitment to protest politics. In 1971 and in 1986, 75 percent of the former student activists continued to use the means of political protest to achieve political objectives. There was also continuity in the institutional politics of the activists and nonactivists; however, the nonactivists were maturing into citizenship at a more delayed rate than the activists.

The real strengths of the 1980s study are the multidimensional measures of citizenship, the comparison with a national sample of white males in the same age and education cohort, and a general model for citizenship participation. The activists scored higher than other groups on every dimension of active political participation. They also scored lowest on the passive dimension of voting and patriotism. Activists were not sunshine patriots. Citizenship comprised more than voting and waving the flag. The activists were heavily involved in institutional and noninstitutional politics. They may not have entered the political arena with the same passionate intensity of their youth, but that difference may have reflected the decline of mass insurgency as much as individual preference. Many of the student government leaders were also ideal citizens, heavily involved in all forms of active institutional politics. As mostly conservative Reagan supporters, they were motivated by a different ideology, group commitments, and political issues.

The members of the random sample who were involved in neither protest politics nor student government were marginal citizens. It is fortuitous that a national sample of adult white males held very similar political views and had about the same level of political participation as the random sample. The comparison provides a bench mark for how different the activists and former student government leaders were. Although it was not the intent of the research, the results do suggest why women and people of color are so critical of this generation of white males. The political orientations were not just different but oppositional. The exception was the white activists' cohort.

Both the activists and the student government heads were involved in politically oriented interest groups. They were likely to have a significant and continuing impact on the political system through their group involvements. For example, in Walsh's (1988) analysis of the mobilization of citizens after the near meltdown at Three Mile Island, sixties activists were the key organizers in about half of the affected downwind communities. They used their acquired political skills to achieve collective goals.

A unique characteristic of this study is the possibility of comparing the subsequent politics of African American and white activists. White activists had the same high level of involvement as the African American generation. Both the black and white students were involved in the same local protest community. Their life choices were different. Yet they shared the characteristic of ideal citizenship. The next chapter will draw out the similarities and differences between the black and white members of the activists' generation.

# 5

# AFRICAN AMERICAN AND WHITE ACTIVISTS TWENTY-FIVE YEARS LATER

This chapter will explore the differences between the African American and white *activists*. Although they were in the same movement, their social origins were quite different, and their subsequent life choices after college also varied. First, the dissimilarity in precollege and college experiences will be examined. Second, the differences in adult life choices between African American and white activists will be presented. Major variations existed for the levels of completed education, occupational sector, occupational values, religious orientation, political involvement over the life cycle, and current involvement in organizations. Despite these differences, the subsequent adult politics were almost identical. It will be shown that the African American and white activists did not diverge significantly in their political attitudes and behavior. They were equally progressive and exercised a high level of citizenship. This is an amazing finding given their subsequent histories and structured opportunities. The almost identical politics twenty-five years later speaks to the enormous impact of participation in the civil rights movement, life choices, and new political challenges.

Third, before the major factors that explain the internal variation in the adult politics of African American and white activists in the 1970s are analyzed, the analysis of a ten year follow-up will be reviewed. One of the advantages of longitudinal research is that it provides an opportunity to compare patterns of results over time. The earlier work (Fendrich 1977) is partially correct but needs to be modified given subsequent events and additional information.

Fourth, causes of variation among activists in each of the major dependent variables will be reported. Given the comparative political homogeneity among the activists, there is less variance to be explained than there is when comparing activists to nonactivists. Nevertheless, there are important differences among activists that can be explained. Not all the activists were extremely progressive in their political views, nor were they involved in every type and level of political participation. What accounted for this internal variation? Did precollege backgrounds, like the socioeconomic status of their parents, have any long-range effects? What about college experiences? Did jobs in the public sector, economic success, marital status, religious commitments, acquisitiveness, or social-change values determine who was likely to oppose the prevailing ideology that undergirded the Reagan administration's policies? What determined complete citizenship? Were the long-term history of political involvement and the extent of organizational involvement more, or less, important than other life choices? Lastly, the chapter will end with a discussion of the problems involved in coping with the conservative era.

## DIFFERENCES BETWEEN AFRICAN AMERICAN AND WHITE ACTIVISTS

Appendix Table A.10 reports the differences between the African American and white activists. The means and standard deviations for both groups and the probabilities associated with an analysis of variance between blacks and whites are presented on the major independent variables.[1] The two groups were approximately the same age, with whites being slightly older (47.21) than the African Americans (46.47). The social origins were quite dissimilar. The median levels of education, occupational status, and income for the African American parents were much lower. Their fathers, or heads of household, completed 10.76 years of schooling, had an occupational prestige score of 44.53, and earned on average $8,940 a year in the early 1960s. For whites their fathers averaged about one year of college, had prestige scores of 78.17, and earned $13,500. The differences in the three measures of social status of the parents were statistically significant.

The whites were not dissimilar from white activists in other studies, having emerged from the highly educated middle class. The social origins of the African Americans were unlike those of the white groups. The lower social origins of African Americans from the striving working class document the strong commitment to education in the African American community, despite relatively modest resources. The lower social origins also highlight the importance of an ethnic group segment of the working class in bringing about social change through political insurgency. Comparing the upward mobility of fathers and sons, the African American activists jumped from 44.53 to 88.33. The upward mobility for whites was less dramatic, moving from 78.17 to 89.75. Thus in one generation the gap in socioeconomic status was closed, with the African Americans and whites having the same level of occupational status. This rapid change was the result of the civil rights movement, the ambition of African American activists, and the subsequent pressure from the federal government to open opportunities for well-qualified African Americans.

While attending the universities, African American activists were less likely to major in the social sciences than the whites. Twenty-seven percent of African Americans, compared with 75 percent of the white activists, majored in the social sciences. Only 4 percent of the white activists majored in the more vocational non-arts-and-sciences programs like education, social work, or business, whereas 41 percent of the African Americans did. Part of this difference was due to the vocational emphasis that was traditionally built into black universities, and part was due to sons of the striving working class seeking a "practical" education.

During the early 1960s the social sciences in U.S. universities were noted for their liberal and slightly reformist orientation toward domestic policies. There were many advocates of specific programs to extend and improve the New Deal. The white activists were more thoroughly exposed to this liberal ideology (Fendrich 1977). The differences in educational exposure were related to political differences in the early 1970s (Fendrich 1977). Social science majors were further to the left ten years later.

After receiving their undergraduate degrees, whites were much more likely to continue advanced academic and professional training. The two major factors that accounted for the significant difference were race and the incomes of their parents. In the early 1960s graduate education was not nearly as accessible for African Americans as it was for whites, who could take better advantage of the expanding opportunities for educational advancement. Family resources also played a significant role. Those activists who came from more economically secure families were more likely to go on to graduate school. Only 17 percent of the whites did not go beyond an undergraduate degree, compared with 41 percent of African Americans. Seventy-nine percent of the white activists and 55 percent of the African Americans held at least a master's degree. Both groups were highly educated, but whites were more so.

The occupational sector and occupational values emphasizing extrinsic rewards were significantly different for the two groups. Whereas 31 percent of the African American activists held jobs in the private sector of the economy, only 17 percent of the white activists did. This is consistent with the findings from the 1970s which indicated that some African Americans valued private-sector employment. Neither the background characteristics nor the advanced graduate education can explain this difference. African Americans were striving "to be all they could be" and looked forward to breaking down past barriers to employment and economic success in the private sector. White activists, because of preparation and choice, preferred public-sector employment early in their careers and remained in public employment.

African American and white activists were equally committed to wanting to be agents of social change. However, the African Americans placed a significantly higher value on the extrinsic rewards of money, prestige, and security. The average score for African Americans was 6.78; it was 5.96 for whites. It is easy to understand why African Americans, being from the striving working class and the first generation into solid middle-class positions, would place a high value on money, status, and security. These were scarce commodities in the African American community.

Breaking down the measure of extrinsic rewards to the single issue of money reveals that African American activists were more acquisitive than their white counterparts.[2] Not only did they value money more, but they also earned more. Although not significantly different statistically, the average income for African American activists was $38,460, compared with $32,502 for white activists.[3] These findings are consistent with the research of the Geschwenders (1973) and Gurin and Epps (1975). African American activists were ambitious young adults pounding on the doors of American institutions, demanding to be let in. Because they came from economically depressed backgrounds caused by a history of racial oppression, striving and achieving economic success were goals consistent with the movement's objectives. African Americans could feel proud about their striving for economic success. The major differences that account for variation in incomes among the activists were the value placed on extrinsic rewards, the amount of advanced education, and working in the private sector or a high government post.

The differences in marital status between African American and white activists also is noted. The white activists were slightly more likely to be living in nuclear families and had fewer children. African

Americans married earlier and were more likely to be currently divorced. Ninety-two percent of the whites were married, compared with 76 percent of the African Americans. During the period of political insurgency of the late 1960s, the white activists delayed marriage and raising children. The African Americans started families earlier; however, in a society where one-half of first marriages ended in divorce, they were at a point in their marriage cycle that put them at greater risk. Divorce rates were also higher for African Americans.

The African Americans were significantly more religious than whites. Sixty-nine percent attended church at least two or three times a month, compared with 13 percent of whites. Sixty-three percent of the white activists never attended church. No white activist was a born-again Christian, but 35 percent of the African Americans were. Clearly, the whites were nonreligious, having a secular orientation. For African Americans churches performed a number of functions. Not only did they provide religious worship and guidance but they were also a center of local community life and an originator of political action (Jaynes and Williams 1989). For African Americans, social affiliation with black churches remained a powerful force. One former activist commented in an interview that black churches kept the middle class and working class bound together.

The dissimilarities in religious orientation contributed somewhat to explaining the difference in organizational involvement. The measure of organizational involvement took into consideration both the number of organizations and the level of participation.[4] Both African American and white activists continued to be highly active. The average score for African Americans was 33.74, compared with 29.88 for whites. Generally, what these scores reflect is a moderate level of involvement in a number of organizations plus contributing time and serving as an officer in a few. Membership was concentrated in civil and human rights organizations, liberal single-issue groups, the Democratic party, and, for African Americans, black church organizations. African Americans frequently belonged to dual organizations like black social work and national social work organizations. The scores on organizational involvement were significantly higher than for the nonactivists.

In a 1991 interview, one former black activist explained that he was not involved directly in political organizations, but that he devoted his free time to build volunteer organizations among black college students. As an administrator in a black university he started programs that included (1) adopting less fortunate families and providing food and basic necessities on a year-round basis, (2) Becoming-A-Man, a program consisting of tutoring fourth- to ninth-grade boys and providing scholarships, (3) assisting the elderly with cleaning, transporting, and visiting programs, and (4) establishing 48 Hours, through which an African American male spent forty-eight hours as a volunteer with a fatherless child over a period of weeks.

Although African Americans had higher levels of organizational involvement, whites had a history of more intense political activity. White activists scored significantly higher on the measure of political involvement over the life cycle than African Americans did. During the political insurgency that occurred during the Johnson and Nixon presidencies, political involvement was a central part of the daily lives of white activists. They experienced intense periods of political opposition and protest during the height of the antiwar movement. In an interview, one activist said he still felt a strong sense of guilt about Vietnam. He was a speaker at a conference of Vietnam Vets Against the War that Jane Fonda helped to organize, and he contributed a chapter to a book opposed to the war. Yet he personally knew many Vietnamese friends who were deserted when the United States withdrew. The war ended, but his friends suffered, leaving him a sad legacy.

African Americans tended to get more involved politically under two sets of conditions: when Democratic presidents were elected, or when they felt betrayed by the political system (Gurin, Hatchett, and Jackson 1988), as during the Reagan presidency. Regardless of race, employment in the public sector contributed significantly to the centrality of political involvement for activists. Public-sector employment provided more opportunity and fewer sanctions against being politically active.

The first wave of this research in the mid-1970s analyzed the adult politics of the African American and white activists on radicalism and a short three-item measure of participation in protest politics.[5] An analysis of variance between race and the two dependent variables, as well as a more elaborate model (Fendrich 1977), reported that African Americans were much less likely to hold radical attitudes or engage in protest behavior than whites. For example, the average score on radicalism for whites was 50.09; for African Americans it was 39.26. For protest behavior, the average score was 6.50 for whites, compared with 5.05 for African Americans. The major conclusion was that white activists were maintaining a stronger commitment to a socialist ideology and protest politics because they were initially motivated by a stronger ideological commitment. In contrast, African American student protest behavior was part of a larger movement with a more pragmatic or practical purpose. They were protesting to open opportunities for themselves and other black Americans.

The findings and conclusions were valid during the period of political insurgency. White activists continued to engage in political insurgency largely because of their opposition to the Vietnam War. They were radicalized. African American activists were less active in protest politics as they successfully took advantage of new career opportunities that opened as a result of the civil rights movement. Neither co-opted by the available opportunities nor enamored of militant black separatism, African Americans were evolving into a powerful ethnic group.

## THE MIDLIFE POLITICS OF THE ACTIVISTS

In the 1980s a new political reality confronted both African American and white activists. The conservative counterrevolution successfully established the political agenda and put into place its loyal followers from the 1960s. There was a massive counterattack on the advances generated by political insurgency and liberal politics between 1964 and 1974 (Domhoff 1990). In the face of this opposition, the political attitudes and behavior of the African American and white activists became remarkably similar. Their politics remained progressive and oppositional. Although they were not as prosocialist as they were in the early 1970s, there was no difference between them in their radical sentiments.[6] Both groups were in solid disagreement with the Reagan administration's policies. On a scale of 6 to 30, where 30 represents strong and complete disagreement with Reagan, the white average score was 24.38, compared with 24.18 for African Americans. Their scores were almost identical on measures of complete political participation or ideal citizenship. The average for whites was 47.96; for African Americans, 48.71.[7] These scores were significantly higher than those from nonactivists from both racial groups. The only political variable on which the African Americans and whites varied significantly was political self-identification. The average score for African Americans was 6.25, or slightly to the left of moderate Democrats. The average score for whites was 7.79, placing them further to the left. This difference, although significant, was modest in comparison with that shown by white males of the same age and education, who were conservatives.

If racial distinctions cannot account for variations in the midlife politics of former activists, what can? Here the analysis turns to the background and life choices that significantly affected the adult politics of activists. Appendix Table A.11 reports the regression analysis for the three measures of political sentiments—radicalism, opposition to Reagan, and political identification—and the measure of complete activism or ideal citizenship. Looking first at radicalism, we see that three factors had strong independent effects on prosocialist sentiments. Among the activists, those who were older were the most radical. This means either that the older members of the activists' generation were the least influenced by the new conservative, procapitalist shift, or that as activists gained more political experience during midlife they saw the necessity of radically restructuring American institutions. I favor the first interpretation over the second because older activists did not have a stronger history of political involvement or organizational participation, which would be related to political experience.[8] Those most strongly committed to being agents of social change in their life's work were also more radical. Since wanting to improve institutions by reducing social inequality and expanding democratic participation is consistent with a socialist ideology, it is not surprising that activists who desired this role were the farthest to the left ideologically. The third independent factor that determined prosocialist sentiments was earning a lower income. The higher the income, the more people have vested interests in a status quo, procapitalist economy. Lower-income activists had a stronger desire to radically reform it.

Among the activists, two factors explain who had the strongest opposition to the Reagan administration. Those who least valued money, status, and security were the most opposed to the Reagan administration's policies. During an era when greed was considered a virtue (Phillips 1990), opposition from those who cared the least about material success should come as no surprise. However, the second factor is somewhat startling. Those activists with the most advanced graduate or professional education were the least critical of the Reagan administration. Note that this does not mean they strongly supported Reagan's policies; it means they were less outspoken in their criticism. The intense oversocialization into a professional position may have produced a reluctance to strongly criticize those in authority (Jacoby 1987). For example, during the Vietnam War, the educated upper middle class supported the government's policies the longest (Goertzel 1976).

Among the activists, two factors explain the variation in political self-identification. Regardless of race, those who attended church the least identified themselves farther to the left. The least religious, or more secular, were self-identified as leftist. Regular churchgoers were also the least radical and least opposed to the Reagan administration's policies. Apparently active church involvement moderated the political sentiments of the activists' generation. Possibly the regular churchgoers were more likely to believe that their fate lay partially in the hands of a supernatural power rather than in collective politics. Lower incomes were again significantly related to a leftist ideology among the activists. Activists making incomes above $50,000 had less ideological inclination to identify themselves as leftists. Those few making less than $10,000, and others making under $30,000, had stronger New Left sentiments.

What about good citizenship? Who among the activists were the most active in all levels of political participation? A different pattern emerges. Race, age, college experiences, most life choices after college, and ideology did not account for much of the variation in citizenship levels among activists. The two strongest independent factors were having maintained a history of political involvement and active participation in social organizations. It is logical that the most politically active would have a history of political involvement, since past patterns of behavior reinforce current political participation. Moreover, it is clear that the greater the group participation and involvement in civic culture, the more likely it is that the members will be ideal citizens. Citizenship is not sustained by ideological commitment, intellectual prowess, ethnic identity, or prestigious jobs and advanced education; it is sustained by getting involved collectively. This finding is identical to that of McAdam (1988). The best predictors of contemporary activism are the number of political organizations to which activists belong and their history of political activism after college. In other words, activism does not persist in a vacuum: it must be structurally reinforced. Lastly, being raised in families with lower incomes and, to a lesser extent, having less prestigious parents had a significant direct effect among activists.[9] Among activists the disadvantage of less privileged backgrounds contributed to more intense political participation. Here is a hidden advantage of a working-class or lower-middle-class social origin. Activists from less privileged backgrounds saw the practicality of remaining active citizens. Politics may not be the only game in town; however, the activists from disadvantaged backgrounds saw its necessity.

## SUMMARY OF FINDINGS

By comparing the activists it was possible to see the stark differences in the social origins between blacks and whites and to record the extraordinary upward mobility of African Americans. As activists they came from the striving working class, and because of their ambition and talents, the civil rights movement, and liberal reforms they were able to achieve socioeconomic parity in just one generation. The social origins of the white activists and their intellectual exposure in college significantly contributed to their becoming active in protest politics and developing the ideology of the New Left. Both groups were highly educated, but the privileges of class origin and being white contributed to greater education achievements for whites.

African Americans were more interested and successful in achieving material success than their white counterparts, and they also placed a greater value on money, status, and security than white activists. An erroneous conclusion could be drawn that the African American activists cashed in or sold out their political commitments because of their acquisitiveness. However, this is inconsistent with their political values and commitments. The economic emphasis and success of African Americans more accurately reflects the long-range objectives of escaping the economic oppression of racial discrimination. African Americans were like earlier waves of upwardly mobile Jewish Americans; they could both be proud of their economic achievements and maintain their political liberalism.

African Americans remained highly involved in the civic culture and stood out from white activists in their religious involvement in black churches, which provided many important organizational resources for the black community. But the centrality of political involvement was greater for white activists because of their intense political involvement during the period of antiwar political insurgency.

One of the more remarkable findings is the similarity in the political sentiments and behavior of African American and white activists. Compared with their nonactivist counterparts, they were more oppositional in their political sentiments and more active as citizens. Nevertheless, there were internal distinctions among activists. Some of the factors that explain variations between activists and nonactivists also account for differences among activists. The oppositional sentiments can best be explained by the activists' values and commitments. Those who wanted to be agents of social change and were nonacquisitive held more radical and oppositional beliefs. Those who espoused more secular values identified farther to the left. Lower income was also associated with being farther to the left. Similar patterns were found in Chapter 4. What was unique about political sentiments is that the older members of the cohort tended to be more to the left. They were the least affected by the conservative era.

Background factors, race, or ideology did not have a major impact on the variation in citizenship among activists. Ideal citizenship was sustained by active participation in civic organizations and by a history of political involvement since leaving college. These findings are similar to those of McAdam's (1989a) research. Interestingly, former activists from less privileged backgrounds, regardless of race, remained more active as adult citizens. They recognized more acutely that collective advancements are the result of unified political struggles and that these group gains can best be maintained by remaining highly active politically.

## COPING WITH THE CONSERVATIVE ERA

Another observation from this longitudinal study parallels the work of Doug McAdam (1988), who reports the stresses among former activists. To claim that activists are good citizens is not to claim that oppositional politics has not taken its toll. There were signs of mental health problems, substance abuse, and other personal tragedies. For example, in this study a leading black female activist showed strong signs of mental stress and substance abuse during an interview. This was confirmed by others who remained in contact with her. A second female activist had severe mental problems and was last seen as a "bag lady" at the Philadelphia airport. Another former white civil rights activist lost his teaching position at a predominantly black high school because of charges of providing alcohol to minors leveled against him by female students. He eventually was cleared of any wrongdoing, but, disappointed with the administration's handling of the case, he quit teaching at the high school and went on to teach computer programming at a vocational tech school.

Delayed careers, or careers marked by heavy political commitments and lower incomes, also generated stress, particularly when the activists became isolated from a supportive political group. The 1980s were particularly stressful. One former activist volunteered, "There are no rewards in politics; I tend to escape into music, hobby diversions, and passive consumerism." Another isolated former activist, who was in the process of developing a bioecological political perspective, said the following:

> The real global problems are transcendental over politics. Except for the eight hundred million Chinese, the capitalists and Communists alike are not prepared to stop population growth or curtail the deadly pollution and despoiling of the planet. The tragic destruction of life support is the issue, not conventional politics.
> Where is the "New Left" now? Maybe some of all political persuasions have rubbed off on me and any minute now it will all come into focus. As far as I can see the lines will be drawn very differently soon. And although my socialized self reacts in a humane way to suffering, my biological and reasoning self says the family with defective genes who has eight kids is as much the enemy of my world of books and culture as the racist redneck of the sixties was to me then. I am waiting for the historical moment to inform me of which way to go. I remain open-minded. However, idealism has been replaced by survivalism and I'm not insulated by middle-class finances, comforts, and manners or pretensions—or by illusions about security provided by a corrupt Pentagon.

Still a third stated,

> Can you understand that I had to sign a loyalty oath in order to be a substitute teacher in 1986? Do you realize that none of the academic staff at FSU has lifted a finger to assist me since 1962?
> The academics at FSU always ask for my input to *their projects*. But they never ask me: "Jerry, how is it with you now? How might we help you make a contribution to society? What can we do to nurture your blossoming and your fulfillment?" (emphasis added)

One former black activist complained that today's black students "don't give a damn about getting an education or furthering civil rights." Another stated in an interview that his two children thought he was lying when he mentioned his intense involvement in the civil rights struggle: "They couldn't believe things were that bad." These are atypical responses but are a real part of the unvarnished record.[10]

Despite the conservative 1980s, the political identities and commitments of African Americans and white civil rights activists were firmly established and deeply embedded. One white's only regret was not being more involved in the struggle. He made this statement despite the fact that his conservative father never forgave him and cut him out of the family inheritance.[11] Although not falling directly in the sample, Judith Benninger Brown is another example. Judith was a national merit scholar at the University of Florida in Gainesville. As a graduate student she came to Tallahassee to join in the movie theater protest and was arrested. She stayed in Tallahassee to work with Patricia Stephens-Due on a CORE-sponsored voter registration project in a northern Florida county where blacks outnumbered whites. She gave up a Ford Foundation Fellowship to continue her activism and was arrested again trying to register black voters. Altogether the project staff was arrested twenty-five times, had thirty-five convictions, and accumulated over two years of jail time. In 1968 Judith co-authored a paper entitled "Toward a Female Liberation Movement," which was credited with helping to start the women's liberation movement. The paper has been published in nine anthologies. She eventually became an attorney and was an ardent supporter of equal rights for minorities and women. She died June 1, 1991, and was considered a heroine for her civil rights activities.[12]

Spurgeon McWilliams, now a medical doctor, is another example. He was a black protester; when asked if he would do it all over again, he answered, "in a heartbeat." Bernard Hendricks, another activist, recalled what it was like and how things had changed:

> I, along with students from FAMU and FSU, participated in a sit-in demonstration at McCrory's five-and-dime store. We were arrested, handcuffed, marched through the streets and jailed. For trying to buy a hamburger, they detained 17 of us for three days and three nights in a solitary confinement cell built for two. It was the most horrifying experience of my life...After returning to Tallahassee in 1983, I was curious to see if things had changed. They had changed, drastically, in the positive. Those days in the '60s were depressing, yet, from an historical perspective it was a great experience, and for that I am grateful.[13]

This book is also about people like Betty Daniels who, when interviewed twenty-five years later, stated, "I can't say I marched or took part in a sit-in. Only a few of my classmates were courageous enough to do that. I gained courage from the successes 25 years ago. Back then, I was afraid to speak out, but I would not hesitate to do it now."[14]

# 6

## CONCLUSIONS: TAKING STOCK

This research extends and clarifies previous work on the life choices and politics of 1960s activists. Fitting together various pieces of the puzzling question of what happened to 1960s activists provides a clearer picture than any single but limited research project. Having information on African Americans puts into sharper relief some of the generalizations about long-term activism. Finally, a twenty-five-year time frame and comparable groups help to clarify issues of moderation of youthful politics or the continuation of distinct generational units.

Sufficient time has elapsed and enough evidence has accumulated from the research of a small number of independent studies to make tentative generalizations about the impact and importance of student protest politics. There have been studies of African American and white civil rights activists, university reform, and antiwar and right-wing student activists (Braungart and Braungart 1988, 1991; DeMartini 1983; Fendrich and Krauss 1978; Fendrich and Smith 1980; Fendrich and Tarleau 1973; Jennings 1987; Jennings and Niemi 1981; McAdam 1988, 1989a; Nassi and Abramowitz 1979; Tripp 1987; and Whalen and Flacks 1989). The greatest clarity of generational unit differences occurs when the activist groups are compared with the baseline of upper-middle-class whites who did not participate in student protest and are now the mainstream of this cohort. Some generalizations apply to all activist groups from the 1960s cohort, other generalizations only apply to white leftists or African Americans, and one only applies to those students from the 1960s who were the youth wing of the radical right. In taking stock, I will address some widely held misconceptions and summarize the major findings, starting with all activists and then focusing on specific groups.

### CLARIFYING MISCONCEPTIONS

One advantage of accumulated longitudinal research is that it gives one the opportunity to put aside myths and false claims and develop a clear understanding of the causes and consequences of student protest. One of the major misconceptions about student protesters is their alleged privileged or, as conservatives would say, their elitist, backgrounds. This misconception arose from almost exclusive studies of white activists at elite universities. In these settings activists frequently did emerge from highly educated, economically secure, liberal backgrounds. But these students did not start the student movement. This myth should be put to rest. Black youths from working-class families were the first and the most consistently active student protesters. They inspired a small number of white middle-class idealists to get involved. They also were the spark that initiated later fires of insurgency in other segments of the population. The major point is that privileged white college students will become involved in the second phase of a social movement, initiated by groups frequently outside the university. Massive student protest is not willed into being by an isolated, academic elite.

A second popular cultural myth is that the activists of the 1960s became just like the acquisitive, marginally political members of their same generation. Accounts of individuals who have sold out or films, books, and op-ed portrayals of moderate ex-radicals serve to depoliticize the movement's goals and participants. The message is that protest politics need not be taken seriously. The cumulative findings clearly indicate that this popular myth is false.

Another myth advanced by neoconservatives is that leftists from the 1960s evolved into political extremists and continue to pose a threat to democratic institutions. The student left is portrayed as consisting of totalitarians who, because of their visceral hatred of democracy, are out to destroy America. Independent research refutes this. The truth is about 180 degrees different from the myth. For example, a white activist declared, "I consider myself part of the extreme left and consider Soviet Communism and Fascism as extreme right, where institutions dominate and supersede the individual. Socialism means people power over institutions." The beliefs most widely shared by the 1960s student left concerned broadening democratic participation, not destroying democracy. Richard Flacks (1988) describes the left's commitment to democratic procedures and principles. The central thrust of the movement was to promote the democratization of institutional life and the empowerment of people at the level of communities, workplaces, and neighborhoods. The work remains largely unfinished. However, the high level of organizational and political involvement of former activists suggests that attempts to create democracy are proceeding quietly in communities throughout the United States.

The last misconception concerns the origin and life cycle of social movements. There is the implicit assumption of a movement's "immaculate conception": each new wave of political insurgency is perceived to have a unique origin. Recent scholarship (McAdam 1988; Taylor 1989) has questioned this assumption. It is more probable that new movements emerge from the somewhat tattered but intact legacy of old movements. They do not have a natural history, springing into life, becoming troubled youths, reaching maturity, and finally dying. Therefore the decline of political insurgency during the 1980s is not a sign of the death of 1960s movements. Movements do not fade away, but remain alive in their carriers and in organizations. Taylor (1989) refers to "abeyance structures" that sustain movements during hard times. An abeyance is a holding pattern of groups which continues to mount some type of challenge even in an unreceptive political environment. Continued effectiveness depends on resources and opportunities. As they age, activists train new potential leaders: for example, Martin Luther King, Jr., and the Southern Christian Leadership Conference (SCLC) benefited from the help of the old liberal left (Branch 1988). Most significantly, action feeds consciousness rather than the reverse. What McAdam (1988) refers to as an "impulse to action" is less an impulse than it is an existential commitment that has been tested and reinforced over the life cycle.

## Major Findings: All Activists

Karl Mannheim's thesis that distinctive generational units will emerge from intense youthful politics is sustained. Activists made exceptional life choices about education, careers, values, and commitments because of their student activism. Regardless of race or left or right political ideology, these generalizations apply. The choice of maintaining political commitment and political action was the structuring principle for their other life choices. Compared with nonactivists, they also had exceptionally high levels of education and occupational concentration.

During the 1960s Lubell (1968) commented that the major dividing line between activists and nonactivists was the economic identification between those who looked to the public purse and those who looked to the private purse. The trend was more complicated than Lubell thought. Activists were located in the politicized segment of the "new class," who produced and distributed knowledge and culture and were involved in the organization and education of people. They were sometimes referred to as the "intelligentsia" and were considered distinct from other new class members who generated technical knowledge in the hard sciences, engineering, and other fields (Gouldner 1979). Their work in education, human services, law, or political institutions and organizations served collective political purposes as much as it served any individual desire for more material success or the formal needs of their employers. The politicized activist units within the new class had strong ideological differences among themselves and with other new class members who were not politically centered. This made it impossible for this class to act in any unified way to extend its class interest (Brint 1984; Kriesi 1989). What is important about this particular structural location is the relative significance of this class segment in defining future problems and policies that would emerge at the economic, political, and cultural levels. Their partial control of knowledge and knowledge systems provided the opportunity to be intellectual gatekeepers for the key issues in policy making. One African American activist commented that a major achievement was gaining knowledge and control over bureaucratic policy and procedure.

Outside of work, the activists' political orientation was different from the nonactivists'. They claimed that intense political participation in social movements was the major structuring set of events in their lives, and they sustained a history of political involvement in a wide variety of causes and organizations. Politics was driven by a sharper ideological focus, whether it was race, the New Left, or establishing a golden conservative era. They remained highly active citizens, both in the civic culture and in political institutions. They were committed to political struggles for the long haul. In general, they were more politically active than student government leaders from the 1960s who were preparing to play adult roles in institutional politics and much more active than typical college graduates.

Like the other members of their age and education cohort, the activists experienced the consequences of the subsequent era of political conservatism. Indeed, beginning with their 1964 support of Barry Goldwater for president, the right wing's youth worked diligently to capture the presidency, not only from Democrats but also from the Eastern Establishment. Over the years they built a conservative infrastructure consisting of magazines, journals, think tanks, political action committees, and the religious right. They selected conservative candidates and helped to defeat their political enemies until they reached national power with the election of Ronald Reagan. By the thousands, they marched into Washington and, according to Blumenthal (1990), sought to create a "movement state," turning departments and bureaus into war zones.

Left-wing and African American activists confronting this new political reality fought back defensively at the local and national level with few allies and resources. But despite the new political reality, there is generational unit continuity. Activists did not merge into some nondistinctive mass of middle-class professionals. In a conservative era, they maintained what Jennings (1987) called "relative and equivalent political continuity." The activist generation's ongoing position relative to other generations and the generation unit's position relative to other units in the same generation remained constant. There also were consistent and predictable responses to new political stimuli not present at the generation's inception.

## MAJOR FINDINGS: AFRICAN AMERICANS

The causes and consequences of African American involvement in the civil rights movement were different than for white leftist students from the 1960s. Although there were only two follow-up studies of African Americans, the findings are remarkably similar. The distinction between activists and nonactivists was not as sharp in the African American group. First, a majority of black students participated in protest: in contrast to whites, they were not a select subgroup of the black student body. Second, the civil rights movement affected those who were not directly involved by providing opportunities, changing an ethnic orientation, and strengthening the African American community. Thus student protest did make a difference, with activists being more active adult citizens, but the contrast between white activists and the noninvolved was much sharper.

The African American activists' generation was highly motivated and had high aspirations and ability. They achieved extremely high levels of education, and their upward mobility from the working class was significant. They concentrate in the knowledge and human service industries where job opportunities and advancement were better. The generation was confident in its ability to influence political decisions and maintained a strong commitment to a collective action strategy. Its members were highly active in organizations and were ideal citizens.

There was not a significant shift in their political orientations over time. They tended to be liberal, New Deal–oriented Democrats. They believed it was the government's responsibility to ensure economic security for everyone, and they were deeply concerned about the fate of other less fortunate African Americans. They were not, however, prosocialist in their view. Nor was their racial ideology black nationalist or integrationist. They had a strong sense of ethnic group solidarity, yet their political views represented a pragmatic rather than a utopian view of American society. Rather than wishing for a promised land, they worked collectively inside and outside the African American community to build a better society brick by brick.

The major difference for African Americans when compared with white activists is that they were empowered. In contrast to the right wing, they did not gain national power, but, in contrast to leftist activists, they have strong national and local organizations and were a significant power bloc in the Democratic party. To avow that African Americans were empowered is neither a claim that they held a proportional share of power nor a statement of the permanent arrangement with the white governing class. African Americans lost much ground during the Reagan and Bush administrations. Nevertheless, they could make legitimate claims and occasionally won significant benefits in bargaining and negotiating over domestic policy issues. Political victories in electing candidates continued to add up. In the 1980s they used the noninstitutionalized means of protest more extensively (Jaynes and Williams 1988).

The empowerment of the black activists had many causes. They took advantage of the programs created during the liberal revival between 1964 and 1974. In contrast to white leftists, they also had a natural constituency of African Americans to represent. The most significant consequence of local movement centers during the civil rights era was that the centers were a base for building a strong civic and political culture in black communities. Both Button (1989) and Morrison (1987) document the legacy of the civil rights movement in contemporary communities and the active civil and political institutions that have survived. In a highly ethnically stratified country like the United States, major changes occurred. The institutions that perpetuated a system of personal and political domination of African Americans were broken by the challenges of the black movement. There was greater opportunity for individual and collective upward mobility for an ethnic community that had the social infrastructure to press forward.

## MAJOR FINDINGS: WHITE LEFTISTS

Research and journalistic reports on 1960s activists have focused on white leftists. Some estimate that as many as three million college students were radicalized during this period. They did not start out as radical leftists, rather, they were radicalized by their participation in social movements and the subsequent negative responses from government officials and institutional authorities. The political turmoil during the late 1960s and early 1970s reinforced their beliefs and created a New Left. In an adult society that shifted to the right in the 1980s, with their nonactivist counterparts becoming conservatives, they moderated their radical self-identification and prosocialist beliefs but remained quite distinct as a group. In the 1980s their political behavior did not have the same white-hot intensity of either their college years or their early adulthood. But the change was not so much due to maturation as it was to the decline in insurgency and the issues that create massive protest. If the various follow-up studies had been completed during an economic depression or a major war, the intensity of protest politics may have been much greater.

Clearly the student radicals made life choices after college that sharply distinguished them from the nonactivists in their generation. They delayed careers and marriages. They chose occupations and occupational values that emphasized a strong ethic of social responsibility and a desire to bring about social change. Their adult lives were not dominated by the acquisitive values that characterized their nonactivist counterparts. As a result, they earned significantly lower incomes. Their lives remained focused on politics, which requires collective action, rather than on individual achievement and success. Student activism had a pervasive influence on subsequent personal and political decisions. White activists also had weak or nonexistent religious affiliations. In this regard, their conservative critics have correctly pegged them as secular humanists.

Tip O'Neil, former Democratic speaker of the U.S. House of Representatives, once said, "All politics is local." This statement applies to white leftists in two important respects. They practiced various forms of citizenship participation at the local level and were highly active in civic and political institutions and organizations. A second, and possibly more telling, aspect of local politics is that it encompassed the political influence of white leftists. In contrast to African Americans, who were empowered and who had strong national organizations and a major role in the Democratic party, and in contrast to the right-wing students, who gravitated to national power during the 1980s, the political power for this distinctive generational unit of leftists was more limited. They were not a major collective force in either the Democratic or Republican party. They did not build a national third party effort to the left of the Democratic party, and they even lacked a strong national organization such as the NAACP that could claim their allegiance and represent their interests. Rather, the leftist activists were somewhat scattered and disunified in a variety of local groups and organizations (Flacks 1988).

What can account for the limited political localism of white leftists, particularly white male leftists? One factor is a form of American exceptionalism. In contrast to Japan and many European and Latin American countries, in the United States there is no link to a national leftist party like the Social Democrat or Socialist parties. When the students were youthful activists, they had only token adult support, in contrast to the local movement centers in the African American community and the affluent right wing in the Republican party that sponsored YAF. Thus leftist activists had to develop their political objectives with little adult support or sponsorship. Second, leaders of the student left despised organization building and the necessity of bureaucratic structure and procedures implied in building a strong national organization. SDS had the potential to evolve into a strong national organization encompassing the New Left, but the leaders chose not to develop a centralized, bureaucratically structured organization. Instead the emphasis was on "participatory democracy," a form of political participation without a strong organizational structure and formal roles of authority. In short, the ideological blinders of a radical egalitarian political style were counterproductive in the long run, leaving SDS in shambles.

Not only did the New Left lack adult sponsorship, a political party, and a strong national organization, but it also lacked a natural built-in political constituency. The African American activists' generation had the constituency of the larger black population in the United States. The New Right had like-minded college students as part of its constituency and a number of single-issue, right-wing groups waiting to be organized into the Republican party. Leftists had partial success in organizing segments of the intelligentsia to win political elections in university-dominated communities, and some limited success in union building for white-collar and blue-collar workers (Flacks 1988). But without a strong political base or constituency, the limited gains could not be sustained over the long haul. Leftists were more effective when they joined and supported existing liberal and progressive organizations. The one exception for the New Left may be women, who went on to organize segments of the women's movement into strong national and local organizations.

The long-term impact of the left-wing student movement on the larger society did not spring from a well-organized power base. Lacking the resources of African American local movement centers and lacking elite sponsorship of the right-wing students, their base, such as it was, consisted of liberal intellectuals who survived the era of McCarthyism. They took the critiques of society by the liberal left seriously and set out to change themselves and society. They broke the bondage of a restrictive middle-class culture that emphasized individual success, acquisitiveness, trust and reliance on authorities, and religious affiliation. They valued and practiced their hard-won individual and political freedoms. Their new life-styles, political commitments, and values persisted in individuals and small groups that supported and valued a more open, democratic, and egalitarian society.

## THE RADICAL RIGHT

During the 1960s the Young Americans for Freedom (YAF) had about the same membership base and distribution across college campuses as the Students for a Democratic Society (SDS); twenty-five years later YAF's historical development was exceptional. They were instrumental in capturing the presidency and assuming national power and prominence during the Reagan years. The research on the long-range development of the student right wing is extremely limited. However, there is no doubt that the students who founded the organization in William F. Buckley's living room went on to national positions of influence in the Republican party. There is also no question that many members from the right-wing generational unit moved to Washington, D.C., to work in various federal bureaus. In their early years they were on the outside looking in and they lost many political battles. In the long run, however, their substantial elite sponsorship and heavy emphasis on building a conservative infrastructure paid off.

If the sole issue in determining the long-range effectiveness of the youthful 1960s movements is gaining power, then the achievements of the youthful right wing clearly indicate that they were the most successful. They developed an elaborate ideology and had significant adult sponsorship. With the election of Ronald Reagan, they felt it was their time to lead the country. Yet, because of internal and external difficulties, there are serious questions of whether this group will be able to sustain its power (Blumenthal 1990). The Iran/Contra exposure seriously weakened the far right. When Reagan began to talk disarmament with Gorbachev, the right felt betrayed. Supply-side economics proved to be unworkable. The issue of success of this right-wing movement is still the center of debate.

## GOOD CITIZENSHIP

Social movements include in their objectives changing the "means" as well as the "ends" of politics. For the left, changing the access and processes by which democracy is practiced was as important as gaining political power (Flacks 1988). The youthful right wing was successful in using the political system to gain power. The left wing was more concerned about changing the system to make it more consistent with ideals for democratic practices. The New Left wanted people to take a direct role in political institutions by becoming more active as citizens. Making history by practicing good citizenship was as important to the left as gaining control over resources and decision making in major institutions.

One of the strengths of this research is its detailed examination of the various components of good citizenship. Consistent with classical democratic theory, good citizenship is defined as actively participating in various types and levels of politics. In the world of work, a frequently asked question is, "Have you done something good lately?" The implication is that no one can simply rest on past performance. The expectation is to maintain high standards in ongoing work. The same question is relevant when considering citizenship. Good citizenship is simply maintaining an active presence in the political process. By the 1980s, neither African American nor white civil rights activists had gained national power, but they were good citizens. The African American activists were good citizens on all four dimensions of active participation. The only dimension that separated the former protesters from those who did not protest as students was the protest dimension of citizenship. Those who protested twenty-five years earlier were still more likely to use the means of noninstitutional politics to achieve their political objectives. Twenty-five years later white activists were equally as good citizens as the African American activists' generation. The white group scored higher on each dimension of active citizenship than its white nonactivist counterparts. Thus student activism had a pervasive effect on adult political activism. The two other major components that explain good citizenship are a history of political involvement over the life course and the number and extent of organizational involvements.

A major academic industry has emerged bemoaning the lack of citizen participation in the United States. Book after book warns its readers about falling rates of political participation, declining civic culture, and growing cynicism on the part of the public. Political researchers (Almond and Verba 1963; Campbell et al. 1960; Key 1961; Lipset 1960; Gamson 1975) have known for a long time that the actual level of political participation falls far short of normative ideals. A number of scholars have criticized our political institutions and offered prescriptions for improving democratic participation (Dahl 1989; Milbrath and Goel 1977; Bellah et al. 1985; Wolfe 1989; Gans 1988).

However, suggestions on improving democratic politics have many shortcomings. They are neither realistic nor consistent with past descriptions of political development and change in the United States (Gamson 1975). As long ago as 1939 Dumond argued that "the presence of a Negro minority, first as slaves, then as free men, has always provided the acid test of American Democracy" (White 1964:15). The activists in this study were jailed, beaten, harassed, and verbally insulted by hostile crowds and authorities. Some students were suspended or expelled from school. From the state governor on down, white officials uniformly and vigorously applied legal sanctions and publicly expressed their hostility toward the demonstrators. The White Citizens Council actively opposed the demands for equal rights and justice. The KKK marched. Vigilante groups terrorized leaders by firing shots into homes and businesses. In a nation that had claimed to be a democracy for almost two hundred years, the students and community activists were fighting a vicious system of apartheid. The day-to-day experience of black citizens was far removed from the democratic ideal, and many whites were determined to keep it that way. Activists put democracy to the acid test.

How can we account for this discrepancy between the political ideal and the practice of opposing democracy? Although I am sympathetic with the critics of the inadequacies of contemporary politics, I find prescriptions for improvement somewhat anemic. Recommendations to improve representative democracy do not fully appreciate how democracy grows and is sustained in a hostile political environment. Frequently recommendations are excessively individualistic. In addition, the conventional critiques of civil apathy have a conformist bias: an implicit theory of progressive socialization into institutional politics. This learning theory inadequately addresses the biographical facts of political participation. To understand enduring political commitments, we must give far more credit to the formative influence of conflict and protest, strife, anger, repudiation, and occasionally even violence.

The conformist vision of young citizens being gradually inducted into responsible civic roles is naive. We supposedly learn good government lessons in civics classes and practice them individually as adults. In fact, we do not develop and blossom into full citizenship one by one. We join the political community by twos and threes, or in large groups. In protest movements, sizeable groups can be recruited at one time. As Martin Luther King, Jr., discovered, "By twenties and thirties and forties, people came forward to join our army" (1963:59). Political identities and commitments originate in collective political experiences, not the other way around. The problem is not the political apathy of individuals but the poverty of collective opportunities to act democratically to achieve collective goals.

So how does good citizenship develop, grow, and sustain itself? One of the main ways to improve the democratic process and viable democratic institutions is to actively oppose those who control big government and big economic institutions. The dramatic and far-reaching changes occurring in Russia and Eastern bloc countries have their origins in oppositional groups of citizens from the civic culture. Sometimes we witness, at great personal risks, citizens joining massive demonstrations and street protests to demand freedom and a democratic form of government. This is not a novel observation on the constitution of modern civic culture. Robert Coles (1967) very explicitly confronted the necessity of protest in his pioneer study of moral development among children and parents active in school desegregation efforts in the early 1960s. But these insights are unassimilated and virtually ignored in the social science literature on civic culture. It is ironic that scholars who debate and bemoan the low levels of political participation do not recognize what Thomas Jefferson understood. The secret for sustaining democracy frequently lies in the active, collective opposition to the state. That is why the 1960s activists' generation became ideal citizens. To claim otherwise is like being a staunch supporter of the Flat Earth Society.

The intersection of biography and history gives a clear message. In one generation starting with harsh oppression, the civil rights activists changed into informed, active, and demanding citizens. They are a living record of what democracy is about.

# EPILOGUE: CURRENT DILEMMAS AND FUTURE PROSPECTS

The historic role that African Americans will play politically is determined in part by the past gains and current dilemmas they face. Morris (1984) argues that before the civil rights movement African Americans were controlled by a tripartite system of domination. Personal, economic, and political freedoms were denied by the system of segregation, economic oppression, and political oppression. The civil rights movement successfully challenged personal and political oppression, but it was unable to significantly change economic domination. Morris ends his book with the critical question of whether the organization, leadership, tactics, and philosophies of the civil rights movement are appropriate for bringing about basic economic change or whether a whole new set of structures and tactics is needed.

Jesse Jackson is an example of a new tactical approach. He exploited the "window of opportunity" provided by the failure of Reaganomics. Despite his personal flaws, drawbacks, and past political mistakes, Jackson offered the most original populist program as a Democratic presidential candidate. His threat to the Democratic party's establishment was similar to Senator Huey Long's threat to the reelection of President Roosevelt in 1936. Long forced Roosevelt to take more decisive action in order to recover economically from the depression.

African Americans face a number of continuing dilemmas (Gurin, Hatchett, and Jackson 1988). Their support for a liberal government oriented toward collective gains runs counter to the basic conservative nature of elite rule (Domhoff 1990) and middle-American beliefs about individual responsibility and models for success. The fluctuating but endemic white racism can be used by one or both political parties to win elections. In past and current elections African Americans have been used as a convenient symbolic community for politicians to condemn. As a numerical minority blacks also lack the voting numbers to be a telling influence in most federal elections or state races. Although it grew since 1984, Jesse Jackson's white support in 1988 came from a small percentage of white voters (Gurin, Hatchett, and Jackson 1988). Other black candidates have found it equally difficult to gain white support.

To avoid the problem of being taken for granted by the Democratic party, African Americans could decide to mount a major third party effort. They would not win, but the result would significantly weaken the Democratic party. Yet the Democratic party is the most likely to revive policies that would be appealing to many African Americans. A revived Democratic party that pushed strong programs to rebuild the physical and human infrastructure, improve schools, provide affordable housing, and guarantee black businessmen contracts and black workers jobs at decent wages would be particularly attractive.

African Americans also face dilemmas in the work world. They are dissatisfied with artificial job ceilings, the limited effectiveness of public-sector jobs, and the almost insidious infection of conservative mandates in public policy making. Moving up has its cost. One activist bitterly complained about highly placed African Americans, "They are as dull as cornflakes and quite comfortable in their do-nothing jobs." When probed further, he made clear that his comments applied to "token blacks" who do not rock the boat. They do not make policy in their jobs, and frequently they perform meaningless tasks like organizing the next meeting. Yet, when a new policy is implemented that adversely affects the disadvantaged, their acquiescence as the "minority representative" serves to legitimate the policy by white policymakers. Those who protest too loudly find they are out of the movers-and-shakers policy loop. African American officials must be squeaky clean and not too controversial if they want to be "successful."

White activists also face a number of dilemmas or contradictions. Like African Americans, they are too small in number to play a decisive role in national politics. And there is the dilemma of supporting a revived Democratic party that emphasizes a corporate state strategy. Whalen and Flacks (1989) wisely observe that the New Left during the 1960s took the corporate state to be the permanent feature of American political reality and embarked on a campaign to criticize the weaknesses of corporate liberalism. To revive support for a business-dominated corporate-state coalition would contradict past positions. Yet, paradoxically, when the climate for social reform diminished with the decline of corporate liberalism, there was less room for positive experimentation to advance a vision of a democratic transformation. The left has fewer opportunities under the conservative counterrevolution.

The ideology of the New Left also poses a dilemma. The commitment to participatory democracy and a shared belief that elite oligarchies dominate all organizations have prevented the New Left from building a national organization, let alone a third party. Flacks (1988) is in sympathy with the supporters of a participatory democracy perspective. Organization building defines one's identity, restricts freedom of thought, infringes on private space, limits personal options, defines personal priorities, and limits freedom of personal action. In general, organization building reduces individual freedom without increasing capacities to be politically effective (Flacks 1988:196–97). If this view is widely shared, the New Left, as an agent of change, will be consigned to the dustbin of history. Personal freedoms must always be balanced to achieve collective goals. Just as peace activists must engage in conflict with authorities, so also it is necessary for individuals to sacrifice personal autonomy to gain shared freedoms. Moreover, personal freedoms are created and sustained by collective actions that are generated by social movements.

The more successful movements are bureaucratically structured (Gamson 1975). One activist described his frustration at attending a regional conference of a progressive group. One entire day of a precious weekend was spent in the fruitless argument over being radically egalitarian by having conveners instead of section organizers and discussants. Although the spirit of participatory democracy was being sustained, the effectiveness of the organization was diminished. Future waves of leftists might learn from the failures of the New Left as well as the successful organizational achievements of African Americans.

Another major dilemma the New Left will confront is whether to support the leading political candidates that represent the interests of neoliberals or to support candidates who represent either a disadvantaged segment of society, such as third world peoples and women, or a populist coalition. Presidential candidates like Michael Dukakis, Gary Hart, Richard Gephardt, and Bill Clinton demonstrate a vision and awareness of neoliberal political concerns. They discuss the challenges of a postindustrial society, the important potential usages of the knowledge industry, technology, rational economic planning, and administrative competence. As neoliberals, however, they suffer a major flaw: they have no soul. Despite Hubert Humphrey's tragic decision to support President Johnson's war, through much of his political career he maintained deep New Deal, liberal roots. He had a strong sense of compassion for the less fortunate in society that neoliberals do not share.

If the New Left decides to support a third world candidate like Jesse Jackson or a white populist, they will be faced with a coalition that does not share many of their political beliefs and is downright conservative on the issues of crime, drugs, and civil liberties. Moreover, a new brand of political populism would threaten some of the special privileges and advantages of the educated, professional new class. For example, university-based members might lose control over the management of knowledge systems because of changing entrance standards and course requirements, lose control of their work environment, and find they have a lesser share of state and federal budgets.

Whites also face work dilemmas. They, like African Americans, face job ceilings. One ex-radical, now a well-placed government bureaucrat, said, "Powerful gatekeepers comprised of senior bureaucrats and elected officials do not trust outspoken progressives from the activist era. Political styles and commitment must conform to the expectations of the inner circle that exercise real power." He claimed to be five steps lower than he should be on the career ladder. He was in charge of a major state welfare program, and confided that he fired his two most progressive staff. He liked them personally, but complained they did not know how to effect change and had naive ideas about the distribution of power. As a result, they caused him problems. He also boasted that he could get results on policy issues, but the arguments had to be cast in conservative rhetoric. For example, he sold the state legislature on welfare programs by arguing their merits in terms of short- and long-term cost cutting, privatizing part of social services, getting welfare recipients working, and having less direct state agency intervention. As a hard-nosed pragmatist, he expanded his program for welfare mothers from $2 to $30 million. The number of welfare mothers working rose from 1.5 percent to 25 percent. He convinced the legislature to waive community college tuition costs and in so doing enabled thousands of welfare mothers to attend college. The ideas of Machiavelli are as pertinent to his job as those of Martin Luther King, Jr.

Most activists have one or more proud accomplishments. They helped to win an election, strengthened an organization, made their work environment more humane, or expanded a needed social service.

Yet the conservative onslaught diminishes their hard-fought gains. One complained, "Social services are stingy, demeaning and a fraud. People in need do not get adequate assistance. A mother of two can't live on $234 a month. Agencies like to select their clients and avoid the seriously mentally ill, those desperate for childcare or substance abuse treatment programs." A common complaint of teachers is that educational institutions have sunk into dull complacency. Another activist summarized his political analysis by saying that the state ought to be smashed.

Despite the good citizenship, two more personal themes emerged from the interviews with activists. Like the title of Ronald Reagan's autobiography, they ask, "Where's the rest of me?" and they wait. This first theme expresses that something is missing. A former, emotionally richer self who was willing to take big risks is lost. Memories of the 1960s are of intense, socially rewarding experiences for a righteous cause. A song, poem, political event, or visit with an old friend stirs quixotic feelings, but the spirit cannot be captured and sustained in everyday life. In addition, activists wait for the historical moment that will again radically shake up and rearrange social institutions and personal lives. They experienced a dramatic historical moment in their youth, and their sense of history tells them that current collective illusions will again be challenged. Like a reserve army, they are ready to be called into action, but they personally worry about biological clocks running down before the troops assemble.

Because of the high level of democratic activism, the activists' generation is likely to be in the thick of emerging struggles. The ubiquitous problems associated with the federal debt crisis and the end of the cold war will provide African Americans and the New Left many opportunities to clarify decisions that must be made to resolve existing dilemmas. The activists' future is intertwined not only with the future of institutional politics but also with the emergence of new social movements. As in the 1930s and 1960s, future waves of protest will create economic and political disruptions to the point that political leaders will be forced to change the direction of public policy and possibly open the door for social reforms.

# APPENDIX

The tables in this appendix report the unstandardized (*b*) and standardized (*beta*) regression coefficients. The standardized coefficients allow for easier comparisons between variables. Student's *t* distribution statistics and their one-tailed observed significance levels are reported. The descriptions of the variables are included in the text of the chapters and the notes. An independent variable was included in the regression analysis if it could account for at least 1 percent of the variance in the dependent variable under analysis. The adjusted $R^2$ or coefficient of determination is reported in the regression tables to reflect a closer fit to the population. $R^2$ is a measure of goodness of fit of a particular model. The number of subjects in each analysis reflects the numbers sampled which are reported in Chapter 1. The exception is the reduced samples of activists reported in Chapter 5, which are twenty-four white male activists and fifty-one African American male activists. In isolated cases of missing values for a particular variable the average score is assigned.

TABLE A.1
Regression Analysis of African American Separatism and Nationalism in 1973

| Independent Variables | Dependent Variables | | | |
| --- | --- | --- | --- | --- |
| | Black Separatism | | Black Nationalism | |
| | b | beta | b | beta |
| 1. Gender | — | — | 1.520 | .063 |
| 2. Age | — | — | -.314 | -.108 |
| 3. Major | .135 | .117 | — | — |
| 4. GPA | — | — | — | — |
| 5. Student activism | .056 | .136* | .694 | .133* |
| 6. Graduate education | — | — | 1.540 | .146* |
| 7. Private-sector preference | — | — | .400 | .094 |
| 8. Occupational status | .023 | .197** | .132 | .090 |
| 9. Marital status | — | — | — | — |
| 10. Current income | — | — | .041 | .006 |
| 11. Extrinsic rewards | .079 | .100 | — | — |
| 12. Level of satisfaction | -.095 | -.157* | — | — |
| Adjusted R square | .090** | | .081** | |

\* = .05
\*\* = .01

TABLE A.2
Regression Analysis of African American Political Attitudes in 1973

| Independent Variables | Dependent Variables | | | | | | | |
|---|---|---|---|---|---|---|---|---|
| | Political Identification | | Personal Efficacy | | Alienation | | Radicalism-Conservatism | |
| | b | beta | b | beta | b | beta | b | beta |
| 1. Gender | — | — | .147 | .018 | — | — | -1.945 | -.174* |
| 2. Age | -.071 | -.127* | — | — | — | — | — | — |
| 3. Father's occupation | — | — | .010 | .056 | — | — | — | — |
| 4. Father's income | — | — | — | — | .231 | .084 | — | — |
| 5. Major | .182 | .067 | 1.146 | .239** | — | — | — | — |
| 6. GPA | .537 | .183* | — | — | — | — | — | — |
| 7. Student activism | — | — | .071 | .041 | — | — | — | — |
| 8. Graduate education | — | — | — | — | .134 | .046 | .415 | .087 |
| 9. Marital status | -.222 | -.103 | — | — | — | — | — | — |
| 10. Career choice | — | — | -.102 | -.033 | — | — | .224 | .052 |
| 11. Private-sector preference | — | — | -.153 | -.108 | — | — | — | — |
| 12. Current income | — | — | .446 | .183* | — | — | -.664 | -.196** |
| 13. Extrinsic rewards | — | — | -.255 | -.077 | — | — | -.611 | -.133* |
| 14. Political organizations | — | — | .745 | .126* | — | — | — | — |
| 15. Other organizations | — | — | .200 | .064 | -.315 | -.117 | — | — |
| 16. Black nationalism | — | — | — | — | .079 | .277** | .193 | .417** |
| 17. Level of satisfaction | — | — | .273 | .109 | — | — | -.312 | -.090 |
| Adjusted R square | .040* | | .143** | | .090* | | .254** | |

* = .05
** = .01

TABLE A.3
Regression Analysis of African American Political Behavior in 1973

| Independent Variables | Dependent Variables | | | |
| --- | --- | --- | --- | --- |
| | Institutional Politics | | Protest Politics | |
| | b | beta | b | beta |
| 1. Gender | — | — | 1.550 | .083 |
| 2. Age | -.096 | -.249** | — | — |
| 3. Major | — | — | .011 | .010 |
| 4. GPA | .108 | .053 | — | — |
| 5. Student activism | .102 | .148* | .004 | .011 |
| 6. Graduate education | .017 | .012 | .061 | .077 |
| 7. Marital status | — | — | -.102 | -.117* |
| 8. Occupational status | .025 | .130* | -.006 | -.054 |
| 9. Current income | .021 | .021 | .037 | .066 |
| 10. Extrinsic rewards | — | — | -.041 | -.053 |
| 11. Political organizations | .430 | .184* | .343 | .251** |
| 12. Other organizations | .176 | .141* | .024 | .033 |
| 13. Political identification | .062 | .089 | — | — |
| 14. Radicalism-conservatism | .039 | .138* | — | — |
| 15. Level of satisfaction | -.108 | -.109* | — | — |
| 16. Personal efficacy | .045 | .114 | .019 | .080 |
| 17. Black nationalism | .002 | .018 | .015 | .194** |
| Adjusted R square | .274** | | .192** | |

\* = .05
\*\* = .01

TABLE A.4
Regression Analysis of African American Political Behavior in 1988

| Independent Variables | Dependent Variable Political Behavior | |
|---|---|---|
| | b | beta |
| 1. Head of household's occupational status | .003 | .006 |
| 2. Head of household's education | -.191 | -.027 |
| 3. Age | .462 | .119* |
| 4. GPA | -1.151 | -.064 |
| 5. Student activism | .444 | .087 |
| 6. Graduate education | -.266 | -.039 |
| 7. Extrinsic rewards | -.386 | -.045 |
| 8. Social-change values | .656 | .111* |
| 9. Occupational status | .069 | .055 |
| *Black Nationalist Attitudes* | | |
| 10. Support for mainline groups | .015 | .006 |
| 11. Support for black nationalism | .114 | .047 |
| 12. Black community control | .094 | .033 |
| 13. Distrust of public officials | .472 | .171** |
| 14. History of political involvement | .998 | .345** |
| 15. Reagan opposition | .437 | .128* |
| 16. Civil rights organizations | 1.016 | .232** |
| 17. Political organizations | 1.275 | .381** |
| 18. Liberal organizations | .091 | .022 |
| 19. Radicalism-conservatism | .121 | .071 |
| Adjusted R square | .686** | |

\* = .05
\*\* = .01

TABLE A.5
Regression Analysis of White Political Attitudes in 1971

| Independent Variables | Dependent Variables | | | | | | | | | |
|---|---|---|---|---|---|---|---|---|---|---|
| | Power Distribution | | Efficacy | | Alienation | | Political Identification | | Radicalism-Conservatism | |
| | b | beta | b | beta | b | beta | b | beta | b | beta |
| 1. Age | .023 | .192* | -.156 | -.201* | — | — | -.037 | -.065 | -.263 | -.100 |
| 2. Head of household's occupation | -.004 | -.149 | — | — | — | — | — | — | — | — |
| 3. Head of household's education | — | — | — | — | — | — | — | — | .134 | .024 |
| 4. Head of household's income | -.016 | -.058 | — | — | — | — | .086 | .068 | -.643 | -.109 |
| 5. Major | .026 | .037 | 1.112 | .250* | — | — | .107 | .033 | .061 | .004 |
| 6. GPA | .047 | .068 | — | — | — | — | — | — | — | — |
| 7. Parents' activism | .106 | .083 | .028 | .004 | — | — | — | — | — | — |
| 8. Religious involvement | — | — | — | — | .86 | .169 | .210 | .037 | .341 | .013 |
| 9. Student activism | .129 | .172 | .519 | .110 | — | — | 1.061 | .310* | -1.635 | -.053 |
| 10. Graduate education | — | — | .031 | .018 | — | — | .018 | .014 | .428 | .268* |
| 11. Marital status | -.217 | -.267* | -.032 | -.006 | -.234 | -.042 | -.349 | -.094 | .117 | .020 |
| 12. Income | -.043 | -.140 | — | — | — | — | -.253 | -.180* | -1.667 | -.096 |
| 13. Occupation | — | — | .014 | .049 | -.028 | -.092 | .023 | .114 | -.738 | -.112 |
| 14. Occupational sector | .048 | .114 | — | — | .423 | .146 | .340 | .176 | 2.604 | .287* |
| 15. Sector preference | .023 | .091 | — | — | .071 | .040 | .024 | .021 | .005 | .009 |
| 16. Extrinsic rewards | — | — | -.355 | -.130 | -.457 | -.154 | -.224 | -.113 | -1.954 | -.210* |
| 17. Political organizations | .082 | .079 | 1.342 | .206* | — | — | .644 | .136 | 3.068 | .139* |
| 18. Other organizations | — | — | .243 | .075 | -.674 | -.193* | — | — | — | — |
| Adjusted R square | .194** | | .106* | | .125** | | .440* | | .535** | |

* = .05
** = .01

TABLE A.6
Regression Analysis of White Political Behavior in 1971

| Independent Variables | Dependent Variables | | | |
|---|---|---|---|---|
| | Institutional Politics | | Protest Politics | |
| | b | beta | b | beta |
| 1. Age | -.021 | -.050 | -.023 | -.085 |
| 2. Head of household's occupation | — | — | — | — |
| 3. Head of household's education | .101 | .106 | — | — |
| 4. Head of household's income | -.070 | -.078 | .026 | .045 |
| 5. Major | .432 | .178 | — | — |
| 6. Parents' activism | .253 | .058 | .538 | .188* |
| 7. Religious involvement | -.100 | -.020 | — | — |
| 8. Student activism | .488 | .189 | .591 | .352** |
| 9. Graduate education | .066 | .069 | — | — |
| 10. Marital status | -.288 | -.103 | -.234 | -.128 |
| 11. Income | .079 | .075 | -.185 | -.267** |
| 12. Occupation | .028 | .183 | .002 | .023 |
| 13. Occupational sector | .176 | .120 | .095 | .099 |
| 14. Sector preference | .023 | .026 | .053 | .092 |
| 15. Extrinsic rewards | — | — | -.270 | -.276* |
| 16. Political organizations | .810 | .228* | .837 | .361** |
| 17. Other organizations | .153 | .087 | — | — |
| 18. Power distribution | — | — | .306 | .136 |
| 19. Political identification | .015 | .020 | .137 | .278* |
| 20. Political efficacy | .133 | .245* | — | — |
| 21. Alienation | -.028 | -.055 | .054 | .164* |
| 22. Radicalism-conservatism | — | — | .012 | .122 |
| Adjusted R square | .177* | | .508* | |

\* = .05
\*\* = .01

TABLE A.7
Regression Analysis of White Political Attitudes in 1986

| Independent Variables | Dependent Variables | | | | | |
| --- | --- | --- | --- | --- | --- | --- |
| | Political Identification | | Radicalism-Conservatism | | Reagan Opposition | |
| | b | beta | b | beta | b | beta |
| 1. Age | — | — | — | — | — | — |
| 2. Head of household's occupation | — | — | — | — | .071 | .172* |
| 3. Head of household's education | — | — | .763 | .156* | .235 | .072 |
| 4. Head of household's income | — | — | -.349 | -.062 | — | — |
| 5. Major | .581 | .180* | 1.300 | .118 | -1.915 | -.272* |
| 6. GPA | — | — | .776 | .054 | -.681 | -.074 |
| 7. Student activism | .768 | .213* | 1.020 | .083 | -.924 | -.117 |
| 9. Graduate education | -.114 | -.088 | -.285 | -.064 | .299 | .106 |
| 10. Occupational sector | .094 | .043 | 1.287 | .171* | -.419 | -.087 |
| 11. Extrinsic rewards | -.227 | -.104 | -.315 | -.043 | .878 | .186 |
| 12. Social-change values | .210 | .165* | .774 | .178* | -.643 | -.232* |
| 13. Occupation | — | — | .099 | .073 | — | — |
| 14. Income | -.240 | -.226* | -.962 | -.265* | -.039 | -.017 |
| 15. Marital status | — | — | — | — | 1.387 | .126* |
| 16. Political involvement | .089 | .125 | .047 | .019 | — | — |
| 17. Liberal organizations | .110 | .163* | .143 | .062 | -.111 | -.075 |
| 18. Progressive organizations | .064 | .048 | 1.027 | .221* | -.165 | -.055 |
| 19. Conservative organizations | -.219 | -.222* | -.592 | -.176* | .699 | .325** |
| Adjusted R square | .529*** | | .574*** | | .571*** | |

\* = .05
\*\* = .01
\*\*\* = .001

TABLE A.8
Regression Analysis of White Complete Political Activism in 1986

| Independent Variables | Dependent Variable | |
|---|---|---|
| | Complete Activism | |
| | b | beta |
| 1. Age | -.396 | -.202* |
| 2. Head of household's education | .413 | .079 |
| 3. Major | .088 | .058 |
| 4. GPA | -1.449 | -.095 |
| 5. Student activism | .535 | .041 |
| 6. Graduate education | .481 | .102 |
| 7. Occupational sector | 1.295 | .161 |
| 8. Social-change values | 1.189 | .257* |
| 9. Occupation | .144 | .099 |
| 10. Income | -.376 | -.097 |
| 11. Marital status | -2.144 | -.116 |
| 12. Political involvement | .898 | .345** |
| 13. Liberal organizations | .548 | .222* |
| 14. Progressive organizations | .199 | .040 |
| 15. Reagan opposition | -.238 | -.143 |
| 16. Political identification | .521 | .143 |
| 17. Radicalism-conservatism | -.063 | -.059 |
| Adjusted R square | .465*** | |

\* = .05
\*\* = .01
\*\*\* = .001

TABLE A.9
Regression Model for Citizenship

| Independent Variables | b | beta |
|---|---:|---:|
| Family Resources | | |
| Head of household's education | 1.215 | .243** |
| Head of household's occupation | .030 | .056** |
| Family income | .953 | .193** |
| College Experience | | |
| Major | 2.878 | .270** |
| GPA | -.385 | -.031** |
| Student activism | 1.859 | .040** |
| Postcollege Experience | | |
| Graduate education | -1.760 | -.287** |
| Occupation | .290 | .272** |
| Occupational sector | .076 | .011 |
| Occupational values | 2.069 | .389** |
| Income | -.669 | -.180** |
| Age | -.530 | -.379** |
| History of Political Involvement | .997 | .426** |
| Organizational Involvement | | |
| Liberal organizations | .263 | .112** |
| Conservative organizations | -.354 | -.100** |
| Progressive organizations | -2.539 | -.136** |
| Adjusted R square = .616** | | |

** = .01

## TABLE A.10
### Analysis of Variance by Race

| Variables | African American Activists | | White Activists | | Probability |
|---|---|---|---|---|---|
| | $\bar{x}$ | S.D. | $\bar{x}$ | S.D. | |
| 1. Age | 46.47 | 2.65 | 47.21 | 4.71 | N.S. |
| 2. Head of household's education | 10.76 | 1.78 | 12.88 | 2.40 | .01 |
| 3. Head of household's occupation | 44.53 | 26.88 | 78.17 | 15.22 | .001 |
| 4. Head of household's income | $8,940 | $10,094 | $13,500 | $9,836 | .05 |
| 5. Major | 1.86 | .83 | 2.71 | .55 | .001 |
| 6. GPA | 2.31 | .68 | 2.46 | .83 | N.S. |
| 7. Graduate education | 1.65 | 1.90 | 3.46 | 2.34 | .001 |
| 8. Occupational sector | 3.02 | 1.27 | 3.63 | 1.10 | .05 |
| 9. Occupational prestige | 88.33 | 6.49 | 89.75 | 8.19 | N.S. |
| 10. Extrinsic rewards | 6.78 | 1.36 | 5.96 | 1.43 | .05 |
| 11. Social-change values | 9.00 | 2.12 | 8.79 | 2.23 | N.S. |
| 12. Marital status | 2.49 | .86 | 2.75 | .61 | N.S. |
| 13. Number of children | 1.59 | .87 | 1.54 | .83 | N.S. |
| 14. Church attendance | 2.96 | .87 | 1.54 | .83 | .001 |
| 15. Born-again Christian | 1.64 | .48 | 2.00 | .00 | .001 |
| 16. Political involvement over life cycle | 15.13 | 3.88 | 17.17 | 4.53 | .05 |
| 17. Organizational involvement | 33.74 | 8.01 | 29.88 | 6.56 | .01 |
| 18. Individual income | $38,460 | $15,240 | $32,502 | $18,780 | N.S. |

TABLE A.11
Regression Analysis of the Political Attitudes and Behavior for African American and White Activists

| Independent Variables | Radicalism-Conservatism | | Reagan Opposition | | Political Identification | | Complete Activism | |
|---|---|---|---|---|---|---|---|---|
| | b | beta | b | beta | b | beta | b | beta |
| 1. Race | -1.061 | -.081 | — | — | .867 | .168 | — | — |
| 2. Age | .551 | .203* | .174 | .137 | .072 | .102 | — | — |
| 3. Head of household's education | — | — | — | — | — | — | — | — |
| 4. Head of household's occupation | -.011 | -.035 | — | — | .004 | .055 | -.022 | -.057 |
| 5. Head of household's income | — | — | — | — | — | — | -1.107 | -.181* |
| 6. Major | — | — | .423 | .082 | — | — | — | — |
| 7. GPA | 2.132 | .167 | .660 | .110 | .467 | .162 | — | — |
| 8. Graduate education | -.714 | -.169 | -.531 | -.268* | — | — | — | — |
| 9. Occupational sector | — | — | — | — | — | — | .159 | .018 |
| 10. Occupational status | — | — | -.008 | -.014 | .048 | .025 | -.015 | -.009 |
| 11. Extrinsic rewards | -.810 | -.124 | -.966 | -.316** | -.161 | -.095 | — | — |
| 12. Social-change rewards | 1.175 | .270* | .315 | .154 | .051 | .045 | .610 | .118 |
| 13. Marital status | -1.303 | -.111 | — | — | — | — | — | — |
| 14. Number of children | -.285 | .044 | -.276 | -.090 | -.058 | -.034 | — | — |
| 15. Church attendance | -1.163 | -.135 | -.707 | -.175 | -.970 | -.433** | — | — |
| 16. Born-again Christian | — | — | — | — | — | — | — | — |
| 17. Political involvement over life cycle | — | — | .007 | .007 | — | — | -.624 | -.024 |
| 18. Organizational involvement | — | — | — | — | — | — | 1.146 | .436*** |
| 19. Individual income | -.758 | -.223* | -.120 | -.076 | -.056 | -.179 | .583 | .408*** |
| 20. Radicalism-conservatism | — | — | — | — | -.194 | -.221* | — | — |
| 21. Reagan opposition | — | — | — | — | — | — | .251 | .099 |
| 22. Political identification | — | — | — | — | — | — | -.386 | -.085 |
| Adjusted R square | .261*** | | .176* | | .225** | | .526*** | |

\* = .05
\*\* = .01
\*\*\* = .001

# NOTES

## PROLOGUE

1. For a fuller discussion of the media portrayal of activists, see Gitlin (1987) and McAdam (1989a).

2. For a detailed discussion of these two psychological theories, see Turner and Killian (1972).

## CHAPTER 1

1. How much race relations have changed was shown by the thirtieth anniversary of the sit-in, when the four men were invited back to Greensboro. They were served at the same seats with a hearty breakfast and were greeted by Aubrey Lewis, a black vice president of Woolworth, who in 1960 would have been denied service. "I'm proud you had the courage to open the doors for a movement," Lewis said. AP story, *Tallahassee Democrat*, February 2, 1990, p. 3a.

2. For a critique of the atmosphere and quality of administration on black college campuses, see Miles (1971).

3. There are many sources that describe the struggle by black students to create separate organizations and mixed effects of the effort (Branch 1988; McAdam 1988; Morris 1984; Newfield 1966). For an excellent account of the sit-in movement, see Mayer's introduction to Proudfoot's (1990) *Diary of a Sit-In*.

4. The number is taken from McAdam (1982). In a personal communication he stated that the number of movement actions was probably much higher than he reported. Hard information was frequently lacking.

5. Popular sources and folklore tend to reserve for white ethnics or, more recently, Oriental Americans the values of hard work, financial sacrifice, and commitment to maximizing opportunities for their children. But these same characteristics apply to the black working class. Instead of focusing on the so-called pathologies of the black underclass, researchers should explore the unstable and shrinking opportunities to maintain stable black working-class families. In coding the occupations of parents, I was struck by how many of the occupations no longer exist. This idea is consistent with Bluestone and Harrison's (1982) deindustrialization of America thesis.

6. More sophisticated analysis using the full range of scores on measures of socioeconomic status and on activism also demonstrates only a slight relationship between education, occupation, and income on political activism. The respective correlations were $-.02$, $-.02$, and $.09$. These data contrast sharply with data showing the upper-middle-class backgrounds of most early waves of white activists. Although whites attending college in Tallahassee came from better-off families, there was no significant relationship between family socioeconomic status and student protest. For a more detailed sense of the cultural and ideological backgrounds and commitments of white civil rights activists, see Hayden (1988), King (1987), and McAdam (1988).

7. Although it was not the intent of the research to explain the antecedent conditions that distinguished college activists from nonactivists, a regression analysis explained about 30 percent of the variation in the level of political activism. The strongest direct relationships were major in college, political activism of parents, different primary goals while attending college, and age. The results are comparable to results of other studies on the antecedents of student activism. If there had been more questions on friendship and organizational networks, the amount of variance explained would have increased. For example, I noted in my dissertation research that civil rights activists generally did not volunteer to participate in the civil rights struggle by themselves. They came in twos and threes. For high-risk activists there must be some kind of support group (McAdam 1989a).

8. This last comment is important. Tilly (1978) argues in his analysis of social movements that powerful groups in society are mobilized offensively to head off any challenges. The police department and bus company could have been anticipating a bus boycott and already rehearsed their response.

9. Although no leaders were killed in Tallahassee, there were very real fears. A few years earlier, in 1951, Harry T. Moore, the field director of the state NAACP, and his wife were murdered when their home was bombed on Christmas Day. Moore was a vigorous leader of the NAACP, building the organization and attacking segregation and violence toward blacks on several fronts. No one was ever arrested for the bombing and murder (Hemmingway 1989).

10. Both Garrow (1986) and Branch (1988) document the extent to which the federal government and state agencies worked in a coordinated fashion to discredit Martin Luther King, Jr. For a general discussion of how the government attempts to hinder social movements, see Gary Marx (1979).

11. One of the best analyses of the emerging cultural influences on bright progressive students during the early 1960s is Todd Gitlin's *The Sixties* (1987). He demonstrates the effects of existential movements and the "beat generation" on the thinking and actions of a number of college students.

12. Scholars on resource mobilization emphasize the free dinner as one of the small selective incentives in the formative stages of social movements. Experienced organizers have frequently commented that a "free" lunch or dinner with a new or potential member can result in hundreds of hours of free labor committed to a movement that involves personal risks.

13. The president of FSU died of a heart attack at the age of fifty-three. It was widely believed in the university community that the pressure to fire faculty and expel students created unbearable strain.

14. The dramatic change in the governor's stance has been attributed in part to two sociologists, Lewis Killian and Charles Grigg, who met with the governor and his staff prior to the speech. As a former governor of Florida, LeRoy Collins is an interesting case study of dramatic change. As governor, he ran as a segregationist, opposed the bus boycott, restricted students to campus during a protest period, and thought the civil rights protests were caused by outsiders. But after the 1964 Civil Rights Act was passed, he served President Johnson as head of the Community Relations Service. He ran for the U.S. Senate and lost the Democratic nomination because he represented President Johnson during the Selma march and expressed strong liberal views. He reports a conversation his wife had during his Senate campaign: "My wife was once accosted on the street by an old friend who said, 'We just can't support Roy this time because of the way he believes.' 'Well,' my wife said, 'he just believes in liberty and justice for all, don't you?' There was no answer." (Collins 1989:23).

15. On March 4, 1961, five CORE members sought counter service at a number of department stores. At one store two of the CORE leaders were threatened and harassed by a small group of whites. As the blacks were leaving, Benjamin Cowins was attacked and beaten to the ground. Both leaders were arrested and jailed. Cowins was convicted of fighting and suspended by FAMU. Rabby (1984) reports that a sense of guilt prevailed in the black community because once again young people were taking a costly stand for the whole community.

16. The president may have been fortunate. In a black student protest movement in the 1920s students at FAMU set fire to several dormitories to protest the school's emphasis on industrial education at the expense of the liberal arts (Neyland 1989).

17. The critical role that African American women played in the civil rights movement has not been fully documented. Rabby (1984) does a good job for the movement in Tallahassee, and Robinson (1987) describes the importance of women in Montgomery. In a personal communication, Aldon Morris indicated that the critical leadership role of women during the earliest phase of protest was more widespread than originally recognized. See also McAdam (1989b).

18. This was a very common pattern during the student protest era. For a discussion of the repressive tactics of authorities, see Marx (1979).

## CHAPTER 2

1. The total number of research subjects was limited. Fifty white male activists were identified from arrest records, names of protesters in the campus and city newspapers, and knowledgeable local informants. Initially the study included women; however, they were too difficult to trace without extensive research funds. Other studies (Demerath, Marwell, and Aiken 1971) suggest that during the transition period between the integrated civil rights movement and the beginnings of the women's movement female activists were exploring a wide variety of alternatives, moving from place to place, making it extremely difficult to trace them.

2. The response rates for the samples were twenty-eight (58 percent) for the activists, thirty-one (62 percent) for the student government leaders, and thirty-six (72 percent) for the politically noninvolved. These figures represent the number of questionnaires returned from the total sent. However, the quality of addresses was not the same for the three groups. Twelve questionnaires sent to activists and two sent to student leaders were returned by the post office. If the response rates are based only on those who received questionnaires, they are 73 percent for activists, 66 percent for student government leaders, and 72 percent for the noninvolved. Using Chi-square, I found no statistically significant difference in the response rate among the three groups.

3. Scores of 3 were given if students were active for six months or more. A score of 2 was assigned to those arrested, 1 if they participated in protest demonstrations, and 0 if they were inactive. In his critique of student activism research, Kerpelman (1972) states that one of the major shortcomings is inadequate measurement, which does not tap the range of student commitment to the protest movement. I designed an index to include a range of commitment.

Early in the questionnaire three filter questions were used to discourage respondents from exaggerating any commitment.

4. In general, the procedures were those recommended to insure a high response rate (Dillman 1974). An attractive questionnaire outlined with the school colors was sent. Two additional follow-ups were mailed; however, funds were lacking to send a final wave by certified mail. Out of a total of 606 questionnaires, 315 were sent to a random sample of the student body (approximately 11 percent), 95 to student government leaders (81 percent), and 196 to those with arrest records (50 percent). Out of the total sample, 96 questionnaires were returned by the post office. Thus, 510 may have received the questionnaires. If this figure is used to compute the response rate, the figure is 37 percent. The rates for the three groups were as follows: random sample, 34 percent; student leaders, 42 percent; and arrested, 40 percent. The lower rate for the random sample was due to the sampling procedures. Instead of using alumni office records, I used actual grade rosters; then university records were used to trace the former students. There were three major reasons for the lower responses from the black samples. First was the quality of record keeping at the two universities. FAMU lacked the resources and technology to keep accurate, up-to-date records. I also included black females in the samples. Women changing from their maiden to married last names made them more difficult to trace. Lastly, African Americans have common surnames, making it very difficult to trace subjects using indirect sources. For example, the Florida Department of Motor Vehicles had listings for sixty-six R. Williams between forty-five and forty-eight in the Miami area.

5. For the second study additional measures were used. The original measure of occupational values did not tap those occupational values associated with wanting to be an agent of social change, so a measure of social-change values was added. Since I was interested in the responses to the conservative 1980s, I developed a measure to determine the extent of agreement with the Reagan administration's performance in handling the nuclear arms race, environmental issues, civil rights, poverty programs, the national budget and deficit, and tax cuts for wealthy individuals and corporations.

6. In comparison with other studies tracing activists from the mid- to late 1960s (Jennings 1987; Marwell, Aiken, and Demerath 1987), I was slightly less successful in finding the subjects but slightly more successful in getting their cooperation in completing the questionnaire.

7. If this particular line of reasoning actually depicted the adult response of most activists, it would be impossible to do this type of longitudinal study. Former activists would not be traceable, and those few who were found would be alienated from social science research and uncooperative in responding. Fortunately, my research as well as others' has found that this is not the modal or predominant pattern for activists. Available information does reveal that a

small fraction of ex-activists was temporarily or permanently disillusioned. In Tom Hayden's *Reunion* (1988), he describes how he retreated from political involvement temporarily after the trial of the Chicago Seven. A few snapped under the pressure, like the murderer of Al Lowenstein, an ex-activist who was convinced the CIA had implanted transmitters in his teeth. One of the most active white students in this study shifted his focus to sexual freedom issues in California. His backside appeared in national publications along with others enjoying nude swimming in California.

8. Jennings (1987) refines Mannheim's ideas on generational continuity. He develops three types of continuity: absolute, relative, and equivalent. *Absolute* refers to individuals holding the same political attitudes and exhibiting the same forms of political behavior as they move through time. The generational unit is isolated from outside forces. *Relative* continuity is maintaining distinctive characteristics relative to other dissimilar generational units within the same cohort over time. *Equivalent* continuity refers to how generational units are forced to respond to new political stimuli and events (such as the conservative 1980s) that were not present at the generation's inception.

9. Although there is no evidence of official involvement, it is alleged that a group of southern businessmen put out a contract to have King assassinated (Clarke 1982).

10. The report created a strong controversy, with many black scholars disagreeing with Moynihan's analysis. See Billingsley (1968), Blackwell (1975), and Staples (1971).

11. For a review of the concept of symbolic racism, see Pettigrew (1985).

12. A personal friend who was a white civil rights attorney in Mississippi told me that the experience was so intense at the psychological level that he identified himself as a black man for two years after the Mississippi experience.

13. The daily student newspaper, the *Florida Flambeau*, contained a number of letters to the editor and comments within articles that reflected students' disapproval of the local civil rights protest.

14. For a further discussion of the legitimation crisis, see O'Connor (1973) and Wolfe (1977).

15. So much ground was lost in federal courts during the 1980s that Congress was persuaded to pass a Civil Rights Restoration Act in 1990. It was vetoed twice by President Bush, but a modified version was approved in 1991.

# CHAPTER 3

1. Occupation is considered the best single determinant of a person's status. The Nam and Powers index compares favorably to other measures of individual economic status or prestige. See Powers (1981).

2. The occupations or career choices of the graduates were classified along a continuum, ranging from those chiefly offering rewards of money and status in the private sector to those offering the opportunity to provide a humanistic service and/or work independently. The categories were (1) proprietors, managers, officials, and salespersons in the private sector, (2) private-practice professionals such as doctors and lawyers, (3) government workers, (4) teachers and education professionals, and (5) those in social service and creative occupations. Respondents' occupations were coded into these five categories.

3. Tripp (1987) in his follow-up study of black activists from the University of Michigan finds about 40 percent of the subjects in the private sector, 40 percent working for government agencies, and another 18 percent working for nonprofit organizations. His subjects graduated from one of the best northern universities more than five years after the subjects of this study. Both the prestige of a University of Michigan degree and the later time period for entering the job market may have contributed to increased job opportunities in the private sector.

4. In activism individuals in a group generally challenge authorities through a series of actions. The social behaviors are frequently intense and occur in hostile settings. Three indices were used to develop a scale of student activism for the FAMU graduates. They were given a score of 1 if they actively demonstrated or protested as students, and a score of 2 if they were arrested during a demonstration. If they were active in the civil rights movement six months or longer, they were given a score of 3. The range of scores on student activism was from 0 to 6. In the 1973 survey of FAMU alumni, sixty-nine, or 37 percent, did not participate. Young men were significantly more involved than women: among the men, 73 percent protested; among the women, 48 percent. The significant, yet lower, level of participation by young black women reflects the traditional sex-role division of that period and male attitudes that black women needed to be protected. Seventeen, or 9 percent, limited their actions to a demonstration or protest. Nine, or 5 percent, did not claim they participated; however, their names were on the arrest records. Twenty-four, or 13 percent, either were active six months or more, or demonstrated and were arrested. Thirty-four, or 18 percent, were active six months or more and demonstrated, and finally, thirty-three (18 percent) demonstrated, were arrested, and were active six months or more.

5. Advanced education and training occurred during a period when opportunities were beginning to open for African Americans. Florida A&M

University is also noted as having one of the highest rates of students going on to graduate education among predominantly black colleges and universities.

6. If the oral histories of numerous activists can serve as a guide, it is likely that the time-consuming and intense protest activity could have cut into valuable study time and therefore resulted in the slightly lower grade point averages of activists.

7. These data are comparable with data in Tripp's (1987) survey. He studied sixty-six activist students who were equal opportunity students enrolled in the University of Michigan in 1969. On measures of education he found that 46 percent of the men and 48 percent of the women earned their undergraduate degrees in education and the social sciences and only 11 percent in the hard sciences. For FAMU students, 43 percent of the males and 53 percent of the females majored in education and the social sciences. Fourteen percent majored in the hard sciences. Among the former FAMU students, 38 percent received advanced degrees, compared with Tripp's study, where 37 percent received advanced degrees.

Tripp (1987) found that a higher percentage of his subjects had received a doctorate or equivalent degree ten years later. Among the Michigan students, 22 percent had received doctorates, compared with 8 percent of the FAMU respondents. Three factors can probably account for the difference. Opportunities to attend graduate school grew for minorities during this period; therefore, Tripp's respondents could have taken fuller advantage of expanding opportunities. An undergraduate degree from the University of Michigan was also likely to receive a more detailed and favorable screening by graduate admissions committees. Third, the University of Michigan was located in the center of the knowledge industry that traded in educational and funding resources, requirements, application procedures, criteria, and references to support seeking an advanced degree. In contrast, FAMU was located closer to the periphery in the early 1960s.

8. Open-ended comments on a questionnaire from an activist who was arrested during the protest demonstrations.

9. Open-ended comment from an arrested activist.

10. These findings differ from findings of earlier research on white activists from the 1960s. Former white activists were more likely to remain single, be divorced, or be married without children. Moreover, those whites with fewer family obligations maintained greater levels of political involvement (Fendrich 1977; McAdam 1988; Whalen and Flacks 1989).

11. This finding contrasts with findings from follow-up studies (Fendrich 1977; McAdam 1988) on white activists.

12. Gurin and Epps (1975) developed a similar scale to measure black nationalism. They, like other researchers, found that black nationalism was a coherent ideology that was multidimensional. In this study on each of the items on the black nationalist scale there were five possible responses from strongly agree to strongly disagree, from strongly approve to strongly disapprove, and from strongly trust to strongly distrust. Undecided or "not sure" responses were excluded. Except for the two items on CORE and SNCC, the subscales are highly intercorrelated.

13. The reasons for the strong support of SNCC and CORE are straightforward. A CORE chapter in Tallahassee spearheaded the protest between 1960 and 1963. Moreover, the FAMU graduates were part of the activists' generation when these two organizations were at the height of their effectiveness.

14. This tapped both party identification and conservative-progressive placement on a political continuum. Respondents were given twelve alternatives for political self-identification: Very Conservative, Conservative Republican, Conservative Democrat, Moderate Republican, Independent, Moderate Democrat, Liberal Republican, Liberal Democrat, New Left, Socialist, Radical, and Anarchist.

15. The personal efficacy scale consisted of five items. Examples were "Public officials don't care much what people like me think," "Sometimes politics and government seem so complicated that I can't really understand what's going on," and "Voting is the only way that people like me can have any say about how the government runs things." The scores ranged from strongly agree to strongly disagree.

16. The alienation scale was composed of five items with a range of scores from strongly agree to strongly disagree. Examples of items were, "The government serves the interest of a few organized groups, such as business and labor, and isn't very concerned about the needs of people like myself," and "As the government is now organized and operated, I think it is hopelessly incapable of dealing with all the crucial problems facing the country today."

17. There were five responses to each of the fourteen items, ranging from strongly agree to strongly disagree. The items contained both pro and con statements. The range of scores was from 14 to 70, with the midpoint being 42. High scores indicated a more radical orientation to politics. The scale was found to be both reliable and valid by its authors.

18. There were four responses, ranging from frequently to never. The range of scores was 5 to 20. High scores indicated high levels of political behavior. The questions were phrased to elicit responses on political activities during the past two years.

19. The correlation between institutional and protest politics was $r = .277$.

20. The two groups were not identical. Some responded in 1973 but not in 1988, and some responded in 1988 but not in 1973. I checked the smaller number that responded to both surveys in 1973 and 1988 with the 1988 respondents. They were almost identical on twenty-four different variables. Thirty-four percent of the larger sample were females, compared with 36 percent for the smaller sample. The same pattern held for the comparable age (46.7 versus 46.8 years), occupational status (86.6 versus 85.1), level of student activism (2.54 versus 2.53), disapproval of the Reagan administration (24.10 versus 23.92), and, most importantly, the major dependent variable of complete citizenship (42.18 versus 42.97). When the regression analysis was run for the smaller sample that participated in both 1973 and 1988, the results were almost identical. The same amount of variance in political behavior was explained (56 versus 55 percent), and the same pattern of major direct effect occurred. The only slight difference was that age had a stronger direct effect for the smaller sample. In sum, the results for the analysis were not materially affected by using the larger $N$ of 114 instead of the smaller $N$ of 64.

21. The percentage of females in 1973 was 41; it was 34 in 1988.

22. This was a recurring theme among the black activists who were interviewed.

23. Because of the question's wording it was difficult to determine whether the declines in distrust were due to more blacks holding these positions or to improvements among white public officials. In many communities the growing political power of the African American community resulted in more control over police behavior (Flacks 1988).

24. Another indication of reformist or mainline support was the extent of church attendance. Seventy-six percent reported attending church at least two or three times a month. African American churches continue to be an important center for social organizational involvement.

25. The best predictors of this strong sense of ethnic identity were the former students who had been the most active in the civil rights movement; those who were active in civil rights organizations; those who valued money, status, and security in their jobs; and those who were not living in intact nuclear families. When ten variables were entered into a regression equation to explain the variance in the composite measure of black nationalism, 16 percent of the variance was explained. The results were highly significant.

26. Eight variables were entered into the regression equation to explain the variation in political self-identification: head of household educational level, the four dimensions of black nationalism, age, student activism, and a history of political involvement since college. In contrast to the 1973 findings, the amount of variance explained increased from 4 to 8 percent. The two variables that had

the strongest direct effect on a leftist political self-identification were student activism and a desire for black community control.

27. The same amount of variance in radicalism (25 percent) was explained in 1988. The strongest direct effects on radicalism were the level of black nationalism and marital status. Those least married had the strongest nationalist sentiments. Blocked opportunities no longer were a strong determinant of support for a socialist-oriented political economy.

28. The four active dimensions of political behavior were highly intercorrelated: the intercorrelations varied from .49 to .84. Each dimension was also highly correlated with complete activism, with correlations ranging from .76 to .93.

29. If this percentage seems high, it should be remembered that there are numerous local elective offices, such as precinct captain and water management district officer, as well as county, city, and school board positions. There are also a number of appointed positions that require informal lobbying and pressure to gain the appointment. Running for and/or winning public office is particularly common in the South (Jaynes and Williams 1989).

30. The mean and standard deviation for the activists' generation were 12.386 and 2.839. The comparable scores for the national sample were 9.585 and 2.607.

31. The degree of organizational involvement was measured by the number of organizations and the level of participation in each organization. Civil rights organizations included the NAACP, the SCLC, the Urban League, the Rainbow Coalition, and human rights groups. Political organizations included political party organizations, church or religious groups that had a political focus, and business and professional organizations that pursued special-interest politics.

# CHAPTER 4

1. As recent studies show, the declining proportion of middle-class citizens in the population becomes most apparent as the younger generation is unable to advance like its fathers. See Myles, Picot, and Wannell (1988).

2. Data on educational levels were gained from the questionnaires and the depths of mothers' commitment indicated in interviews.

3. Two factors strongly affected the level of education. The first was the educational level of the parents; the second was the level of political activism of the students while in college. A regression analysis was able to account for 28 percent of the variance in educational levels.

4. In 1971 there were no questions that tapped what activists positively valued in their work. Rosenberg's (1957) extrinsic rewards scale was used. In the later follow-up, it became clear that activists wanted to be agents of social change in their occupations or professions.

5. Other studies have found a disproportionate number of white activists who went on to teach college in the social sciences (Braungart and Braungart 1991; Whalen and Flacks 1989).

6. The African American activists' generation did not have the same problem. They were exemplars in their community and had a wider range of potential spouses who share their political views.

7. In a comparison with national samples of whites in 1972 and 1974, the white college graduates had significantly higher levels of political efficacy and political trust (Abramson 1977).

8. Only one of the former white civil rights activists identified his full-time occupation as a revolutionary.

9. If these figures seem high, it should be remembered that the period between 1969 and 1971 was the peak of protest politics.

10. The $F$ ratio for the analysis of variance for the three groups was 28.35 and significant beyond the .001 level.

11. The characteristics that did change were not different for the full and reduced samples. For example, in 1971 the average age was 32.93. Fifteen years later the average ages for the full and reduced samples were 47.65 and 47.68, respectively. The white cohort was fifteen years older, and the full and reduced samples were not different from each other. The 1971 and 1986 samples had the same levels of education for parents, major in college, grade point average, student activism, and location in the private or public sector of the economy. The means and standard deviations were not different. For example, for the $n$ of 88, the mean and standard deviation of activism was 2.11 and .81. For the $n$ of 71 the figures are 2.06 and .83.

12. The lack of upward occupational mobility for African Americans compared with whites is another indication that the major gains for African Americans occurred as a result of the civil rights movement and have been stalled during the conservative era.

13. Eighteen different choices in the type of organizations were provided. The correlation between the number of organizations and activism was $r = .50$ and was highly significant. So was the correlation between intensity of membership and activism ($r = .56$). The activists' participation went beyond receiving a newsletter or membership. Activists were more likely to volunteer hours of service and to be officers in organizations.

14. The support for the Democratic party doubled since 1971. The surge reflects changes in the party, changes in the activists, and no third party alternative.

15. A factor analysis of eighteen different types of organizations using ordinary least squares and varimax rotation identified the three clusters.

16. The specific types of liberal groups were civil rights organizations, the Democratic party, professional interest groups, liberal political action groups, and prochoice, environmental, public interest, human rights, and aid groups like Hands Across America. The conservative groups were the Republican party, religious political organizations, business political organizations, conservative PACs, and antiabortion groups. The progressive groups were the Rainbow Coalition and antinuclear, peace, and feminist groups. For each group a respondent could indicate the level of involvement: not active, receive newsletter, contribute money, member, contribute two or more hours of work a month, hold an office or position.

17. The $F$ ratio was 9.69, and significance for the analysis of variance on liberal groups was less than .001. The comparative figures for conservative and progressive groups were 4.96, and 7.41 and less than .01, respectively.

18. For a more detailed discussion, see Fendrich and Turner (1989).

19. The exceptions were that the FSU students were from the South and a higher percentage were the sons and daughters of military personnel.

20. The analysis of variance for the three groups on the Reagan scale was highly significant, with an $F$ ratio of 28.24 and significance beyond the .0001 level.

21. The analysis of variance for the three groups on political involvement was significant, with an $F$ ratio of 4.00 and a probability less than .05.

22. The mean scores for the activists, student government leaders, and random samples were 8.167, 11.333, and 10.912, respectively. The analysis of variance was highly significant, with an $F$ ratio of 18.14 and a probability less than .0001.

23. The $F$ ratio was 4.63; the probability was less than .05.

24. The $F$ ratio and probability for political communication were 6.85 and .01, respectively. The $F$ ratio and probability for party and campaign politics were 3.59 and .05, respectively. The $F$ ratio and probability for local politics were 4.63 and .05, respectively. Lastly, the $F$ ratio and probability for protest politics were 13.36 and .0001, respectively.

25. In the analysis of variance for complete activism, the $F$ ratio and probability were 8.23 and less than .001.

26. The pattern for African Americans was different. The student protesters in the African American generation were significantly different on the measure of protest politics than those who were not student demonstrators. On the other three dimensions of political participation the blacks who were not student activists were about as active as adults.

27. The six identical items were voting, working with others to solve a local problem, contacting officials, forming a group to work on a local problem, taking part in party activities or a political campaign, and persuading others how to vote.

28. The average age for the General Social Survey and the random sample were 47.28 and 48.67. The father's average education was 12.1 and 11.8. The incomes were $34,335 and $37,412. In the General Social Survey 25 percent were Democrats and 63 percent were Republicans. For the random sample the percentages were 26.5 and 52.9.

29. On the six-item scale, lower scores indicated more participation. The mean and standard deviation for the national sample were 12.3 and 2.73; the respective means and standard deviations for the activists, student government leaders, and random sample were 9.54, 9.23, and 11.32 and 3.23, 3.07, and 3.00. Both the activists and student government leaders were significantly more active as citizens.

30. The proportional weights assigned were 1 for the activists, 2 for the student government leaders, and 140 for the random sample.

31. The unweighted but disproportional regression analysis accounted for 47 percent of the variance.

32. The analysis of liberal, conservative, and progressive organizations with the four active dimensions of citizenship revealed that those active in liberal organizations were more active in local politics, were better political communicators, and were more involved in party and campaign politics than the other two groups. Those belonging to progressive organizations scored the highest on protest politics. Members of conservative organizations scored the highest on the passive political dimension of voting and waving the flag. Conservative group members scored somewhat higher on party politics than the progressives but much lower than the progressives on local, communication, and protest politics.

33. The concept of the radical center is used by Gerald Marwell to describe the long-range consequences of student activism. The *radical center* refers to deep commitments stemming from religious, family, or organizational ties. Activists from the radical center were not the sons and daughters of socialists and Communists of the 1930s, nor were they necessarily exposed to an intellectually oriented leftist ideology. Therefore, they were radical but not leftist. (Personal communication with Gerald Marwell.)

34. The term *myth* is appropriate. The ideology of the Reagan era was "free enterprise," but the government, representing the dominant interest of the rich and powerful, moved from a tax-and-spend policy to a borrow-and-spend policy. The full effects of this policy are still being felt.

# CHAPTER 5

1. There were twenty-four white male activists and fifty-one African American male activists. The African American females were not included in the comparisons because of the absence of data on white female activists.

2. The analysis of variance on the item measuring the importance of money earned for one's job was significant beyond the .01 level. African Americans had a mean score of 2.37 and whites a mean score of 1.87 on a scale of one to three.

3. Taking into account wage increases between 1986 and 1988, one can say that African Americans still earned more than whites.

4. The respondents were provided with a list of organizational categories and two open categories in which they could list additional organizations. For each organization they could indicate that they were not active, received a newsletter, contributed money, were a member, volunteered two or more hours a month, or served as an officer. The scores ranged from 0 to 120.

5. The measure of radicalism was the same Nettler and Huffman scale used throughout the study. The measure of protest combined the three items of participating in political campaigns, taking part in protest demonstrations, and engaging in any political action that could lead to arrest. For more details, see Fendrich (1977).

6. The mean score on radicalism for whites was 38.04, compared with 35.33 for African Americans. Their respective standard deviations were 11.87 and 7.80.

7. Although not reported here, on each of the four separate scales constituting complete activism—political communication, campaign and party politics, local politics, and protest politics—there were no significant differences between black and white activists.

8. Being older was also related to opposing the policies of the Reagan administration and identifying farther to the left, but the relationships were not statistically significant.

9. Lower socioeconomic origin was not an indirect reflection of the influence of race. When race was included in the regression equation, the

relationship between coming from families with lower incomes and good citizenship remained the same.

10. This research had no way of determining whether the activists had more or fewer mental health difficulties than the nonactivists. For some insight into the counseling and therapeutic needs of 1960s activists, see Kupers (1990).

11. Interview with activist. His family reaction was confirmed by another activist who remains his friend.

12. Obituary, *Tallahassee Democrat*, June 1991.

13. This quote was taken from the *Tallahassee Democrat*'s writers. When the newspaper got wind of the story, it assigned reporters to do its investigative reporting on the consequences of the movement. I cooperated by providing some names of respondents they could interview (Lindstrom 1988).

14. Ibid.

# REFERENCES

Abramson, Paul R. 1977. *The Political Socialization of Black Americans: A Critical Evaluation of Research on Efficacy and Trust*. The Free Press.

Alford, Robert R., and Roger Friedland. 1975. "Political Participation and Public Policy." *Annual Review of Sociology* 1:429-79.

Almond, Gabriel A., and Sidney Verba. 1963. *The Civic Culture, Political Attitudes and Democracy in Five Nations*. Princeton University Press.

Alwin, Duane F., Ronald L. Cohen, and Theodore M. Newcomb. 1991. *Political Attitudes over the Life Span: The Bennington Women after Fifty Years*. University of Wisconsin Press.

Ash, Timothy G. 1990. "The Revolution of the Magic Lantern," *The New York Review of Books*, January 18, pp. 42-50.

Astin, Alexander. 1970. "Determinants of Student Activism." In *Protest: Student Activism in America*, ed. Julian Foster and Durward Long. William Morrow.

Baird, Leonard L. 1970. "Protests: A Study of Student Activism." In *Protest: Student Activism in America*, ed. Julian Foster and Durward Long. William Morrow.

Barnet, Richard J., and Ronald E. Muller. 1974. *Global Reach: The Power of the Multinational Corporations*. Simon and Schuster.

Bell, Daniel. 1967. *Marxian Socialism in the United States*. Princeton University Press.

———. 1976. *The Cultural Contradictions of Capitalism*. Basic Books.

Bellah, Robert N., et al. 1985. *Habits of the Heart: Individualism and Commitment in American Life*. Harper & Row.

Billingsley, Andrew. 1968. *Black Families in White America*. Prentice-Hall.

Blackwell, James E. 1975. *The Black Community: Diversity and Unity*. Dodd, Mead.

Blauner, Robert. 1972. *Racial Oppression in America*. Harper and Row.

Bloom, Jack M. 1987. *Class, Race, and the Civil Rights Movement*. Indiana University Press.

Bluestone, Barry, and Bennett Harrison. 1982. *The Deindustrialization of America*. Basic Books.

Blum, R. H. 1970. *Society and Drugs*. Jossey-Bass.

Blumenthal, Sidney. 1990. *Pledging Allegiance: The Last Campaign of the Cold War*. Harper-Collins.

Boston, Thomas D. 1988. *Race, Class and Conservatism*. Unwin Hyman.

Bowles, Samuel, and Herbert Gintis. 1982. "The Crisis of Liberal Democratic Capitalism: The Case of the United States." *Politics and Society* 11, 2:51–93.

Branch, Taylor. 1988. *Parting the Waters*. Simon and Schuster.

Braungart, Margaret M., and Richard G. Braungart. 1988. "The Life-Course Development of Left- and Right-Wing Youth Activist Leaders from the 1960s." Paper presented at the 11th Annual Scientific Meeting of the International Society of Political Psychology, Secaucus, New Jersey.

———. 1991. "The Effects of the 1960s Political Generation on Former Left- and Right-Wing Youth Activist Leaders." *Social Problems* 38:297–315.

Brink, William, and Louis Harris. 1966. *Black and White*. Clarion Books.

Brint, Steven. 1984. " 'New Class' and Cumulative Trend Explanations of the Liberal Political Attitudes of Professionals." *American Journal of Sociology* 90:30–71.

Burnstein, Daniel. 1988. *Yen! Japan's New Financial Empire and Its Threat to America*. Simon and Schuster.

Button, James W. 1989. *Blacks and Social Change: Impact of the Civil Rights Movement in Southern Communities*. Princeton University Press.

Campbell, Angus, et al. 1960. *The American Voter*. John Wiley.

Carey, J. T. 1968. *College Drug Scene*. Prentice-Hall.

Carlson, Jody. 1981. *George C. Wallace and the Politics of Powerlessness*. Transaction Books.

Carmichael, Stokely, and Charles Hamilton. 1967. *Black Power*. Vintage Books.

Clarke, James. 1982. *American Assassin: The Darker Side of Politics*. Princeton University Press.

Cole, Leonard A. 1976. *Blacks in Power: A Comparative Study of Black and White Elected Officials*. Princeton University Press.

Coles, Robert. 1967. *Children of Crisis: A Study of Courage and Fear*. Little Brown.

Collier, Peter, and David Horowitz. 1989. *Destructive Generation: Second Thoughts about the Sixties*. Summit Books.

Collins, LeRoy. 1989. "Past Struggles, Present Changes and the Future Promise for Civil Rights in Florida and the Nation." In *The Civil Rights Movement in Florida and the United States*, ed. Charles U. Smith. Father and Son Press, Tallahassee.

Cruse, Harold. 1967. *The Crisis of the Negro Intellectual*. William Morrow.

Dahl, Robert A. 1989. *Democracy and Its Critics*. Yale University Press.

Davis, James Allan, and Tom W. Smith. 1987. *General Social Survey*. Roper Center for Public Opinion Research.

Delevan, Virginia. 1960. "Editor and Friends Land in Jail for Talking to Negroes." *Florida Flambeau*, March 15.

DeMartini, Joseph R. 1983. "Social Movement Participation: Political Socialization, Generational Consciousness and Lasting Effects." *Youth and Society* 15:195–223.

Demerath, N. J., III, Gerald Marwell, and Michael T. Aiken. 1971. *Dynamics of Idealism*. Jossey-Bass.

Dillman, Don A. 1974. "Increasing Mail Questionnaire Response: A Four-State Comparison." *American Sociological Review* 39:744–56.

DiPrete, Thomas A., and David B. Grusky. 1990. "Structure and Trend in the Process of Stratification for American Men and Women." *American Journal of Sociology* 96:107–43.

Domhoff, G. William. 1990. *The Power Elite and the State*. Aldine De Gruyter.

Edsall, Thomas B. 1984. *The New Politics of Inequality*. Norton.

Feagin, Joe A., and Harlan Hahn. 1973. *Ghetto Revolts*. Macmillan.

Fendrich, James M. 1977. "Keeping the Faith or Pursuing the Good Life: A Study in the Consequences of Participation in the Civil Rights Movement." *American Sociological Review.* 42:144–157.

———. 1983. "The Elite Policy Response to Race and Ethnic Relations in Capitalist Societies." *American Behavioral Scientist* 26, 6 (July/August):757–72.

Fendrich, James M., and Ellis Krauss. 1978. "Student Activism and Adult Left-Wing Politics: A Causal Model of Political Socialization for Black, White and Japanese Students of the 1960s Generation." In *Research in Social Movements, Conflict and Change*, ed. Louis Kriesberg 1:231–255. JAI Press.

Fendrich, James M., and Charles U. Smith. 1980. "Black Activists: Ten Years Later." *The Journal of Negro Education* 49:3–19.

Fendrich, James M., and Alison T. Tarleau. 1973. "Marching to a Different Drummer: The Occupational and Political Orientations of Former Student Activists." *Social Forces* 52:245–53.

Fendrich, James M., and Robert W. Turner. 1989. "The Transition from Student to Adult Politics." *Social Forces* 67:1049–57.

Feuer, Lewis S. 1969. *The Conflict of Generations*. Basic Books.

Flacks, Richard. 1970. "Who Protests: The Social Bases of the Social Movement." In *Protest: Student Activism in America*, ed. Julian Foster and Durward Long. William Morrow.

———. 1971. *Youth and Social Change*. Rand McNally.

———. 1988. *Making History*. Columbia University Press.

Gamson, William A. 1975. *The Strategy of Social Protest*. Dorsey.

Gans, Herbert J. 1988. *Middle American Individualism*. The Free Press.

Garrow, David J. 1981. *The FBI and Martin Luther King, Jr.* Norton.

———. 1986. *Bearing the Cross*. William Morrow.

———. 1987. "Introduction" to Jo Ann Gibson Robinson, *The Montgomery Bus Boycott and the Women Who Started It*. University of Tennessee Press.

Gerth, Hans H., and C. Wright Mills. 1946. *Max Weber: Essays in Sociology*. Oxford University Press.

Geschwender, Barbara N., and James A. Geschwender. 1973. "Relative Deprivation and Participation in the Civil Rights Movement." *Social Science Quarterly* 54:403–411.

Geschwender, James A. 1971. *The Black Revolt*. Prentice-Hall.

Gitlin, Todd. 1980. *The Whole World is Watching*. University of California Press, Berkeley.

———. 1987. *The Sixties*. Bantam Books.

Goertzel, Ted. 1976. *Political Society*. Rand McNally.

Gouldner, Alvin. 1979. *The Future of Intellectuals and the Rise of the New Class*. Seabury.

Greene, W. 1970. "Where are the Savios of Yesteryear?" *New York Times Magazine* July 12, 1970 6:6-10.

Gurin, Patricia, and Edgar Epps. 1975. *Black Consciousness, Identity and Achievement*. John Wiley.

Gurin, Patricia, Shirley Hatchett, and James A. Jackson. 1988. *Hope and Independence: Blacks' Response to Electoral and Party Politics*. Russell Sage.

Gutterbock, Thomas M., and Bruce London. 1983. "Race, Political Orientation and Participation." *American Sociological Review* 48:439-53.

Haines, Herbert H. 1988. *Black Radicals and the Civil Rights Mainstream, 1954-1970*. University of Tennessee Press.

Hamilton, Charles V. 1981. "On Black Leadership." *The State of Black America, 1981*, ed. James D. Williams, 239-65. National Urban League.

Harrison, Bennett, and Barry Bluestone. 1988. *The Great U-Turn*. Basic Books.

Hayden, Tom. 1988. *Reunion: A Memoir*. Random House.

Heilbroner, Robert. 1990. "Seize the Day." *New York Review of Books*. Feb. 15, 1990. pp. 30-31.

Hemmingway, Theodore. 1989. "The Rise of Black Student Consciousness in Tallahassee and the State of Florida." In *The Civil Rights Movement in Florida and the United States*, ed. Charles U. Smith. Father and Son Press, Tallahassee.

Horton, Myles, Judith Kohl, and Herbert Kohl. 1989. *The Long Haul: An Autobiography*. Doubleday.

Hout, Michael. 1984. "Occupational Mobility of Black Men: 1962 to 1973." *American Sociological Review* 49:308-23.

Isaac, Larry, and William Kelly. 1981. "Racial Insurgency, the State and Welfare Expansion: Local National Level Evidence from Postwar United States." *American Journal of Sociology* 86:1348-86.

Jacoby, Russell. 1987. *The Last Intellectuals*. Basic Books.

Jaynes, Gerald D. 1986. *Branches without Roots: The Genesis of the Black Working Class in the American South, 1862–1882*. Oxford University Press.

Jaynes, Gerald D., and Robin M. Williams, Jr. 1989. *A Common Destiny: Blacks and American Society*. National Academy Press.

Jennings, M. Kent. 1987. "Residues of a Movement: The Aging of the American Protest Generation." *American Political Science Review* 81:367–82.

Jennings, M. Kent, and Richard G. Niemi. 1981. *Generations and Politics: A Panel Study of Young Adults and Their Parents*. Princeton University Press.

Keniston, Kenneth. 1968. *Young Radicals*. Harcourt Brace Jovanovich.

Kerpelman, Larry C. 1972. *Activists and Nonactivists: A Psychological Study of American College Students*. Behavioral Publications.

Kesey, Ken. 1962. *One Flew over the Cuckoo's Nest*. Viking Press.

Key, V. O. 1961. *Public Opinion and American Democracy*. Alfred A. Knopf.

Killian, Lewis M. 1975. *Impossible Revolution, Phase II*. Random House.

———. 1984. "Organization, Rationality and Spontaneity in the Civil Rights Movement." *American Sociological Review* 49:770–83.

Killian, Lewis M., and Charles U. Smith. 1960. "Negro Protest Leaders in a Southern Community." *Social Forces* 38:253–57.

King, Martin Luther, Jr. 1957. "Facing the Challenge of a New Age." *Phylon* 18:25–34.

———. 1963. *Why We Can't Wait*. Harper and Row.

———. 1964. *Stride Toward Freedom*. Harper and Row.

King, Mary. 1987. *Freedom Song: A Personal Story of the 1960s Civil Rights Movement*. William Morrow.

Kriesi, Hanspeter. 1989. "New Social Movements and the New Class in the Netherlands." *American Journal of Sociology* 94:1078–1116.

Kupers, Terry. 1990. "The Sixties Radical at Midlife." *Socialist Review* 20:81–94.

Landry, Bart. 1987. *The New Black Middle Class*. University of California Press, Berkeley.

Leadership Conference on Civil Rights. 1982. *Without Justice: A Report on the Conduct of the Justice Department in Civil Rights in 1981–82*. Washington, D.C.

Lemann, Nicholas. 1991. *The Promised Land*. Alfred A. Knopf.

Lindstrom, Andy. 1988. "Positive Reaction." *Tallahassee Democrat*, December 18.

Lipset, Seymour Martin. 1960. *Political Man: The Social Bases of Politics*. Doubleday.

Lipset, Seymour Martin, and Everett Carl Ladd, Jr. 1972. "The Political Future of Activist Generations." In *The New Pilgrims: Youth Protest in Transition*, ed. Philip G. Altbach and Robert S. Laufer. David McKay.

Lubell, Samuel. 1968. "That Generation Gap." *Public Interest* 13:52–60.

McAdam, Doug. 1982. *Political Process and the Development of Black Insurgency, 1930–1970*. University of Chicago Press.

———. 1988. *Freedom Summer*. Oxford University Press.

———. 1989a. "The Biographical Consequences of Activism." *American Sociological Review* 54:744–60.

———. 1989b. "Gender Differences in the Causes and Consequences of Activism." Paper presented at the American Sociological Association meetings, 1989, San Francisco.

Maidenberg, M., and P. Meyer. 1970. "The Berkeley Rebels: Five Years Later." *Public Opinion Quarterly* 24:477–78.

Mankoff, Milton, and Richard Flacks. 1972. "The Changing Social Base of the American Student Movement." In *The New Pilgrims: Youth Protest in Transition*, ed. Philip G. Altbach and Robert S. Laufer. David McKay.

Mannheim, Karl. [1928] 1972. "The Problem of Generations." In *The New Pilgrims*, ed. Philip G. Altbach and Robert S. Laufer. David McKay.

Marger, Martin N. 1987. *Elites and Masses*. Wadesworth.

Marwell, Gerald, Michael Aiken, and N. J. Demerath. 1987. "The Persistence of Political Attitudes among 1960s Civil Rights Activists." *Public Opinion Quarterly* 51:359–75.

Marx, Gary. 1967. *Protest and Prejudice: A Study of Belief in the Black Community*. Harper & Row.

———. 1979. "External Efforts to Damage or Facilitate Social Movements: Some Patterns, Explanations, Outcomes and Complications." In *Dynamics of Social Movements*, ed. Meyer Zald and John D. McCarthy, 94–125. Winthrop Publishing.

Matthews, Donald, and James Prothro. 1966. *Negroes and the New Southern Politics*. Harcourt, Brace & World.

Mauss, A. L. 1971. "On Being Strangled by the Stars and Stripes." *Journal of Social Issues* 27:183–202.

Meier, August, and Elliot Rudwick. 1973. *CORE: A Study in the Civil Rights Movement*. Oxford University Press.

Milbrath, Lester W., and M. L. Goel. 1977. *Political Participation*. Rand McNally.

Miles, Michael W. 1971. *The Radical Probe*. Atheneum.

Miller, James. 1987. *Democracy Is in the Streets: From Port Huron to the Siege of Chicago*. Simon and Schuster.

Mills, C. Wright. 1956. *The Power Elite*. Oxford University Press.

_____. 1959. *The Sociological Imagination*. Oxford University Press.

Moore, Douglas. 1960. "New Trespass Laws Strongly Protested." *Journal and Guide*, March 5.

Morris, Aldon D. 1984. *The Origins of the Civil Rights Movement: Black Communities Organizing for Change*. The Free Press.

Morris, Eugene 1990. "Woman's Bus Ride Launched City Boycott." *Tallahassee Democrat*, January 15. p.1.

Morrison, Minion K. C. 1987. *Black Political Mobilization: Leadership, Power and Mass Behavior*. SUNY Press.

Moynihan, Daniel Patrick. 1965. *The Negro Family: The Case for National Action*. U.S. Government Printing Office.

Myles, J., G. Picot, and T. Wannell. 1988. *Wages and Jobs in the 1980s: Changing Youth Wages and the Declining Middle*. Labour Market Activity Survey. Statistics Canada.

Nam, Charles B. 1963. "Methodology and Scores of Socioeconomic Status." Working paper No. 15, U.S. Bureau of the Census. U.S. Government Printing Office.

Nam, Charles B., and E. Walter Terrie. 1981. "Measurement of Socioeconomic Status from United States Census Data." In *Measures of Socioeconomic Status*, ed. Mary G. Powers. Westview Press.

Nassi, A. J., and S. I. Abramowitz. 1979. "Transition or Transformation? Personal and Political Development of Former Berkeley Free Speech Movement Activists." *Journal of Youth and Adolescence* 8:21-35.

Nettler, G., and J. Huffman. 1957. "Political Opinion and Personal Security." *Sociometry* 20:51-66.

Newcomb, Theodore M. et al., 1967. *Persistence and Change: Bennington College and Its Students after 25 Years*. John Wiley.

Newfield, Jack. 1966. *A Prophetic Minority*. New American Library.

Neyland, Leedell W. 1989. "The Tallahassee Bus Boycott in Historical Perspective: Changes and Trends," In *The Civil Rights Movement in Florida and the United States*, ed. Charles U. Smith. Father and Son Press, Tallahassee.

O'Connor, James. 1973. *The Fiscal Crisis of the State*. St. Martin's Press.

Orcutt, James, and James Fendrich. 1980. "The Decline of the Protest Movement: An Analysis of Students' Perceptions." *Sociological Focus* 13:203–19.

Orum, Anthony M. 1973. *Black Students in Protest*. American Sociological Association.

Parenti, Michael. 1986. *Inventing Reality*. St. Martin's Press.

Peterson, Richard E. 1970. "The Scope of Organized Student Protest." In *Protest: Student Activism in America*, ed. Julian Foster and Durward Long. William Morrow.

Pettigrew, Thomas F. 1985. "New Black-White Patterns: How Best to Conceptualize Them." In *Annual Review of Sociology*, ed. Ralph H. Turner and James F. Short. Annual Reviews Inc.

Phillips, Kevin. 1969. *The Emerging Republican Majority*. Arlington House.

———. 1990. *The Politics of Rich and Poor*. Random House.

Piven, Francis Fox, and Richard A. Cloward. 1971. *Regulating the Poor*. Pantheon.

———. 1979. *Poor People's Movements*. Vintage.

———. 1985. *The New Class War*. Pantheon.

Powers, Mary G. 1981. *Measures of Socioeconomic Status*. Westview.

President's Commission on Campus Unrest. 1971. *Report of the President's Commission on Campus Unrest*. U.S. Government Printing Office.

Proudfoot, Merrill. 1990. *Diary of a Sit-In*. 2nd Edition. University of Illinois Press.

Pynchon, Thomas. 1990. *Vineland*. Little Brown.

Rabby, Glenda. 1984. *Out of the Past: The Civil Rights Movement in Tallahassee, Florida*. Dissertation, Department of History, Florida State University.

Riesman, David 1950. *The Lonely Crowd*. Yale University Press.

Ripley, Pete. 1990. "Commentary." *Tallahassee Democrat*, February 18.

Rivers, Larry E. 1989. "The Rise of Social Consciousness within the Black Community and the Crusade for Social Change in Leon County, Florida, 1956–57." In *The Civil Rights Movement in Florida and the United States*, ed. Charles U. Smith. Father and Son Press, Tallahassee.

Robbins, Tom. 1980. *Still Life with Woodpecker*. Bantam Books.

Robinson, Jo Ann Gibson. 1987. *The Montgomery Bus Boycott and the Women Who Started It*. University of Tennessee Press.

Rosenberg, Morris. 1957. *Occupations and Values*. The Free Press.

Rustin, Bayard. 1965. "From Protest to Politics: The Future of the Civil Rights Movement." *Commentary* 39:25–31.

Sale, Kirkpatrick. 1973 *SDS*. Random House.

Sawyer, Mary R. 1987. "Harassment of Black Elected Officials: Ten Years Later." Voter Education and Registration Action, Inc., Washington, D.C.

Searles, Ruth, and J. Allan Williams. 1962. "Negro College Students' Participation in the Sit-Ins." *Social Forces* 50:215–19.

Sears, David O., and Carolyn L. Funk. 1990. "The Persistence and Crystallization of Political Attitudes over the Life-Span: The Terman Gift Children Panel." Paper presented at the annual meeting of the American Sociological Association, August.

Smith, Charles U. 1961. "The Sit-Ins and the New College Student." *Journal of Intergroup Relations* 2:223–29.

———. 1989. *The Civil Rights Movement in Florida and the United States*. Father and Son Press, Tallahassee.

Smith, Charles U., and Lewis M. Killian. 1958. "The Tallahassee Bus Protest." Field Reports on Desegregation in the South. B'Nai B'Rith.

Smith, Robert C. 1982. *Black Leadership: A Survey of Theory and Research*. Institute for Urban Affairs and Research. Howard University.

Staples, Robert. 1971. *The Black Family: Essays and Studies*. Wadesworth.

Swank, Duane, and Alexander Hicks. 1984. "Militancy, Need and Relief: The Piven and Cloward AFDC Caseload Thesis Revisited." *Research in Social Movements, Conflict and Change* 6:1–29.

Taylor, Verta. 1989. "Social Movement Continuity: The Women's Movement in Abeyance." *American Sociological Review* 54:761–75.

Tilly, Charles. 1978. *From Mobilization to Revolution*. Addison-Wesley.

Tripp, Luke S. 1987. *Black Student Activists: Transition to Middle Class Professionals.* University Press of America.

Turner, Ralph H., and Lewis M. Killian. 1972. *Collective Behavior.* Prentice-Hall.

U.S. National Advisory Commission on Civil Disorders. 1968. *Report of the National Advisory Commission on Civil Disorders.* Bantam.

Useem, Michael. 1984. *The Inner Circle.* Oxford University Press.

Verba, Sidney, and Norman Nie. 1972. *Participation in America: Political Democracy and Social Equality.* Harper & Row.

Verba, Sidney, Norman Nie, and Jae-on Kim. 1971. *The Modes of Democratic Participation: A Cross-National Comparison.* Russell Sage.

Vogel, David. 1989. *Fluctuating Fortunes.* Basic Books.

Walker, Daniel. 1968. *Rights in Conflict.* Grosset and Dunlap.

Walsh, Edward J. 1988. *Democracy in the Shadows.* Greenwood Press.

Walters, Ronald W. 1988. *Black Presidential Politics in America: A Strategic Approach.* SUNY Press.

Warren, Robert Penn. 1965. *Who Speaks for the Negro?* Random House.

Weinberg, Ian, and Kenneth N. Walker. 1969. "Student Politics and Political Systems: Toward a Typology." *American Journal of Sociology* 75:77–96.

Whalen, Jack, and Richard Flacks. 1989. *Beyond the Barricades.* Temple University Press.

White, Robert M. 1964. *The Tallahassee Sit-Ins and CORE: A Nonviolent Revolutionary Submovement.* Ph.D. dissertation, Department of Sociology, Florida State University.

Whyte, William H. 1956. *The Organization Man.* Simon and Schuster.

Wills, Gary. 1988. "The Kennedys in the King Years." *New York Review of Books*, November 10, pp. 10–16.

Wilson, William J. 1978. *The Declining Significance of Race: Blacks and Changing American Institutions.* University of Chicago Press.

Wiltfang, Gregory L., and Doug McAdam. 1991. "The Costs and Risks of Social Activism: A Study of Sanctuary Movement Activism." *Social Forces* 69:987–1010.

Wolfe, Alan. 1977. *The Limits of Legitimacy: Political Contradictions of Contemporary Capitalism.* The Free Press.

———. 1989. *Whose Keeper?* University of California Press.

Wood, James L. 1974. *The Sources of American Student Activism*. Lexington Books.

Zinn, Howard. 1964. *SNCC: The New Abolitionist*. Beacon Press.

# INDEX

## A

"Abeyance structures", 135
Abramowitz, S. I., 34, 133
Abramson, Paul R., 61, 91, 174n
American Civil Liberties Union, 18, 27
Activists: coping with conservative era, 129–130; keeping the faith, 130–131; clarifying misconceptions, 133–135; democratization of institutions, 134; and privileged status, 134; major findings 135–137; and good citizenship, 142–143
Activists, black and white: difference in parental socio-economic status, 120; similarities between, 120–125; major in college, 121; differences in graduate training, 121; similarities in being agents of social change, 122; differences in extrinsic rewards, 122; differences in marital status, 122–123; differences in valuing money, 122; differences in religious involvement, 123; differences in organizational involvement, 123; differences in radicalism in 1971, 124–125; differences in protest politics in 1971, 124–125; differences in life-cycle political involvement, 124; differences in political self-identification in 1980s, 125; similarities in complete activism, 125; similarities in radicalism-conservatism in 1980s, 125; multivariate analysis of political self-identification, 126–127; multivariate analysis of Reagan opposition, 126; multivariate analysis of radicalism-conservatism, 126; multivariate analysis of citizenship, 127; summary of findings, 127–129
Adams, Willie, xxiii
AFDC, 45
African American activists: prediction of activism's consequences, xxii; working-class origins, 4–5, 52; political continuum, 30; aspirations and achievements, 51–55; educational attainment in 1973, 53–54; public

African American activists *continued*:
employment in 1973, 53; male-female differences, 53; incomes in 1973, 54; marital status in 1973, 55; political identification in 1973, 60; political attitudes, 60–62; radicalism-conservatism in 1973, 61–62; political efficacy in 1973, 61; political alienation in 1973, 61; political behavior in 1973, 62; political efficacy, multivariate analysis for 1973, 64; political self-identification, multivariate analysis for 1973, 64; political alienation, multivariate analysis for 1973, 65; radicalism-conservatism, multivariate analysis for 1973, 65; political behavior, multivariate analysis for 1973, 66–67; summary of ten year study, 68–69; educational attainment in 1988, 70; marital status in 1988, 70; occupational status in 1988, 71; public employment in 1988, 71; income in 1988, 71; political self-identification in 1988, 76; radicalism-conservatism in 1988, 76; life-cycle political involvement, 76; political behavior in 1988, 77; as ideal citizens, 83–84; 165n, 169n

African American political attitudes, caution in interpreting, 55–56

African American women, importance of, 27

African Americans: national survey of, 38; limitations on upwardmobility, 52–53; similarity to Jewish Americans, 128; major findings, 137–138; empowerment, 138; and Democratic Party, 138, 146; testing democracy, 143; current and future dilemmas, 145; and the race card, 146; in white controlled employment, 146

Agnew, Spirow T., Vice President, 93

Aiken, Michael T., 7, 34, 40, 86, 113, 165n, 167n

Alford, Robert R., 46

Alienation, 171n *see also* African American activists and white activists and nonactivists

"All politics is local", 139

"All we are saying is give peace a chance", 35

Almond, Gabriel A., 143

Alwin, Duane F., 34

Amnesty International, 102

Anti-Communist hysteria, xxi, 11, 18, 37

Apartheid, 143

"Appropriated memories", 33

Aristotle, 32

Ash, Timothy C., xxi

Astin, Alexander, 89

# B

Background characteristics, of activists, 4–8

Baird, Leonard L., 86

Baker, Ella, 27

Barnett, Richard J., 46

Barry, Marion, xxii–xxiii

Basie, Count, band leader, 25

Beijing, China, xxiii

Bell, Daniel, xix–xx, 34

Bellah, Robert N., 143

Berkeley, "Free Speech" movement, xx

Berkeley, California, xxi

Billingsley, Andrew, 168n

Birmingham, Alabama, 23, 37

Black liberation as result of civil rights movement, 10–11

Black ministers, Tallahassee, xv
Black Muslims, 57, 73
Black Nationalism: dimensions of, 57, 171n; multivariate analysis of, 172n; in 1973, 55–60; multivariate analysis in 1973, 63–64; in 1988, 72–74 *see also* African American Activists
Black Panthers, 40, 57, 73
"Black Power", 35
Black working class, 4
Blackwell, James E., 54, 168n
Blair, Ezell, 2
Blauner, Robert, 63
Bloom, Jack M., 38–39
Bluestone, Barry, 47, 164n
Blum, R. H., 34
Blumenthal, Sidney, 107, 109, 114, 137, 142
Boston, Thomas D., 54
Bowles, Samuel, 47
Braden, Carl, 18
Branch, Taylor, xvi, xxiii, 19, 27, 37, 135, 163n, 165n
Braungart, Margaret M., 34, 133, 174n
Braungart, Richard G., 34, 133, 174n
Breitler, Alan, xii
Brink, William, 38, 59
Brint, Steven, 136
Brown, H. Rap, 57
Brown, Judith Benninger, 131
Buckley, William F., 141
Burnstein, Daniel, 46
Bus boycott, white resistance, 10–14
Button, James W., 138

C

Campbell, Angus, 143
Campbell, Doak, FSU President DOAK, 12
Career choices, continuum, 169n
Carey, J. T., 34
Carlson, Jody, 40
Carmichael, Stokely, 56–57, 63, 72
Carter, Charles, 12
Carter, Jimmy, President, 47
Cason, Sandra, 6
Central Intelligence Agency, 41, 45
Chicago, Illinois, 38–39
Chicago Seven, 43
Churchill, Winston, 39
Citizenship, among African Americans, 78–83 *see also* ideal citizens and good citizenship
Civil rights activists, repressive actions by authorities and vigilantes, xii *see also* anti-Communist hysteria
Civil rights movement, as catalyst, xxi
Civil rights movement: resistance to, 1; degree of student participation, 3; role of churches, NAACP and black colleges, 3
Civil Rights Act, 1964, xiv, xxi, 25, 37, 45
Civil Rights Restoration Act, 1991, 168n
Clamshell Alliance, 89
Clarke, James, 168n
Cleaver, Eldridge, xix
Clinton, Bill, 147
Cloward, Richard, 3, 35, 37, 46, 48, 67
Cohen, Ronald L., 34
Cole, Leonard A., 56
Coles, Robert, 144
Collier, Peter, xxi–xxii, 91, 96
Collins, LeRoy, Governor, 11, 15, 18–19, 165n
Complete activists, xxiii *see also* ideal and good citizenship
Conformists' vision of citizenship, 144
Conoly, G. W., xv

Conservative 1980s, 105
Conservative coalition, dominance of, 45–47
Conservative organizations, 102
Conservative Think Tanks, 47
Consumer Product Safety Commission, 45
Control groups, xii–xiii see also tracking activists
CORE: xi–xii, xiv, 7, 15, 18–19, 21, 27, 57; and the Tallahassee Sit-ins, 14–19; purpose of, 14
Corporate liberalism, 147
Cowins, Benjamin, 165n
Cruse, Harold, 56
Czechoslovakia, xxi

D

Dahl, Robert A., 81, 143
Daley, Richard, Mayor, 43
Daniels, Betty, 131
Davis, James Allen, 81, 104, 111
Delevan, Virginia, 1, 17
DeMartini, Joseph R., 133
Demerath, N. J., III, 7, 34, 40, 86, 113, 165n, 167
Democratic Leadership Council, 102
Desegregating: restaurants and lunch counters, 14–19; movie theaters, 21–25; "white" swimming pools, 23
*Destructive Generation*, xxi
Detroit, Michigan, 38
Dillman, Don A., 167n
Diprete, Thomas A., 71
Disillusionment hypothesis, 32–33
Distinctive generations hypothesis, 33–34
Dixon, Howard, 18
Domhoff, G. William, 45, 47, 125, 146
Dow Chemical, 41

Due, John, 21
Due, Patricia, 21, 23–24, 31 see also Patricia Stephens
Dukakis, Michael, 147
Dupont, Rev. K. S., xv
Durham, North Carolina, 4
Dutschke, Rudi, 32

E

Eastern bloc countries, 144
Edelman, Marian Wright, xxiii
Edsall, Thomas B., 44, 47, 114
Educational level for whites, multivariate analysis of, 173n
Ehrlichman, John, 40
Eisenhower, Dwight, President, xiii
Elite universities, xx
Emerson, Ralph Waldo, 6
Employee Retirement Security Act, 45
Environmental Protection Agency, 45
Epps, Edgar, xx, 4, 52–54, 56, 59, 65, 122, 171n
Equivalent continuity, 137
Ervin, Richard, Florida Attorney General, 12
Existential commitment, 6, 13

F

Fair Housing Act, 1968, 45
FAMU: xi, xxiii, 1, 3–5, 9, 30, 51; faculty, 11–12; secret meetings of black and white students, 13; ROTC at, 16; university officials, 24–25; response rate, 167n
Farrakan, Louis, 73
FBI, xxiii, 42
Feagin, Joe A., 39
Fendrich, James Max, xv, 46, 119, 121, 124, 133, 170n, 175n, 177n

Feuer, Lewis S., xxi
Flacks, Richard, xx-xxi, 5, 7, 34, 37, 46, 60, 65, 86, 88, 90, 94, 98, 133-134, 140, 142, 146-147, 170n, 172n, 174n
Florida Board of Control, 12
Florida Department of Motor Vehicles, 31
Florida Department of Labor, 52
*Florida Flambeau*, 17
Florida Supreme Court, 11
Florida Legislature, 11
Florida Theater, 21
Fonda, Jane, 124
Ford, Gerald, President, 47
"Freedom Now", 35
Freedom Riders, CORE sponsored, 19
Friedland, Roger, 46
FSU: xii, 6-7, 29, 31, 104; protest, 25; response rate, 165n
"Fuck the War", 35
Funk, Carolyn L., 34

# G

Gaines, Mary, 27
Gamson, William A., 46, 143, 147
Gans, Herbert J., 143
Garrow, David J., xvi, 27, 37, 46, 165n
General Social Survey: 176n; comparisons for African Americans, 81; for whites, 111-112
Generational unit continuity, 137, 168n
Gephardt, Richard, 147
Gerth, Hans H., 32
Geschwender, Barbara, 5, 122
Geschwender, James, 5, 25, 33, 122
Gintis, Herbert, 47
Gitlin, Todd, xix, 6, 42-43, 46, 88, 163n, 165n

"Go slow" policy, of adult African American leaders, 21
Goel, M. L., xxiii, 81, 96, 143
Goertzel, Theodore, 126
Goethe, 26
Goldwater, Barry, 35, 136
Good citizenship: multivariate analysis for African Americans, 82; among whites in 1986, 108-111; activists exemplify, 142; summary, 142-144; weakness of theory, 143-144 *see also* African American Activists, White activists, black and white activists
Gore, George W., FAMU President, 12
Gouldner, Alvin, 136
Greene, W., 34
Greensboro, North Carolina, sit-in, 2, 4, 14-15, 163n
Grigg, Charles, 165n
Grusky, David B., 71
Gurin, Patricia, 3-4, 52-56, 59, 65, 77, 81, 122, 124, 145-146, 171n
Gutterbock, T. M., 51

# H

Hahn, Harland, 39
Haines, Herbert H., 4
Haley, Richard, 15, 19
Hamilton, Charles V., 56
Hampton, Henry, xvi
Harris, Louis, 38, 59
Harrison, Bennett, 47, 164n
Hart, Gary, 147
Hartley, Broadus, 9
Hatchett, Shirley, 56, 77, 81, 124, 145-146
Hayden, Tom, 6, 42-43, 164n, 168n
Heilbroner, Robert, 105
Hemmingway, Theodore, 10, 164n
Hendricks, Bernard, 1, 131

"Hey, Hey, LBJ, how many kids have you killed today", 35
Hicks, Alexander, 46
Holloman, Roosevelt, 24
Holtzman, Elizabeth, xxiii
Hoover, J. Edgar, 37-38, 40
Horowitz, David, xxi-xxii, 91, 96
Horton, Myles, 1
House Un-American Activities Committee, 18
Hout, Michael, 71
Howard University, xiii
Hudson, James N., Rev. Dr., xv, 9
Huffman, J., 61
Humphrey, Hubert, 42, 148

## I

Ideal citizens, xxiii *see also* good citizenship, complete activism
"Immaculate conception" theory of social movements, 135
Inter-Civic Council, Tallahassee, xv, 9-12, 15, 27
Intersection of biography and history, 142-144
Intragenerational units, 33
Iran/Contra, 142
Isaac, Larry, 46

## J

Jackson, James A., 56, 77, 81, 145-146
Jackson, Jesse, xxii, 74, 124, 145-146, 148; support for in 1988, 76
Jackson State University, 35
Jacoby, Russell, 126
Jakes, Wilhelmina, xi-xii, 8, 19
Jaynes, Gerald D., 46, 48, 55-56, 62, 77, 81, 83, 173n
Jefferson, Thomas, 144

Jennings, M. Kent, 34, 60, 62, 67, 133, 137, 167-168n
Jesus Christ, 19
Johns, Charley, State Senator, 11
Johnson, Lyndon, President, 35, 37-38, 43, 148

## K

Karinga, Ron, 63
Kelley, William, 46
Keniston, Kenneth, xxi, 5
Kennedy, John F., President, xi, xiv, 35, 37
Kennedy, Robert, 35, 37, 89
Kent State University, 35
Kerpelman, Larry C., 165n
Kesey, Ken, 33
Key research questions, 31-32
Key, V. O., 143
Killian, Lewis, xii-xxi, 9-10, 14-15, 37, 39, 57, 163n, 165n
Kim, Jae-on, 30
King, Martin Luther, Jr., xi, xxi-xxiii, 1, 3-4, 9, 13, 19, 35-36, 39, 56, 68, 74, 106, 135, 144, 148, 168n; letter to jailed students in Tallahassee, 19
King, Mary, xxiii, 164n
Krauss, Ellis, 133
Kriesi, Hanspeter, 136
Ku Klux Klan, 13, 143
Kupers, Terry, 88, 115, 178n

## L

Ladd, Everett Karl, 32, 34
Landry, Bart, 52, 54, 71
Leadership Conference on Civil Rights, 48
Lemann, Nicholas, 37-41, 53, 56, 74
Lewis, John, U. S. Representative, xxiii

Liberal organizations, 102
Liberals, Cold War, 39, 42 see also Kennedy, Humphrey
Lindstrom, Andy, 178n
Lipset, Seymour Martin, 32, 34, 143
London, B., 51
Long, Huey, 145
Longitudinal studies, 29–31 see also tracking activists
Lowenstein, Al, 168n
Lubell, Samuel, 135

# M

McAdam, Doug, xix, xxi, 3, 7–8, 34, 37, 40–41, 46, 57, 60, 82, 87–88, 90, 94, 98, 102, 113–114, 127, 129, 133, 135, 163n–165n
McCain, Franklin, 2
McCain, James, 15
McCarthy, Eugene, 89
McCarthyism, 141
McGovern, George, 89
McKissick, Floyd, 4
McNeil, Joseph, 2
McWilliams, Spurgeon, 131
Machiavelli, 148
Maidenberg, M., 34
"Making history", defined, 66, 142
Malcolm X, 35, 56–57, 72
Mandela, Nelson, 75
Mankoff, Milton, 34
Mannheim, Karl, 33–34, 106, 115, 135, 168n
Marger, Martin N., 67
Marshall, Burke, 37
Marwell, Gerald, 7, 34, 40, 86, 113, 165n, 167n, 176n
Marx, Gary, 37, 42, 56, 67, 165n
Mass arrest of protesting students, 24
Matthews, Donald, xii, xxii, 2–3, 5, 30, 34, 69

Maturation hypothesis, 32
Mauss, A. L., 33
Mayo, William, City Commissioner, 17
Media: 41, coverage of rape trial, 13–14; portrait of activists, ix
Medicaid, 45
Medicare, 45
Meier, August, 14
Meyer, P., 34
Miami Beach, Florida, 14
Milbrath, Lester W., xxiii, 81, 96, 143
Miles, Michael W., 163n
Miller, James, 42, 45, 90–91
Mills, C. Wright, 3, 32, 35, 47, 91
Mine Safety and Health Administration, 45
Montgomery, Alabama, xxi, 4, 8, 12, 36
Montgomery Improvement Association, xv
Moore, Douglas, 2
Moore, Harry T., assassination of, 164n
Moral Majority, 102
Morris, Aldon, xii, 4, 145, 163n, 165n
Morris, Eugene, 8–9
Morrison, Minion K. C., 138
Moscow, 11
Moses, Robert, 41
Moynihan, Daniel Patrick, 37, 40
Muller, Ronald E., 46
Myles, J., 173n

# N

NAACP, 3, 9–10, 27, 74, 79, 140
Nam, Charles, 52, 85
Nassi, A. J., 34, 133
National Guard, 35
National Organization for Women, 102

National Public Radio, xxi
National Student Association, 6
National Traffic Safety Commission, 45
Neoliberals, 147–148
Nettler, G., 61
"New class", 136, 148
New Deal, 45, 121
New Left: 90–91, 113, 128, 136, 139, 142, 147, and participatory democracy, 140; exception of women's movement, 141; and white activists, 146; and ideology, 147 see also white activists
New Right, 140
New York City, 38
Newcomb, Theodore M., 34
Newfield, Jack, 163n
Neyland, Leedell W., 9, 11, 165n
Nie, Norman, 30
Niemi, Richard G., 34, 60, 62, 67, 133
Nixon, Richard, President, xxi, 40, 43, 46
"Nixon's father should have withdrawn", 35
North Carolina A&T University, 2

## O

O'Connor, James, 168n
O'Neil, Tip, 139
Occupational Safety and Health Administration, 45
Oedipal conflict, xxi–xxii
"Off the Pigs", 35
Omnibus Safe Streets and Crime Control Act, 40
Open Housing Act, 1968, xxi
Orcutt, James, xv, 46
Organization building versus political freedom, 147
Organizational involvement, 173n, 175n, 177n
Orum, Anthony, 2, 4, 30

## P

Parenti, Michael, 143
"Participatory democracy", 42, 147
Patterson, Carrie, xi–xii, 19
Pentagon, 42
Persian Gulf, xxi
"Personally acquired memories", 3, 33
Peterson, Richard E., 41
Pettigrew, Thomas F., 168n
Philadelphia, Mississippi, 47
Phillips, Kevin, 39, 43, 48, 77, 92, 107, 114, 126
Picketing, by FAMU students, 22
Picot, G., 173n
Piven, Francis Fox, 3, 35, 37, 46, 48, 67
Plaquemine Parish, Louisiana, xiv
Poland, Jeff, xii
Political behavior, 171n see also African American activists and white activists and nonactivists
Political efficacy, 171n see also African American activists and white activists and nonactivists
Political gladiators, xxiii see also good citizenship and complete activism
Political harassment, xxiii
Political insurgency, consequences of, 45
Political protest, increased for African Americans during the 1980s, 81 see also African American activists
Political self-identification: defined, 171n; multivariate analysis of, 172n see also African American activists and white activists and nonactivists
Poor People's March on Washington, 39
*Poor People's Movements*, 3
Port Huron Statement, 45

Powers, Mary G., 169n
President's Commission on Campus Unrest, 36
Progressive organizations, 102
Protest politics, expansion during the 1960s, 35–44
Prothro, James, xii, xxii, 2–3, 5, 30, 34, 69
Proudfoot, Merrill, 163n
Pynchon, Thomas, 33

R

Rabby, Glenda, xii, xvi, 10–11, 14–15, 17, 19, 20–26, 165n
Radical center, defined, 176n
Radical right, major findings of former YAF members, 141–142
Radicalism-conservatism: 171n, multivariate analysis of, 173n see also African American activists and white activists and nonactivists
Rainbow Coalition, 102
Rape, of FAMU student, 13–14
Reagan, Ronald: 30, 35, 47, 72, 141, 149, counter offensive against civil rights, 48; Governor Ronald, 93
Reagan opposition: among African Americans in 1988, 77–78; among white activists, 106–107
Reaganism, as counter offensive to progressive victories, 44–48
Reaganomics, failure of, 145
Relative continuity, 137
Richmond, David, 2
Riesman, David, 88
Ripley, Pete, 48
Rivers, Larry E., 13
Robbins, Tom, 33
Robinson, Jo Ann, 27, 165n
Rollins, Rev. J. Metz, xv, 9, 12
Roosevelt, Theodore, President, 145

Rosenberg, Morris, 174n
Rubin, Jerry, xix
Rudd, John, Judge, 18, 22
Rudwick, Elliot, 14
Russia, 144
Rustin, Bayard, 67

S

Sale, Kirkpatrick, xxii
Samora, Julian, xiii
San Diego, California, 38
Savio, Mario, xx
Sawyer, Mary R., xxiii
SCLC, xi, 3, 27, 39, 46, 74, 135
SDS, 33, 38, 140–141
Searles, Ruth, 30
Sears, David O., 34
Simon, Tobias, 18
Sit-ins: in the South, 2; support for and opposition against, 5; white resistance, 16
Smith, Charles U., xii, xvi, xxi, 10, 133
Smith, Robert C., 55
Smith, Tom W., 81, 104, 111
SNCC, xxiii, 11, 27, 57
Social Action Committee at FAMU, 13
Social movements: political, xx; counterculture, xx
Southern Conference Education Committee, 18
Speed, Dan B., xv, 12
Stalin, 35
Staples, Robert, 168n
Steel, Rev. C. K., xv, 9, 12–15, 19, 21
Stephens, Patricia, xii, xi, 4, 14–16, 19 see also Patricia Due
Stephens, Priscilla, xi, 14, 23
Street, Wilhelmina, 8 see also Wilhelmina Jakes

Student Activism, hypotheses about consequences of, 32–34
Student government leaders, as ideal citizens in 1971, 98
Student right-wing as adults, 136–137
"Sunshine patriots", 109
Supplemental Security Income, 45
Swank, Duane, 46

## T

Tallahassee, Florida, xii, 6, as a local movement center, 8–14
Tallahassee Chamber of Commerce, 17
Tallahassee Chapter of CORE, one of the first integrated in the Deep South, 14–16
Tallahassee City Commission, 10, 12, 17, 23–24
*Tallahassee Democrat*, 18, 20
Tallahassee Human Relations Committee, xv
Tallahassee Municipal Airport, 19
Talyor, Verta, 135
Tarleau, Alison T., 133
Teague, Sam, Mayor, 22
Terrie, Walter, 52, 85
Thatcher, Margaret, 44
"Thatcherism", 44
*The Big Chill*, xix
*The Civil Rights Movement in Florida and the United States*, xvi
*The Lonely Crowd*, 88
*The Negro Family: The Case for Action*, 37–38
*The Organization Man*, 88
Thomas, Clarence, 72
Thoreau, Henry David, 6
Tilly, Charles, 164n
"To Fulfill These Rights", 37
"Toward a Female Liberation Movement", 131

Tracking activists, 29–31
Tripp, Luke S., 34, 54, 62, 133, 169–170n
Turner, Ralph H., 163n
Turner, Robert W., 175n

## U

U. S. Chamber of Commerce, 47
U. S. Commission on Civil Rights, xiii–xiv, 72
U. S. Commission on Civil Rights, Florida Advisory Committee, 26
U. S. Department of Justice, 48
U. S. Equal Employment Opportunity Commission, 72
U. S. National Advisory Commission on Civil Disorders, 38–39
U. S. Office of Education, xii
U. S. Senate, xv
U. S. Supreme Court, 79
University of Florida, 131
University of Michigan, 34, 169–170n
University of Texas, 6
Upward mobility: African Americans, 50–53; black and white comparisons, 86, 120–121; of whites, 85–86, 99
Urban League, 74
Useem, Michael, 44

## V

Verba, Sidney, 30, 143
Viet Cong, 42
Vietnam Veterans Against the War, 124
Vietnam War, xix–xx, 41, 43, 93, 125
Vigilantes, 13
Vogel, David, 44
Voting Rights Act, 1965, xxi, 37, 45

# W

Walker, Daniel, 143
Walker, Kenneth N., 98
Wallace, George, 40, 47
Walsh, Edward J., 116
Walters, Ronald W., 56
Wannell, T., 173n
War Powers Act, 45
Warren, Earl, Chief Justice, xiv
Warren, Robert Penn, xiv
Washington, D. C., 42; far-right moves to, 141
Watts, Los Angeles, 38
"We must destroy the village in order to save it", 42
"We Shall Overcome", xxi, 37
Weber, Max, 32
Weinberg, Ian, 98
"Welfare queens", 48
West Feliciana Parish, Louisiana, xiv
Whalen, Jack, xx, 34, 60, 88, 90, 94, 98, 133, 146, 170n, 174n
"Where's the rest of me", 149
White activists: progressive beliefs, 6–7; support for, 7; college goals, 8; political continuum, 29; in contrasts to 1930s activists, 43; nonacquisitive values, 90; as new rather than old left, 91; as political gladiators in 1971, 96; as ideal citizens in 1971, 97; support for activist in 1971, 97–98; sharp contrast with their generation, 104; identical levels of protest behavior in 1971 and 1986, 106; as local political activists, 109–110; as party and campaign workers, 109; as political communicators, 109; protest politics in 1986, 111; rejoin Democrat Party in 1986, 114; and life choices, 139; lacking a strong national organization, 140; and the Democratic Party, 146–147; current and future dilemmas, 146–149; and the new left, 146; and work dilemmas, 148
White activists and nonactivists: parental socio-economic status, 86; extrinsic occupational rewards in 1971, 86–87; occupational preference in 1971, 87–88; employment sector in 1971, 87; career paths in 1971, 88; organizational involvement in 1971, 89; marital status in 1971, 88–89; beliefs about power distribution, 90–91; political efficacy in 1971, 91–92; political self-identification in 1971, 92; radicalism-conservatism in 1971, 93; multivariate analysis of power distribution in 1971, 93–94; multivariate analysis of political self-identification in 1971, 94–95; multivariate analysis of alienation in 1971, 94; multivariate analysis of political efficacy in 1971, 94; multivariate analysis of radicalism-conservatism in 1971, 95; multivariate analysis of political behavior in 1971, 96; political behavior in 1971, 96–97; educational levels in 1986, 99; marital status in 1986, 99–100; employment sector in 1986, 100–101; social change values in 1986, 100–101; organizational participation in 1986, 101–102; political party support in 1986, 101–102; income differences in 1986, 101; comparative organization involvement in 1986, 102–103; political self-identification in 1986, 103–104; multivariate analysis of radicalism and conservatism in 1986, 105; political behavior in 1986, 105–106;

White activists and nonactivists *continued:* Reagan opposition, 106–107; multivariate analysis of Reagan opposition, 107–108; levels of patriotism in 1986, 108–109; life-cycle political involvement, 108; good citizenship in 1986, 108–111; compared to national survey, 111–112; on complete activism scale, 111; multivariate analysis of complete activism, 112; multivariate analysis of weighted sample on complete activism, 112–113; as distinctive generational units, 115; major findings, 139–141
White Citizens Council, 13, 16, 143
White liberals, problems with, 21
White nonactivists: college goals, 8; potential conservatism, 43–44; acquisitive values, 90; as Reagan supporters, 106–107, 109; as sunshine patriots, 109; as oppositional, 116
White power structure, 11–13
White radicalization, 40–43
White resistance, national level, 40
White, Robert M., 6, 10–11, 13, 15, 18, 21, 143
White student government leaders, movement to the far right in 1986, 103–104

White's political self-identification, compared to national sample, 104
*Who Speaks for the Negro?,* xiv
William, Whyte, 88
Williams, J. Allan, 30
Williams, Robin W., 46, 48, 55–56, 62, 77, 81, 83, 173n
Willis, Ben, Judge, 22
Wills, Gary, xi
Wilson, William J., 52, 56
Wiltfang, Gregory L., 87
Wolfe, Alan, 143, 168n
Wood, James L., 36
Woolworth's, in Tallahassee, 16
Working-class, African American, 164n *see also* upward mobility
World Leaguers, 35
"Would you trust a crooked Dick", 35
Wright, Zebedee, 10

# Y

YAF, 33, 140–141
Young, Andrew, xxii, 74
Youth movements, opposition to, xxi

# Z

Zinn, Howard, 4

www.ingramcontent.com/pod-product-compliance
Lightning Source LLC
Chambersburg PA
CBHW030137240426
43672CB00005B/157